A
Citizen's
Guide to
GOVERNMENT

A
Citizen's
Guide to
GOVERNMENT

C. Richard Tindal
St. Lawrence College

McGraw-Hill Ryerson Limited
Toronto Montreal New York Auckland Bogotá
Caracas Lisbon London Madrid Mexico Milan
New Delhi San Juan Singapore Sydney Tokyo

**McGraw-Hill
Ryerson Limited**
A Subsidiary of The McGraw-Hill Companies

A Citizen's Guide to Government

ISBN: 0-07-552812-6

2 3 4 5 6 7 8 9 10   W   6 5 4 3 2 1 0 9 8

Printed and bound in Canada

Care has been taken to trace ownership of copyright material contained in
this text. The publishers will gladly take any information that will enable them
to rectify any reference or credit in subsequent editions.

Sponsoring Editor: Gord Muschett
Associate Editor: Margaret Henderson
Developmental Editor: Marianne Minaker
Production Editor: Gail Marsden
Production Co-ordinator: Nicla Dattolico
Cover Designer: Dianna Little
Printer: Webcom

Canadian Cataloguing in Publication Data

Tindal, C. R., date —
    A citizen's guide to government

Includes bibliographical references and index.
ISBN 0-07-552812-6

1. Canada - Politics and government.   I. Title.

JL81.T56 1997   320.471   C97-930370-2

Table of Contents

Preface and Acknowledgements

This is **not** a conventional political science text book. As the title suggests, it is a basic primer on government, intended to encourage greater public understanding, interest and involvement. It is a "Citizen's Guide," designed to inform Canadians about their governments and how they work, and about the fundamental changes underway in the role of government and in key areas of Canadian public policy.

This Guide has also been prepared for use with a General Education course which I have developed and am teaching at St. Lawrence College, Kingston Campus. There is an accompanying Instructor's Manual which complements the use of the Guide for that purpose. It contains learning outcomes and elements of performance, along with case studies, test questions and the like. In addition, each chapter of the Guide (except the first and last because of their introductory or summary nature) concludes with definitions of key terms and concepts (highlighted in *italics* where they first appear in the chapter), points to ponder for class discussion, and suggested additional readings. In preparing both the Guide and the Instructor's Manual, I have drawn upon almost 30 years of experience in teaching government courses at the community college level.

I am indebted to my colleague and close friend, Ian Wilson of St. Lawrence College, for actively encouraging this project and for his many helpful comments and suggestions. Thanks also to the third year class of Human Resource Management students who used the first draft of this Guide in the winter 1996 semester and offered their critique.

For reviewing all or parts of the Guide and providing helpful comments and suggestions, I am also grateful to Sheila Bell of Durham College, Michael Boam of Sheridan College, Tom Chambers of Canadore College, John Fakhouri and Edison Roach of Algonquin College, Garfield Gini-Newman of Vaughan Secondary School, Dean Haggerty, Brien Holmes and Peter Malkovsky of Sir Sandford Fleming College, Karen Moreau-Petti of Niagara College, Barbara Reavely of Mohawk College, Diane Rindall of Red River Community College, Dennis Roughley of Georgian College and Lynne Woolstencroft of Conestoga College.

Staff at McGraw-Hill Ryerson Limited were helpful as usual, including Susan Calvert, Ralph Courtney, Margaret Henderson, Marianne Minaker, Gail Marsden, and especially Gord Muschett.

For those interested in the technical aspects, I prepared this Guide, and provided the publisher with a "camera-ready" copy, using Wordperfect 6.1 for Windows. As a result, I must accept not only the usual responsibility for any deficiencies in the content of the book, but also any shortcomings in its appearance.

Richard Tindal
Inverary, Ontario
January 1997

A
Citizen's
Guide to
GOVERNMENT

Chapter 1

Canada at the Crossroads

Objectives and Highlights

♦ To demonstrate the importance of government in our lives.

♦ To illustrate the fundamental changes underway in the role of government and the challenges they pose for society.

The over-worked cliché which serves as the title of this introductory chapter is usually applied today to describe the threat of Québec separation. We are at the crossroads because of the national unity crisis. If we don't choose the right path, we face the break-up of our country.

We are also told that Canada is at the crossroads in terms of its financial state. Our governments have lived beyond their means for far too long and must now bring their debt under control if we are to avoid a financial catastrophe.

Both of these issues are very important and both are discussed in this Guide. But it is contended that there is another very fundamental way in which Canada is at the crossroads. This concerns the public perception of government and of the role which government should play in our lives. We have been moving from a prolonged period when we probably became too dependent upon government to one in which government is increasingly portrayed as "the enemy." Many of the long-established programs and institutions that helped to define the Canadian identity are under assault or already disbanded. A key purpose of this Guide is to encourage the reader to reflect upon the kinds of changes which are underway and to participate actively in the debate about the future role which our governments should play.

Why Should We Care About Governments?

The answer is simple: we should care because governments deal with the things we most care about. What are those things? The list will vary somewhat, depending on your age, economic status and other characteristics. But it is likely to include most of the items below. Review these items, and rank them according to their importance to you, with #1 being the most important.

1	Jobs
3	Social safety net (UI, welfare, pensions, etc.)
2	Medicare (national health care system)
6	Environment (pollution)
5	Taxation levels
4	Crime (security in home and neighbourhood)
7	Affordable housing
___	Other

If things like these are what concern you, it is hard to imagine not being concerned about governments. Governments have never had all of the answers, and we have relied upon them too much in the past. But they certainly play a key role in addressing issues like these, as the brief summary below will indicate.

1 Jobs

Government is the single largest employer in the country, even with the down-sizing and layoffs of recent times.

Government also influences the creation of jobs by the private sector in a vast number of ways. For example:

♦   The federal government uses its taxing and spending policies and its control over interest rates and the money supply in an attempt to stimulate economic growth while avoiding excessive inflation.

♦ Provincial governments provide essential programs and services, like highways and hydro-electric power, without which economic growth and job creation could not occur. Provinces also use taxing powers to influence the economy, as illustrated by the tax cut introduced by the Ontario Government in the spring of 1996 as a means of stimulating economic growth.

♦ Local governments zone and service land and issue building permits which allow construction and growth to proceed.

♦ *Something to Think About*

Why for the past 15 years has the federal government largely ignored high unemployment, and even contributed to it, while focusing almost all of its attention on fighting inflation? Even with inflation at minimal levels in recent years, why has the government continued to ignore (or even to aggravate) the problem of unemployment, while concentrating on deficit and debt reduction?

Why has the Conservative Government elected in Ontario in June of 1995 preoccupied itself with introducing massive spending cuts, leading to unemployment — all in the name of economic growth and job creation?

We'll attempt to answer these questions in later chapters, especially Chapter 9 which deals with the present state of the Canadian economy and its debt load.

2 *Social Safety Net*

All three levels of government are involved in Canada's comprehensive network of social programs, which have been described as providing coverage "from womb to tomb." The most visible (and controversial) of these programs is welfare. It is still administered (and partially funded) by municipal governments in some provinces, notably Ontario. In fact, Ontario municipalities will be assuming even greater responsibility for welfare as a result of changes announced by the Province in January 1997 and discussed later in this Guide. In most jurisdictions, however, welfare has shifted from the municipal to the provincial level. Whatever the specific arrangements for administration of welfare, the national government pays up to 50% of the costs.

Depending on one's definition, social programs extend to such areas as pensions, affordable housing, support for post-secondary education and medicare — although some of these matters are examined separately in this introductory discussion. Whatever the definition, what is clear is that support for this type of program has been eroding.

In recent years, "welfare-bashing" has become increasingly common, and there is growing public support for government cuts to welfare programs. Pension reform is underway, prompted by the view that we can no longer afford existing levels of support for those seniors who are well off financially. Tuition fees for college and university students are on the rise. There is also talk about the introduction of private educational institutions, which some fear could lead to a two tier system of higher education such as there is in the United States, where only the well-to-do can afford to attend private schools.

In Chapter 10, we will look at whether Canada's social programs have created a "safety net" or a "hammock." We'll also look at how much these programs are being reduced at present and the implications of these reductions.

3 Medicare

One of the key differences between Canada and the United States is our national health care system. Some people even claim that it is one of the features which defines us as a nation.

Health is a provincial responsibility under our constitution, but since the mid-1960s the federal government has provided a substantial portion of the funding for hospital care and physicians' services. This federal funding is now being gradually phased out, causing many people to worry about the loss of national standards in health care in Canada and the eventual collapse of our medicare system. Some provincial premiers have recently challenged the federal government's role in setting national standards, suggesting that the provinces should take over this task. Meanwhile, a discussion document from the Canadian Medical Association in mid-1996 claims that the privatization of Canada's health care system is already underway, pointing out that those able to pay at private clinics can get faster service than those who must contend with long waiting lists in the public system.[1]

Local governments are also involved in health, usually through agencies such as health units. They are also involved in providing or affecting many of the key determinants of health: by ensuring clean water, sewage and waste disposal, well designed neighbourhoods and safe living environments.

♦ Something to Think About

If the main determinants of health are factors such as education, lifestyle and living environment, why do we spend 95% of our "health" dollars on a sickness-care system, centred on doctors and hospitals?

What can **you** do about your health — rather than waiting for government to do something about it?

These issues are explored in Chapter 11.

4 Environment

Here again, all three levels of government are involved. While the federal government passed an *Environmental Protection Act* in 1988, it has left much of the initiative to the provinces. They have created most of the agencies for controlling pollution.

Municipal governments are responsible for such areas as garbage and waste disposal. They also provide policies and facilities which help to minimize water, land and air pollution.

As with medicare, there are now challenges to the role of the federal government with respect to national environmental standards.

---

[1]Elaine Medline, "Public health, private profits," *Kingston Whig Standard,* July 15, 1996.

The opposition is clothed in the language of "harmonization," and is presented as a positive new era of federal-provincial cooperation in environmental matters. The strong support for this approach, however, from right-wing governments like that of Ralph Klein in Alberta, suggest that its primary objective is to reduce environmental regulations. Environmental groups are concerned that harmonization could mean "a race to the bottom" which equalizes to the **lowest** standards currently in existence.[2]

5 *Taxation Levels*

This is perhaps the most obvious evidence of the existence of government, and the one least appreciated by the public. All three levels levy taxes — on every imaginable activity and product.

Under the constitution of Canada:
◆ the federal government has unlimited taxing power;
◆ provinces can levy direct taxes only; and
◆ municipalities can levy only such direct taxes as are authorized by the provinces. The one main taxing power granted to municipalities has always been the tax on real property (that is, land and buildings).

There is a prevailing view (constantly reinforced by business groups and other lobbyists) that Canadians suffer from crushing burdens of taxation almost unheard of in the rest of the world. On the other hand, there is considerable evidence to suggest that business (especially big business) has benefited from very substantial tax breaks and tax concessions over the past couple of decades and has not continued to pay its share of taxes at the same level as ordinary consumers.

However high or fair they are, taxes are the price we pay to enjoy the services provided by governments. Those who portray taxes as somehow wasting money that could have been used for private consumption ignore the positive benefits that we derive from the public goods that we receive from those tax dollars. To take an over-sim-

---

[2]This discussion is based on Rosemary Speirs, "Harmonized environmental rules a recipe for disaster," *Toronto Star*, September 26, 1996.

plified example, lower taxes would leave us with more money to buy a bigger, fancier car — but we might be driving that car over potholes on poorly maintained roads because of lost government revenues from lower taxes. As we will see again and again throughout this Guide, in government everything connects. We need to think about the full implications of the choices we make.

The issue of taxation is explored as part of the discussions in Chapter 9. It examines Canada's economic and fiscal policies and tries to explain why our governments have pursued the priorities they have. It challenges much of the "conventional wisdom" surrounding this subject and suggests some of the options which governments might have (should have?) pursued.

6 Crime

It doesn't matter that the statistics show a decrease in violent crimes in recent years. There is a widespread **perception**, fuelled by sensational media coverage, that violent crime is on the increase. Perception is reality and, as usual, governments are expected to "do something."

For many people, the answer is to get tough on crime, to spend more money on policing, to increase the sentences handed out, and to build more prisons. Efforts to increase law enforcement involve all three levels of government. All levels establish standards of permissible behaviour, through statutes or acts passed at the senior levels and by-laws passed by municipalities. Policing is provided by municipal police forces, by provincial police forces in Ontario, Québec and Newfoundland, and by the RCMP. Infractions of the law are dealt with in provincial and federal courts, and those convicted may spend time in federal penitentiaries or provincial correctional institutions.

Since it costs (depending on the institution) between $50 000 and $80 000 a year to keep someone behind bars, however, increasing the prison population will not help to keep taxes down. Since many prisoners learn far more about crime after they are put behind bars, it is also not evident that longer prison sentences will reduce crime.

As in so many areas of public policy, we need to look beneath the symptoms (the crimes) to the underlying causes if we are to have any real or lasting improvement. There is considerable evidence to suggest that many of the spending cuts now being made by governments in the name of financial restraint will contribute to increased crime in the future — and increased costs in areas such as policing, the courts, the prison system and health care. Experts at a recent conference claimed that money spent on early childhood education and programs dealing with family violence is a better investment than money used to hire police and build prisons. They pointed out that Canada spends $10 billion annually on police services, the courts, legal aid and corrections and yet the overall crime rate continues to increase.[3]

This Guide will try to give you information that "arms you" to make thoughtful judgments about the policy questions facing governments.

7   *Affordable Housing*

The federal government has a major impact on the cost of housing through its interest rate policies. High interest rates not only increase the cost of mortgages, they restrict housing construction, and this can lead to housing shortages which also force up costs. Alternatively, low interest rates — such as we have at present — **can** stimulate the housing market, if consumers have enough confidence about their futures to make the major commitment involved in a house purchase.

Provincial governments provide a variety of controls relating to the housing market, including a standard building code which must be followed in construction. They may build public housing units, subsidize the costs of housing for target groups, or control costs for tenants through rent controls.

Municipal governments directly control the housing industry through their land use controls and policies and their regulatory and inspection activities.

---

[3]Canadian Press, "Investment in prevention pays society dividends," *Kingston Whig Standard*, October 1, 1996.

Are You Convinced Yet?

Even the brief examples above illustrate the important roles played by governments. But you may have had personal experiences which make you sceptical about the intentions of those in government. You may view with suspicion the statement: *"We're from the government; we're here to help you,"* finding it about as believable as "the cheque is in the mail." If you hold this view, you are certainly not alone! When asked which federal political party has concrete solutions to the nation's major challenges, 76% of respondents in the *Maclean's* magazine annual year-end poll said **none**. This finding prompted leading pollster Allan Gregg to conclude that "people increasingly have decided that governments are simply not an important force in their everyday lives."[4]

It is ironic and troubling that Canadians appear to be giving up on their governments at the same time as they are increasingly concerned about the future and about what it will hold for them. Most respondents in the *Maclean's* survey:

♦ expect to have to keep working beyond the age of 65 to support themselves;
♦ believe that many people will never find full time work;
♦ doubt that there will be government assistance in the future for those who lose their jobs;
♦ anticipate that those with money will be able to buy a higher education at private universities; and
♦ grudgingly accept the inevitability of two tier health care.[5]

These concerns are real and understandable, and most of them are addressed in this Guide. Their existence can be interpreted as a failure on the part of government, which is obviously the judgment of many disillusioned Canadians. But their existence also underlines the im-

---

[4]Quoted in Anthony Wilson-Smith, "Future Imperfect," *Maclean's*, December 30, 1996, p. 18.

[5]Joe Chidley, "Reduced Expectations," Maclean's, *op. cit.*, p. 22.

portance of government, since resolution of these concerns will depend to a considerable extent on effective action by government.

Whatever their shortcomings, **we need our governments**. They are the vehicle we use to decide how our scarce resources will be allocated among the wants and needs we have as a society. These decisions are never easy because our wants and needs are always greater than the resources available to fulfil them. Governments manage the conflict inherent in this situation, they provide a wide range of public goods available to the entire population, and they redistribute wealth in an attempt to ensure a minimum standard of living for all. Without the civilizing influence provided by government, we would be reduced to "the law of the jungle" and "the survival of the fittest."

It is true that there are many imperfections in our system of government. Many "ordinary" Canadians feel that the system is not responsive to their needs and concerns. *Democracy*, as Churchill said, *is the worst system — next to all the rest*. We'll look more closely at our system of government and how it operates in the next few chapters. Understanding our system, imperfections and all, is the first step toward bringing about improvements in it.

Why Are We at the Crossroads?

We are at the crossroads because we face some very fundamental choices about the roles of our governments and the relationships they should have with one another and with the Canadian people. We reached this point after going through a number of shifts or pendulum swings, as briefly summarized below.

Historically, we were largely self-reliant. Problems were solved through individual efforts and/or support from families and neighbours. For example:

♦ "Welfare," such as it was, was essentially a form of local charity, largely provided by the church.

♦ Individual landowners maintained the portion of road which ran across the front of their properties.

♦ Barns were raised or homes built with a local "bee" in which members of the community participated.

With the shift from an agricultural and rural society to an industrialized and urban one, individual and community self-sufficiency declined and the role of government increased. The extended family living off the land was replaced by the individual working in a factory and living alone in a city apartment. In response to the new economic uncertainties, the "positive state" developed. Government began to establish minimum standards to protect the public and to enforce numerous rules and regulations.

Ironically, as government moved in, much of the remaining volunteer and community self-help activity died away. When problems arose, the attitude became "why doesn't the government do something about it." The more government did for us, the less people seemed able (or willing?) to look after themselves. Throughout the 20th century (at least until quite recently), we took less and less self-responsibility and relied more and more on government — even as we complained about the size of government and the burden of our taxes.

Notice how inconsistent we are. We show our disillusionment with government by laughing at the cliché: "We're from the government; we're here to help you." Then we react to a problem by complaining: "Why doesn't the government do something!"

After an almost continuous expansion of government throughout the 20th century, the pendulum has reversed itself in the 1990s. What is happening, and why, is a matter of some debate. The prevailing view has been that governments grew too large, became too intrusive, encouraged too much dependency, got into too much debt, and had no choice but to scale back dramatically. Underlying this view is a belief that governments are wasteful (perhaps inherently), take too much in taxes, and are involved in too many activities which could be better left to (and more efficiently handled by) the private sector.

We should applaud all efforts by government to review carefully what they are doing and how they are doing it. It is certainly reasonable for taxpayers in a democracy to look for evidence of value for the dollar spent. If the needs of society can be addressed effectively for less money, we all benefit.

◆ Something to Think About

But is that what is happening today as governments at all levels cut programs and services in an effort to reduce debt and to hold the line of taxes? There is growing concern that many of these actions may be shortsighted and dangerous. Those holding this view believe that governments are not considering (or are insensitive to) the harmful impact on society of these expenditure and program cuts.

A sampling of newspaper clippings from a three week period in late 1996 reveals the following examples of these concerns:

◆ A daily parade of people in wheel-chairs, clutching walkers, hobbling on damaged legs, and breathing with the aid of oxygen tanks can be seen in Metro Hall in Toronto. They are turning up to see if they still qualify to ride Wheel-Trans, the public transit system for people with disabilities. After the Harris Government cut $8.17 million from Wheel-Trans funding last year, Metro Council and the TCC decided that the only option was to change the eligibility criteria to reduce the number of users.[6]

◆ Ontario's top environmental watchdog reports that the provincial government's plan to eliminate, revise or consolidate 50 environmental regulations is putting the environment "in jeopardy."[7]

◆ Provincial cutbacks to the justice system which could total $116 million dollars are blamed for chaos in the court system, with long line-ups for filing documents, long delays in processing documents, and even problems of important documents like court orders being misplaced.[8]

---

[6]Editorial, "Cuts victimizing Wheel-Trans Users," *Toronto Star*, October 20, 1996.

[7]Greg Crone, "Environment in danger," *Kingston Whig Standard*, October 11, 1996.

[8]Tracey Tyler, "Chaos in the court: Cuts hit the civil justice system," *Toronto Star*, October 20, 1996.

♦ Stories are accumulating about delays for up to a year for cataract surgery and hip replacement surgery. Even emergency surgery to repair broken bones are not immune from delay, as in the example of the 72 year old man with a leg broken in two places who was forced to wait in great pain while he was "bumped" for a week, because of too few surgeons, operating rooms and nurses in a busy downtown Toronto hospital.[9]

Even allowing for the possibility that coverage of these stories has been sensationalised as is customary in the media, there is little doubt that government cutbacks are having an adverse impact on the lives of ordinary Canadians.

Perhaps even more troubling is the possibility that many of the cutbacks currently being made, far from saving money, will end up costing the government (and the taxpayers) more money. As will become clear in later chapters, there is considerable evidence to suggest that any short term savings from cutting the social programs which underpin civilized society will be more than offset by increased costs related to such societal ills as unemployment, sickness, poverty, and crime. As Justice Minister Allan Rock told a national meeting of police chiefs, "throwing away the key on murderers won't keep the streets safe if provinces slash social programs that help set kids on the straight and narrow."[10]

Another concern is that governments often appear to look only at the short term when undertaking expenditure cuts. As discussed in Chapter 11, for example, provincial governments are currently cutting hospital beds and closing hospitals in an attempt to bring health budgets under control. Any surplus in hospital beds which **might** exist at the moment, however, reflects the fact that our population is still in its below-average hospital utilization years. One-third of the Canadian population starts turning 50 in 1997, and by their mid-50s people

---

[9]Ellie Tesher, "Readers tell of health care horrors," *Toronto Star*, September 27, 1996.

[10]Canadian Press, "Rock launches counterattack," *Kingston Whig Standard*, August 29, 1996.

make above-average use of hospitals. Not surprisingly, that increased usage continues to climb as they age. Closing too many hospitals now could mean having to reopen at least some of them again within 10 years.[11]

A further challenge when expenditure cuts are being made is that government actions are interconnected and intertwined. **All** implications should be carefully considered before a decision is made, but this is often not the case. Take the example of municipal recreational programs. They are optional; it is up to the municipality how much is provided in this area.

Everything Connects

Faced with budget cutbacks, a council is apt to decide that recreation programs can be dispensed with more easily than "essential" services like roads, water and sewer systems or fire departments.

But, recreation programs that promote fitness can contribute directly to improved health and save money on doctors and hospitals. Recreation programs can also reduce youth crime and policing and court costs. Community policing initiatives often include the establishment of youth centres which provide a range of recreation programs. Every dollar saved on scrapping recreation programs might actually cost more than that in increased sickness or crime costs — if we look carefully at the full implications of what we are doing.

Governments don't seem to look at the big picture, especially if the cost that may arise is in some other agency's budget, or even in another level of government's budget. Why would municipalities spend more on recreation to decrease the federal and provincial spending on sickness care? Because, there is only one set of taxpayers in Canada, you say. But, such changes won't occur until we learn to appreciate the links between actions and to pressure our governments to take a broader view.

---

[11]David K. Foot (with Daniel Stoffman), *Boom, Bust & Echo*, Toronto, Macfarlane Walter & Ross, 1996, pp. 165-167. This issue is one of many fascinating examples of the impact of demographics found in this book.

♦ *Something to Think About*

For example, do we want to have our tax dollars spent on more police officers and prisons to catch and incarcerate young people **after** they have broken the law, or on more pre-school programs and care, more child care support, more recreation programs and youth activities and other initiatives which can keep young people from breaking the law in the first place?

Yes, this is stating the choice in greatly oversimplified (even simplistic) terms. But, we need to know that there are choices, that we don't have to look at problems in only one way. We need to understand the links between government actions and to appreciate that prevention deserves at least as much emphasis as problem solving after the fact.

Becoming Lean But Not Mean

One of the big challenges we face is in maintaining a proper balance as governments go about reducing their role and their involvement in society.

It is all very well for governments to talk about encouraging individual self-reliance, but this can simply be a code word for abandoning individuals to their own devices. It is striking that the vision of the future identified by many Canadians in the previously cited *Maclean's* survey is of "a lean, mean world, where people must fend for themselves against the vagaries of society and the marketplace."[12] Only government, by continuing to play a prominent role, can soften that rather bleak picture.

It is fine for governments to pursue greater efficiency, to talk about operating in a more business-like fashion. But, constant reference to "business plans" and determining "what kind of business you

[12]Chidley, *op. cit.*, p. 22.

are in," doesn't change the fact that government is **not** business. It exists to serve fundamentally different purposes. In many cases, it provides the kinds of services and programs that business does not provide and would not provide — because they are not profitable. Government's role is to serve the public interest, elusive as that might be; whereas business, especially big business, seems increasingly concerned only with maximizing profits for current shareholders. Even though they often say it, it is doubtful that most people would really want government to act just like a business — "making quick decisions behind closed doors for private profit."[13]

The next several chapters of this Guide take a closer look at the structure and operation of our system of government — at the federal, provincial and municipal levels. Building on this foundation, later chapters then return for a closer look at the kinds of decisions governments are making with respect to economic and social policies and programs. While you are encouraged to come to your own conclusions about the appropriateness of what is happening, the "bias" of this Guide is in favour of a continuing significant role for government. The Guide concludes with a chapter which summarizes the insights gained and offers practical tips on how to take more personal responsibility for your own life and for the behaviour of government.

---

[13]David Osborne and Ted Gaebler, *Reinventing Government*, New York, Penguin Books, 1993, p. 22.

Chapter 2

What Are Our Many Governments and What Do They Do?

Objectives and Highlights

♦ To introduce the structure and operation of government at all levels.

♦ To illustrate the varied and valuable services provided by government.

♦ To develop your personal government directory.

Much of the widespread public disillusionment with government probably stems from two main sources: **(1)** citizens aren't sure which level of government is responsible for what, and **(2)** even if they find the right level of government, they don't know who to hold accountable or where to pursue their concern.

A good starting point is a list of names and phone numbers, such as the one you can compile using the *Guide to Government Directory* provided with this chapter. Once completed, it will provide you with a convenient checklist of contacts for your future interaction with government.

Also in this chapter is a whimsical description of *A Day in the Life* of college student Frank N. Earnest, whose adventures serve to illustrate many of the important services and programs provided by the various levels of government in Canada.

We begin with a brief overview of the general structure of government found at the federal, provincial and local levels in Canada.

Introduction

I f Canadians feel over-governed, they have good reason for this sentiment. Most Canadians are under the jurisdiction of at least three levels of government, and often four. These are:

1. The Government of Canada, usually referred to as the federal government.

2. A provincial or territorial government, such as the Government of Manitoba or the Government of the Northwest Territories.

3. A municipal government, such as a village, town, city or township. [In addition, there may be an "upper tier" municipal government, such as a county, regional or district government, found mainly in Ontario, Québec and British Columbia.]

Knowing which level of government looks after what is quite a challenge for Canadians — especially when so many responsibilities are shared among two or more levels. Some indication of this overlap is evident from the brief discussion of various topical issues in Chapter 1. The next several chapters will shed more light on who does what, why responsibilities have become so intertwined, and what the implications are of current efforts to disentangle responsibilities. Before proceeding into these intergovernmental issues, however, let's take a preliminary look at the government structures found at the various levels of government in Canada.

The Federal Government

It is customary to discuss the organization of the federal (and provincial) government in terms of two separate branches, executive and legislative, and how they interrelate. Most texts also identify a third branch of government, the judiciary or court system, about which more will be said later in this Guide.

Chart 1

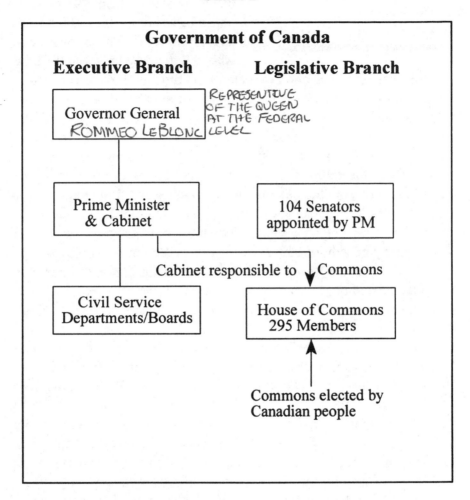

Government of Canada

Executive Branch   **Legislative Branch**

Governor General
ROMMEO LEBLONC

(handwritten: REPRESENTIVE OF THE QUGEN AT THE FEDERAL LEVEL)

Prime Minister & Cabinet

104 Senators appointed by PM

Cabinet responsible to ↓Commons

Civil Service Departments/Boards

House of Commons 295 Members

↑

Commons elected by Canadian people

For many Canadians, their main (and perhaps only) personal inter-action with the federal government occurs approximately every four years[1] when they have an opportunity to elect from their riding one member of parliament (MP) to the *House of Commons.*

---

[1]The maximum term for a parliament is five years (except for a possible extension during an extreme emergency such as wartime), but the party in power usually calls an election toward the end of the fourth year. The timing depends on the party's assessment of when it is most likely to get re-elected.

**Principle of
Representative Government**

The Commons consists of 295 members elected from 295 geographic areas (ridings) into which Canada is divided. These members, who will increase to 301 at the time of the next federal election expected sometime in 1997, are chosen to represent and make decisions on behalf of the Canadian population. This arrangement for *representative government* is found in virtually every democratic governing structure. As will be seen, it is present in the election of legislative assemblies at the provincial level and of councils at the municipal level. It is also found in the election of student unions or student councils in colleges and universities.

Besides its representative role, the House of Commons has two other key roles: **(1)** to pass laws, in the form of statutes or acts, for the governing of Canada, and **(2)** to act as a "watchdog" keeping an eye on the Cabinet and the civil service. The watchdog role of course, is mainly carried out by the opposition parties in the Commons, since members of the governing party are expected to support their Cabinet, not to criticize it.

While the House of Commons receives most of the media and public attention, Canada's Parliament has two Houses. In this *bicameral legislature*, the *Senate* is the upper chamber. It shares the law-making role of the Commons and must also give its approval before a bill can become a law. In addition, it plays a kind of watchdog role by giving "sober second thought" to actions taken by the Commons. This mature reflection was supposed to come from the appointment of leading Canadians from all walks of life, who would bring experience and sound judgment to the task. To be appointed, Senators must be at least 30 years of age, and they hold office until age 75. However, an appointed Senate gradually lost legitimacy as notions of democracy and accountability took hold in the 20th century.

Turning to the executive branch, the *Governor General* represents the Queen in Canada, reflecting the fact that Canada is a constitutional monarchy. The Governor General is appointed by the Queen (but on the advice of the Canadian Prime Minister), to act on her behalf when she is not in Canada. The Queen is the Head of State, whereas the Prime Minister is the head of government. These govern-

The Head of State

ing arrangements distinguish Canada from a republic like the United States, in which there isn't any separate Head of State different from the President.

The Governor General has many official duties, in Canada and abroad. A number of the duties are automatic and simply carry out the "advice" given by the Prime Minister. This is true, for example, of the appointment of Cabinet ministers. Many of the duties are social and ceremonial in nature and could presumably be carried out by the Prime Minister, as they are by the President or other Head of State in countries which are republics. But the Prime Minister is a partisan, political figure, less suited to representing the country as a whole and is sufficiently burdened with other duties. For these reasons, there is much to be said for having a separate Head of State. Moreover, there are a limited number of discretionary powers vested in the Governor General/Queen which are rarely required but can be important in the operation of our system of government. These discretionary duties are explored in a later chapter, but they help to make the position of Governor General more valuable and relevant than is commonly appreciated.

The key members of the executive branch are the *Prime Minister* and *Cabinet*. While the government of Canada consists of the various elements of governing machinery outlined in the preceding chart, when people refer to "The Government," they are usually thinking of the Prime Minister and Cabinet, which highlights the central position they hold. The main responsibilities of the Cabinet include: **(1)** developing policies to deal with the issues facing the country, **(2)** introducing bills to carry through these policies into law, and **(3)** supervising the civil servants who apply these policies and administer the laws on a day-to-day basis.

Given the central importance of the Prime Minister and Cabinet, it is perhaps surprising that they are not directly elected by the Canadian people — although it can be said that they are indirectly chosen. This is true in the sense that by voting for the candidate of a particular party, we are helping to elect members of that party to the Commons.

Normally, the party which elects the most members is deemed to have won the election. The leader of that party will become the Prime Minister of Canada and a number of other victorious candidates from that party will be chosen by the Prime Minister to serve as ministers in the federal Cabinet and to share in running the government.

Principle of Responsible Government

The principle of *responsible government* holds that the Cabinet is responsible to the House of Commons (from which its members come) and can only continue to hold office so long as it is supported by a majority of the members of the Commons. However, when a majority of the members of the Commons belong to the same party as the members of the Cabinet, as is usually the case, this principle ceases to have much practical value. In such a situation, the governing party can normally count on sufficient support in the assembly when required, and will continue to govern until the Prime Minister decides that the time is right to call an election — sometime before the maximum term of five years draws near to completion.

The actual day-to-day work of the government of Canada is carried out by full time employees who are known as the *civil service* or public service. The majority of these employees work for government departments (like Agriculture, Fisheries, Environment, Health and Welfare, Revenue and Transport), and each department is headed by a minister of the Cabinet. Through this structure, the appointed civil servants are answerable to the Canadian people through elected politicians in the Cabinet. Through a long-standing principle of *ministerial responsibility*, ministers are held accountable for the performance of the civil servants within their departments.

The Provincial and Territorial Governments

Canada is a *federation*. A federation is a system in which the functions of government are divided between two or more levels: a national government and provinces or states. In Canada's case, the federation is made up of one national government, ten provincial governments and two territorial governments (the Yukon and the Northwest Territories). A third territorial government will come into existence in 1999, with the division of the NWT into western and eastern Arctic portions. The eastern portion, with a population mainly of Inuit (formerly called Eskimo), will be known as Nunavut. No name has yet been chosen for the new western Arctic territory.

If you understood the structure of the government of Canada, the governing arrangements at the provincial level are much the same.

The public's main participation is again through the election of a representative body, in this case called the *Legislative Assembly* (or National Assembly in the case of Québec). The number of members varies by province and ranges from a high in Ontario of 130 members (soon to be reduced to 103 for reasons explained later) to only 32 in Prince Edward Island and only 24 and 17 in the Northwest Territories and the Yukon, respectively. All provincial legislatures are *unicameral*; there aren't any upper chambers like the Senate found at the national level. The Legislative Assembly has the same responsibilities as the House of Commons: to represent the people, to pass laws, and to act as a watchdog.

The party winning the most seats in the Assembly makes up "The Government," consisting of the *Premier* and Cabinet. The Cabinet is responsible to the Assembly and must have the support of its members; but here again, party loyalty usually ensures that support. The Cabinet has the same key roles as its federal counterpart: to develop policies, introduce laws, and supervise the administration of those laws.

The day-to-day running of the government is again carried out by civil servants, mostly organized in departments headed by Ministers who sit in the Cabinet.

The *Lieutenant Governor* is the official head of the provincial government (representing the Queen). He or she is appointed by the Queen on the advice of the federal government, which really means appointment by the Prime Minister. The roles of the Governor General also apply to the Lieutenant Governor. In addition, one of the traditional roles of the office was to act as an agent of the federal level in "keeping an eye on" provincial actions which might be con-

trary to the national interest. Given the strength of provincial governments today, however, any intervention of this sort by a Lieutenant
Governor would not be tolerated.

The similarity with the structure of the national government is
evident from the chart which follows.

Chart 2

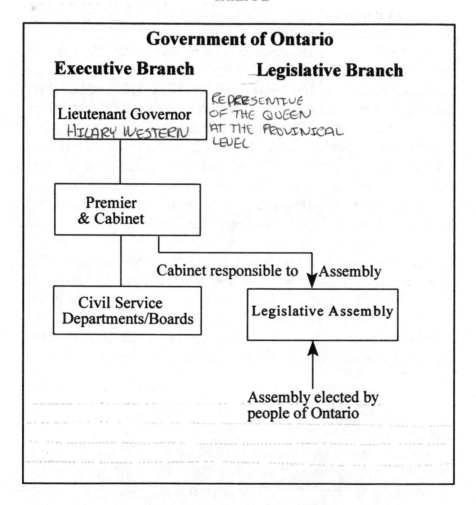

Government of Ontario

Executive Branch   **Legislative Branch**

Lieutenant Governor
HILARY WESTERN

REPRESENTIVE
OF THE QUEEN
AT THE PROVINICAL
LEVEL

Premier
& Cabinet

Cabinet responsible to ↓Assembly

Civil Service
Departments/Boards

Legislative Assembly

Assembly elected by
people of Ontario

Overall, the government of a province operates on the same principles of representative and responsible government, and has much
the same governing machinery — except that:

♦ it has a Legislative Assembly instead of the House of Commons.

♦ it doesn't have any second chamber like the Senate.

♦ it has a Lieutenant Governor instead of a Governor General.

**What's in a Name?
MLA, MPP or MNA**

In all provinces but Ontario and Québec, the members of these assemblies are known as MLAs. Ontario members are officially known as MPPs, even though there is only one Parliament in Canada, and it is a federal institution. Québec members are known as MNAs, or members of the National Assembly. Québec refers to its legislative assembly in this manner to reflect the independent, nation-like status it has attempted to project and assume. However, in spite of the change in name, the Québec assembly operates under exactly the same principles of representative and responsible government.

Government of the Northwest Territories

Another significant difference from the federal governing arrangements is evident with respect to the government of the Northwest Territories, and reflects the influence of its large aboriginal population. Aboriginals make up 60% of the population in the NWT, as compared to only 25% in the Yukon.[2] Governing traditions among aboriginals rest on the achievement of consensus. As a result, while the NWT government observes the principles of representative and responsible government, it operates quite differently. A 24 member Legislative Assembly is elected. The Premier and Cabinet are responsible to the Assembly and only govern with its support. But (and it is a big but), there aren't any political parties. After each election all 24 MLAs chose, by secret ballot, which of them will serve as Premier

---

[2]According to Graham White, "Canada's Most Distinctive Region: The Northwest Territories," in Paul Fox and Graham White (eds.), *Politics: Canada*, 8th edition, Whitby, McGraw-Hill Ryerson Limited, 1995, pp. 182-190, on which this section is based.

and as Ministers. The result is a great deal more discussion of issues among all 24 members and a much less divisive, confrontational style of decision making. While this may sound appealing to Canadians tired of the constant bickering among political parties, these arrangements also mean that it is very difficult for voters to pass judgment on a government's performance. The absence of parties also means the lack of a clear focus of accountability.

Municipal Governments

By comparison to the federal and provincial levels, the organization of government at the municipal level is simpler. There aren't two separate branches, executive and legislative. Nor is there any separate governing group like a Cabinet. Instead, all governing respon-

Council is **the Key**

sibilities are centred on one body — the elected *municipal council*.

The size of the council varies depending on the type of municipality. Small and rural municipalities such as Ontario's villages and townships have only five members. Alberta villages may be governed by as few as three members and the councils of its municipal districts (rural municipalities) normally have between four and nine members.[3] On the other hand, large cities and county and regional municipalities may have 20 members or more. The head of the council is variously known as the mayor, reeve, warden or chair and is either directly elected (in most instances) or chosen by the members of the council.

The council combines both executive and legislative responsibilities. It proposes policies, passes laws (by-laws), appoints staff and supervises their work as well. In other words, it carries out within one body the work that is divided between separate executive and legislative branches at the provincial and federal levels.

---

[3]Jack Masson with Edward Lesage Jr., *Alberta's Local Governments, Politics and Democracy*, 2nd edition, Edmonton, University of Alberta Press, 1994, pp. 90 and 106.

**Election by Ward
or by General Vote**

In smaller municipalities, members of council are usually elected *at large* or by *general vote*. Under this method, they run for office across the whole municipality and voters have an opportunity to choose from among all candidates in selecting their preferences. In larger municipalities, the head of council is still elected at large, but it is common for councillors to be chosen on a *ward* basis. This means that the municipality is divided into a number of separate geographic areas or wards, with one or more councillors elected from each ward. This arrangement is not unlike the process we use in electing members to the provincial legislature or House of Commons from separate ridings or constituencies.

Whether by general vote or by ward, however, councillors are normally elected as independents. Organized parties are not much in evidence at the municipal level in Canada, even though they are common in the United States and Britain. The main exceptions are some of the larger Québec municipalities. Readers may recall the colourful Jean Drapeau whose Civic Party controlled a majority of seats on Montreal's council for almost three decades until he retired in 1986.

Without parties, there is no governing group within a municipal council; nor any official opposition or "watchdog" for that matter. Unlike the Prime Minister or Premier, a big city mayor has no bloc of party votes to call upon in support of measures to be passed. Canadian municipalities are governed by what is often termed a "weak-mayor system," in which the head of council has to rely upon his or her persuasive powers to try to mobilize support for actions to be taken. Even so, many mayors have played a strong leadership role. Examples include David Crombie in Toronto, Stephen Juba in Winnipeg, Allan O'Brien in Halifax and Hazel McCallion in Mississauga.

One of the most colourful mayors in Canadian history has to be Charlotte Whitton, who became the first woman mayor of a major Canadian city with her election in Ottawa in 1951. She held that position until 1956, and then again from 1960 to 1964. Her antics were legendary and well documented, including the time she threatened the Board of Control (Ottawa's executive committee) with a gun — only a cap pistol as it turned out. Typical of her irreverence was the following exchange with the Lord Mayor of London.[4] It was a formal occasion, with the Lord Mayor resplendent in his robes and chains of office and Charlotte wearing a fine gown and a corsage.

Lord Mayor: *"If I smell your flower, will you blush?"*
Charlotte: *"If I pull your chain, will you flush?"*

The day-to-day running of government is handled by staff, the municipal civil service, organized into departments which reflect the responsibilities being exercised by the municipality.

The basic governing structure of a municipality, therefore, consists of just two components — the elected council and the municipal staff, as depicted in the chart below.

Chart 3

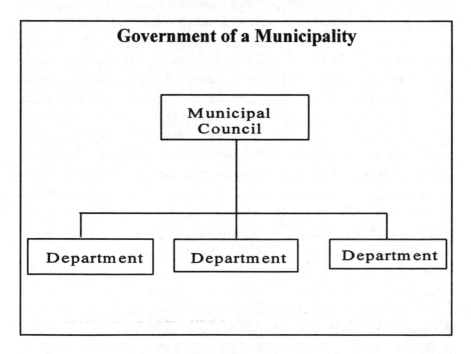

Government of a Municipality

Municipal Council

Department   Department   Department

---

[4]This anecdote has long made the rounds and is repeated in Allan Levine (ed.), *Your Worship* (The Lives of Eight of Canada's Most Unforgettable Mayors), Toronto, James Lorimer and Company, 1989, p. 132.

There are many variations on this basic governing structure, of course, especially in larger municipalities. Two of the most common variations are: **(1)** to establish a number of standing committees of council, to assist the council in discharging its responsibilities; and **(2)** to establish a chief administrative officer (CAO) to act as the senior coordinating officer for all staff matters. These and other governing structures are described in Chapter 5.

While the structure of government in any one municipality is relatively simple, the overall system of municipal government is far from being so. There is only one federal government in Canada, along with ten provincial governments and two territorial governments — soon to be three. In contrast, there are over 4 000 municipalities in Canada, some 800 in Ontario alone. These municipalities are classified into a number of different categories: cities, towns, villages, rural municipalities (also termed townships, parishes, and rural districts), counties, and regional, district and metropolitan municipalities.

In addition, there are thousands of agencies, boards and commissions which also form part of local government in Canada. These bodies include boards of education, health units or agencies, electricity and utility commissions, conservation authorities, police commissions, parks boards, and library boards. Most of these bodies are appointed, not elected, they provide a number of important services that are (or ought to be) closely coordinated with municipal services, and they claim a substantial portion of the revenues raised by the municipalities within their jurisdiction. The result is a local government system characterized by considerable fragmentation and potential confusion, even if the governing arrangements for any one municipality may be relatively simple and straightforward.

Summary: You and Your Governments

So where do you fit into the picture, after this admittedly very brief introduction to the levels of government in Canada?

You and your fellow Canadians decide who will make up these various levels of government through exercising your voting rights.

You get to choose the head of your municipal council and all the council members, or at least the members representing your area if there is a ward system of election. You also elect one member of the legislative assembly in your province or territory, from the particular riding or constituency in which you reside, and you similarly elect one member of the House of Commons. Details on voting and other ways of participating in government are provided in Chapter 8.

Understanding Who Does What

There is no simple way of describing the division of responsibilities among the various levels of government in Canada — especially since many responsibilities are actually shared by two or more levels. Perhaps the simplest approach is to describe a day in the life of a mythical college student in the Township of Bountiful. The story which follows is rather fanciful, but it does serve to illustrate the relevance of government in our lives, something which we too often take for granted or fail to appreciate.

A Day in the Life

Scene 1: A Morning Eye-Opener

The day does not begin well. Our student, Frank N. Earnest, is attempting his morning shave, still rubbing the sleep from his eyes. Suddenly, to his mounting horror, the following things happen:

♦ the water stops running in the sink, and the lights go out.
♦ when he goes to the living room window to see if there has been a power failure in the neighbourhood, he discovers that the road in front of his house has disappeared.
♦ squinting in the early morning light, he realizes that the park across the street has vanished, as has the school down the street.
♦ he races to the phone to call the police — but there is no answer. He gets the same result when he tries to call the fire department.

Frank wakes up in a cold sweat. A dream. It was only a dream. No more anchovies on his bedtime pizza, he resolves.

Frank's wild dream isn't that far-fetched. What it describes is nothing more than the disappearance of a number of the basic services provided by local government. This contrived scenario is just a way of illustrating how important those services are to us in our everyday lives. While most of these services are financed with assistance from the senior levels of government (mainly the provinces), they are provided by municipalities and local boards (such as the school board).

Scene 2: Just a Few Errands

After recovering from this morning adventure, Frank goes about his daily activities.

♦ Still not finished with local governments, he visits the branch library in his neighbourhood to return *Local Government in Canada*, a rivetting story which he had finished late last night.

♦ Back in his car, Frank heads toward the adjacent city of Plentiful. Without even noticing, he leaves a township road and drives for several miles on a county road and then a provincial highway. From there, he goes on to Highway 401 (a federal-provincial highway) and travels the last few miles to the city.

♦ Frank's next stop is to get a new sticker for his license plate. He goes to the Ontario Government building in Plentiful and pauses in the lobby to get his bearings. Looking down the list of offices on the wall by the bank of elevators, he notices:

□ The Assessment Division of the *Ministry of Finance*, where his parents had gone recently to appeal the assessed value of their home. (They had first blamed the municipality, before learning that it was the Province which assessed properties.)

□ The *Ministry of Colleges & Universities*, with which he is familiar from his years as a student.

□ The *Ministry of Community and Social Services* — an office Frank had seen more than he wanted to during a long period of unemployment before he had decided to increase his job prospects by taking a college diploma.

□   The *Ministry of Environment*, to which his father had taken a water sample from the cottage, to have it tested.

□   The *Ministry of Health*, to which he had come earlier this year to get his new photo health card (now a collector's item?).

□   The *Ministry of Labour*, where his uncle had gone for litera-ture on collective bargaining, in anticipation of a union being certified to represent his plant workers.

□   The *Ministry of Municipal Affairs*, which has just begun an investigation into the financial affairs of Bountiful after re-ceiving a petition from concerned taxpayers.

□   The *Ministry of Natural Resources*, from which Frank gets his annual hunting permit.

□   The *Ministry of Solicitor-General*, with which his cousin Marty was familiar, having been an unhappy guest in one of the Province's detention centres.

□   The *Ministry of Transportation* — finally the Ministry he wanted today. This shouldn't take long he thought as he en-tered the elevator, unless the staff are all out on the highways catching unsafe trucks and transports again!

Scene 3: Frank and the Feds

A few minutes later, Frank is on his way again, pleased with the prompt and courteous service he has received. His next stop is the Post Office (an outlet of *Canada Post*, a crown corporation which is part of the Executive Branch of the Government of Canada) where he buys a stamp and mails his income tax return to *Revenue Canada*.

With only a couple of months until the end of his school year, Frank then heads off to the *Canada Employment Centre* of the federal government to check again on job postings. As he reviews the limited listings, he wonders again if he should consider a career in the *Armed Forces* (another part of the executive branch of the federal govern-ment). He has a friend who is getting his university education paid for while in the forces; Frank wants to find out more about what this involves. He wouldn't mind pursuing a university degree after fin-ishing his college diploma, but he would need government financial support to do it. His father recently took an early retirement buy out from the *Department of Fisheries and Oceans*, as part of the downsizing underway throughout the federal government. His parents both seem concerned about keeping up the mortgage payments on the home they purchased a few years ago, complaining about the high interest rate policies of the *Bank of Canada*, another agency of the Executive Branch of the federal government.

A few years ago Frank had thought of a career in the federal civil service. A posting in some foreign embassy of the *Ministry of External Affairs* had seemed exciting and exotic — until embassy bombings and hostage-takings became far too common. The *Ministry of Indian and Northern Affairs* had also interested him, especially with all the land claim disputes flaring up between the federal government and Canada's native peoples. However, Frank had come to terms with the fact that government, including the military, was no longer a promising source of new jobs. Downsizing had become a more familiar term than job security for government workers.

Scene 4: Frank Faces Reality

Shrugging off a vague feeling of discouragement, Frank turns the car toward home and an evening of studying for his government course. Thinking back over the day's activities (and that crazy dream he'd had), Frank is struck by how much government is involved with his everyday life. He resolves to get a better understanding of the various governments affecting him and to work on ensuring that they are serving his needs.

Who Are You Going To Call?

The best starting point for Frank — and you — is to know **where** you are from, "governmentally speaking" and to know **who** your main contacts are and **how** to reach them if you have problems or concerns relating to any level of government. Make up your own special Government Directory using the form on the following page. It may take you a few minutes to track down all of the information you need, but completing this list is your first step in taking responsibility for your relationship with government.

Your Guide to Government Directory

A: MUNICIPAL

1. Name of your municipality   _____

2. Head of municipal council   _____

3. Councillors from your area
   (if elected by wards)   _____

4. Clerk or CAO of municipality   _____

5. Treasurer of municipality   _____

6. Phone # of municipal office   _____

7. Phone # of school board office   _____

8. Director of Education   _____

9. School trustee for your area   _____

10. School principal (if applicable)   _____

B: PROVINCIAL

11. Name of provincial member   _____

12. What political party?   _____

13. Phone # of riding office   _____

14. Location of riding office   _____

C: FEDERAL

15. Name of federal member   _____

16. What political party?   _____

17. Phone # of riding office   _____

18. Location of riding office   _____

Concluding Observations

So far, so good. You now have a general grasp of the various levels of government in Canada, how they are organized in terms of basic governing machinery, and the kinds of services they provide. These governments exist to give us a vehicle through which we can identify and address our collective concerns as Canadians. Human wants and needs are always greater than the resources available to satisfy them. As a result, difficult allocation decisions must be made, decisions about who gets what, when, and how.[5] In democratic societies, it is elected governments that are authorized to make these decisions, subject to the continuing approval of the public in periodic elections. How well our governments fulfil this role is a matter for your personal assessment, but the ensuing chapters will provide you with additional background on which to base that judgment.

Before we take a closer look at the actual functioning of our government systems, however, it is useful to understand more fully how and why responsibilities and power have been shifting back and forth between the various levels of government in Canada. Any such examination directs attention to the constitutional division of power which, in turn, raises questions about Canada's constitution and why we are apparently obsessed with an unsuccessful quest for its amendment. These issues form the basis for the next two chapters in the Guide.

---

[5]Harold Lasswell, *Politics: Who Gets What, When and How*, New York, McGraw-Hill, 1936.

The Last Word

Definition of Terms and Concepts

At Large Elections: [Also known as General Vote elections]
Candidates for office run over the entire municipality and all voters in that municipality choose from among all the candidates — in contrast to ward elections, described below.

Bicameral Legislature:
A legislature with two houses of parliament, an upper chamber and a lower chamber — as in the case of Canada's Parliament.

CAO (Chief Administrative Officer):
The senior coordinating officer who heads up the public service in municipalities which use this system.

Cabinet:
A committee of ministers chosen by the Prime Minister (or Premier) to lead and coordinate the activities of government.

Civil Service:
The employees of the government (at all levels), who are responsible for implementing the decisions of government, administering the laws, delivering the programs and services, and looking after day-to-day operations.

Federation:
A government system in which powers are divided between two or more levels: a national government and provinces or states.

Governor General:
The representative of the Queen, who acts on her behalf as the Head of State for Canada when she is not in this country.

House of Commons:
The lower house in Canada's bicameral Parliament, a body whose members are elected by Canadians from ridings across Canada.

Legislative Assembly:
The provincial equivalent of the federal House of Commons, whose members are elected from ridings across the province.

Lieutenant Governor:
The provincial equivalent of the Governor General with respect to acting as the Queen's representative in the province. The Lieutenant Governor also represents the federal government.

Ministerial Responsibility:
The principle that a minister is responsible for the actions taken by those in the department of government which he or she heads.

Municipal Council:
The governing body elected to exercise the powers granted to a municipality.

Premier:
The head of government for a province, who attains this position (normally) by virtue of being leader of the political party which captures the most seats in the Legislative Assembly in a provincial election.

Prime Minister:
The federal equivalent of a Premier, who attains his or her position in exactly the same way.

Representative Government:
The election of members to represent and make decisions on behalf of the larger population. This principle is reflected in the election of the House of Commons at the federal level, of legislative assemblies at the provincial and territorial level, and of municipal councils at the local level.

Responsible Government:
The principle that the executive branch of government is responsible to, and must be supported by, the legislative branch. More specifically, this principle means that the Cabinet can only continue governing as long as it is supported by a majority of elected members in the Commons or Provincial Assembly.

Senate:
The upper House in the Canadian Parliament, consisting of 104 appointed members.

Unicameral Legislature:
Term to describe a legislature which has only one House, such as is found in all provinces today. In contrast, a bicameral legislature like the Canadian Parliament has two Houses: a House of Commons and a Senate.

Ward Elections:
This occurs when a municipality is divided into geographic areas or wards, with candidates running for office from within these wards rather than over the whole municipality. The latter arrangement is known as election at large or by general vote.

Points to Ponder

1. How long did it take you to compile your *Guide to Government Directory*? With which level of government were you most familiar when you began working on your Directory?

2. Do you now understand how the same voters (including you) elect different members (usually from areas with differing geographic boundaries) to make up governing bodies at the municipal, provincial and federal levels?

3. Try re-enacting the adventures of our student in the "Who Does What" section of this lesson (leaving out the fanciful nightmare). In other words, try to keep track of your activities for one day, noting how many times you come in contact with services, activities or regulations provided by one of our levels of government. The resulting list should help to demonstrate why you need to know more about government.

For Further Reading

A number of short and readable articles on the executive and legislative branches are found in Paul Fox and Graham White, *Politics: Canada*, 8th edition, Whitby, McGraw-Hill Ryerson Limited, 1995, or any of the earlier editions edited by Paul Fox.

A good introduction to the basic machinery and operating principles of government is found in W. White, R. Wagenberg and R. Nelson, *Introduction to Canadian Politics and Government*, 6th edition, Toronto, Harcourt Brace & Company, 1994, Chapter 1. See also James John Guy, *How We Are Governed*, Toronto, Harcourt Brace & Company, Canada, 1995, Chapter 1, for an introductory discussion of various roles of government.

A number of readings on more detailed aspects of the various levels of government will be found at the end of Chapters 5 and 6, which explore these governments in more depth.

Chapter 3

Who's on First?
Intergovernmental Relations in Canada

Objectives and Highlights

♦ To explain the shift from federal to provincial dominance.

♦ To debate the merits of a strong federal government versus strong provinces.

♦ To examine provincial-municipal relations and to assess the impact of recent disentanglement initiatives.

Comics Abbott and Costello had a classic baseball routine entitled *"Who's on First,"* a conversation about names and positions which moved quickly into total confusion and hilarity. Much the same might be said of efforts to describe intergovernmental relations in Canada!

This chapter attempts to bring some clarity and order to this subject by outlining the original division of powers under the constitution and then tracing the main changes in the federal-provincial relationship over the past 130 years. It reveals a striking shift in the balance of power, from a dominant national level to increasingly assertive provinces. It examines the "fend-for-yourself" federalism that has been evolving, with each level attempting to deal with its debt problems by passing the buck to the next level down. Against this background, the chapter explores the main arguments typically advanced in favour of a strong national government and in favour of provinces.

Provincial-local relations are also examined, along with the many parallels between this relationship and that found at the federal-provincial level. While efforts to disentangle and to reduce the overlap between the provincial and local level sound attractive, some cautionary comments are offered about this approach.

Introduction

A s we saw in Chapter 2, Canadians have no shortage of governments supposedly attending to their needs. The result is a complex and confusing picture. It doesn't help that the governments often hide behind each other in trying to evade responsibility for unpopular or controversial situations.

A story which has made the rounds for twenty years or more concerns the "International Conference on the Elephant" — an event to which learned scholars were invited to present a research paper on some aspect of the elephant. The highlights of the Conference featured four papers, from Britain, France, the United States and Canada. They were entitled as follows:

Britain: *The Elephant and the Empire*

France: *The Sex Life of the Elephant*

U.S.:   *How to Build Bigger and Better Elephants*

Canada: *Elephants: A Federal or Provincial Responsibility?*

That says it all. Whatever the issue, Canada usually manages to reduce it to a squabble over jurisdiction. It wasn't supposed to be this way. Sir John A. Macdonald, Canada's first Prime Minister and one of the chief architects of the governing arrangements for the new country, thought that he had allocated powers in such a way that the national level would clearly dominate. Instead, we approach the 21st century with the national government reducing its role and provincial governments increasingly asserting their claims for expanded jurisdiction. What happened to Sir John's plan and what is happening to our federal system? What are the merits of a strong national government and what are the merits of a stronger role for provinces? To answer these questions is the purpose of this chapter.

Shifts in the Federal-Provincial Relationship

The story of the creation of the "Dominion of Canada" is familiar to most people, if only from their high school history classes. The challenge was how to establish a new country out of the separate colonies which then existed — Upper Canada or Canada West (Ontario), Lower Canada or Canada East (Québec), New Brunswick and Nova Scotia. All of the colonies were insistent on maintaining their separate identities and existence in whatever new governing structure might be formed. The solution agreed upon was the establishment of a federal state or federation. This simply means the bringing together of a number of different political communities with a common government for common purposes and separate "state" or "provincial" governments for the particular purposes of each community.[1]

Sir John A. Macdonald reluctantly accepted the idea of a federal system as the price necessary to create the new country. But he also made every effort to create a federation in which the national government was clearly the dominant level. The fact that the discussions leading up to the creation of Canada took place as civil war raged across the border in the United States certainly made an impact. The United States Constitution had attempted to provide for a strong level of state governments. The states had been given all *"residual powers,"* that is, all powers not otherwise specifically assigned to the national or state level. The civil war was being fought over state rights, over which level of government in the United States would predominate. Not surprisingly, the Fathers of Confederation (led by Macdonald) took the view that Canada should avoid any such catastrophe by establishing a federal system in which the national level would clearly prevail.

As we will see, however, Sir John would have been wise to heed the advice of his fellow Scot (and fellow drinker), Robbie Burns who observed that "the best laid plans o' mice and men gang oft aglee" — that is, that plans "often go astray." To see what happened, read on.

---

[1] Eugene Forsey, *How Canadians Govern Themselves*, 3rd Edition, Ottawa, Ministry of Supply and Services, 1991, p. 7.

The Division of Powers

The division of powers for the new federal system was set out in the British North America Act of 1867,[2] particularly in Sections 91 and 92 which outlined the main powers of the national and provincial levels, respectively.

The national government was given (among other matters):

a) a blanket power to make laws for the "peace, order and good government of Canada."

b) 29 examples (later increased to 31 through constitutional amendment) of this blanket power in the form of specific areas of responsibility. These included what were regarded as the most important responsibilities of government, including such areas as money and banking, defence, navigation and shipping, regulation of trade and commerce and criminal law.

c) unlimited taxing power.

d) all residual power — that is, anything "left over" and not otherwise specifically assigned.

e) the power (exercised through the office of Lieutenant Governor in each province) to reserve any provincial bill for consideration by the national government.

f) the power to disallow any provincial act up to one year after its passage.

In contrast, the B.N.A. Act limited the provinces to:

a) 16 specific responsibilities which were then regarded as being of a local or minor nature. These included such matters as municipal institutions, hospitals, and reform schools.

b) direct taxation powers only.

---

[2]This Act was subsequently incorporated within the Constitution Act of 1982, as discussed in the next chapter.

Initial Federal Domination

Sir John A. Macdonald took full advantage of this one-sided division of powers and the national level dominated from 1867 until the closing years of the 19th century. In part, this domination stemmed from the leadership and sense of national vision provided by Sir John A. The railway was extended westward, to link Canada "from sea to sea," immigration policies populated the newly opened western territory, and tariff policies encouraged those in the west and east to buy the products produced by the manufacturing sector which was concentrated in Central Canada. Federal dominance was also reinforced by frequent use of the powers of *disallowance* and *reservation*.

Inevitably, of course, the provincial governments began to assert their rights and to demand that the national government exercise more restraint, especially with respect to the use of the powers of reservation and disallowance. They received support from a series of decisions by the Judicial Committee of the British Privy Council (which was then the final court of law for Canada). These decisions had the effect of restricting the scope of the national government while broadening the scope of the provinces.

It was during the "Roaring Twenties," however, that provincial governments enjoyed their first major expansion in power and importance. By this time, more than 50 years after Confederation, it was becoming apparent that a number of the powers given to the provinces were going to be among the most important responsibilities of government in the 20th century. While earlier economic growth had been stimulated by such national initiatives as railway construction and immigration, the 1920s saw the expansion of highways and the development of mineral wealth — both matters under provincial jurisdiction. In addition, this period saw increased provincial (and municipal) expenditures on education and public welfare.

The provincial momentum was short-lived, however, and various events conspired to promote a resurgence of national domination over the next 30 years. The main influences were:

a) the Depression of the 1930s, which reduced several provinces to near bankruptcy and led the national government to assume a substantial responsibility for relief payments (welfare).

b) the Second World War, in which the extreme centralization of activities brought Canada close to being a unitary state. By the end of the war in 1945, the national government accounted for 82% of all government spending, with the provinces and local governments each spending roughly half of the rest.

c) the post-war management of the economy, which called for national government actions with respect to the promotion of employment, economic growth and stable prices. By this time, most western nations had embraced *"Keynesian economics,"*[3] which was based on the use of government taxing and spending policies (and complementary monetary policies through the banking system) to offset fluctuations in the economy and ensure growth and prosperity.

Post-war Management of the Economy

There were also other factors at work in this post-war period. The national government had built up a highly qualified group of civil servants during the war years and that gave it some extra credibility and "clout" for a time. Beginning during the war years, there had been considerable centralization of finances. The details need not concern us here, but essentially the provinces — in return for substantially enlarged grants from the national level — stayed out of the three major tax fields of corporate tax, income tax and succession duties. This arrangement was intended to ensure better coordination of these tax fields (since both levels of government had been active in them) and to make easier the pursuit of Keynesian economics by the national government.

Another major factor at this time was the expanded use of what became known as the *"federal spending power."* This is the power of the national government to make payments to people or institutions or governments for purposes for which it does not necessarily have

---

[3]So-called because it was based on the writings of British economist John Maynard Keynes.

the power to legislate. During the period of economic growth and prosperity that followed the Second World War, it seemed appropriate that the national government should use its powers to tax wealth wherever it might be concentrated in Canada and then to redistribute that wealth for the benefit of all by supporting various programs. By the 1960s, approximately one-third of the expenditures of the national government were largely based on this federal spending power — for such areas as family allowances, Canada Pension Plan, Old Age Security, Unemployment Insurance, Hospital Insurance, higher education, equalization payments, and regional economic development grants and subsidies.

Many of these areas have been in the news in recent years. In most cases, they have become "an item" because the national government has withdrawn or reduced its financial commitment to these programs, or is contemplating such action. This curtailment of the federal spending power reflects the greatly reduced role which the national government has accepted (and has had forced upon it) in more recent times. What happened to the national dominance which seemed so enduring during the 1930s through the 1950s?

Pendulum Swings to Provinces

To some extent, it was a case of the pendulum having swung so far one way that it inevitably had to swing back (that's why it's called a pendulum). Among the factors contributing to this reversal were the following:

a) Post-war urbanization triggered a big increase in spending by provinces (and their municipalities), putting them in a "revenue squeeze." This led the provinces to demand more grant money from Ottawa or a greater proportion of the three tax fields which had been rented out to, or shared with, Ottawa since the Second World War.

b) As provinces developed highly qualified public services of their own, they were less inclined to defer to the expertise of the national public service.

c) The long period of national dominance had featured Liberal Governments in Ottawa; in fact, the Liberals were in power for 22 consecutive years from 1935 to 1957. John Diefenbaker's upset election victory in 1957 was partly based on an appeal to the "forgotten regions" outside of Central Canada and a promise to pay more attention to provincial rights. It would be 1968 before a Liberal Government again enjoyed a majority in Ottawa, and by then a number of factors made it impossible to resume the old, centralist ways.

d) One of those factors was a marked shift in the position and demands of Québec after 1960. That year saw the election of a Liberal Government under Jean Lesage which introduced a wide range of reforms to modernize Québec society. These reforms were very expensive and the provincial Liberals put increasing pressure on Ottawa for a greater share of the tax fields — demanding what became known as more *"tax room."*

e) Québec's demands fell on responsive ears when the Liberals returned to power in Ottawa with a minority government in 1963. Under Lester Pearson's leadership, the national government presided over an era which became known as *cooperative federalism.* It has been praised for demonstrating the flexibility of federalism, thereby undermining (at the time) the separatist threat in Québec. It has also been condemned for making too many concessions to the provinces, thereby undermining the role of the national government.

f) While the issue of Québec separation has never been far below the surface in the intervening years, it should be noted that there have also been rumblings from other parts of the country as well. Western provinces expressed dissatisfaction with a number of policies of the national government and decried Ottawa's failure to understand the needs of the west. Some organizations advocating western separation appeared and disappeared. At least some of the strong western support for the Reform Party is essentially a western protest vote. Maritime Union has also been discussed from time to time, although the Atlantic provinces have tended to be the most supportive of a strong role for the national government because of their reliance on financial assistance from Ottawa.

g) By the 1980s, there was a general feeling of discontent with the size and prominence of the national government and a fairly widespread viewpoint that further decentralization of power would be beneficial. This view was consistent with the right wing and somewhat anti-government sentiment which had become pronounced by this point in countries such as Britain (under Margaret Thatcher) and the United States (under Ronald Reagan). If "getting government off the backs of people" was the objective, the next best thing was to shift the responsibility for decision making by government as close to the people as possible. By this reasoning, a shift of powers from the national to the provincial level was a step in the right direction.

h) As the 1980s unfolded, even the national government seemed willing to accept (or to promote) a reduction in its role. This was evident in the positions which had been taken by the governments of both Joe Clark and Brian Mulroney. In the case of the latter, Ottawa agreed to some decentralization of powers in unsuccessful attempts to amend the constitution of Canada through the Meech and then the Charlottetown Accords, both discussed later in this Guide.

Perhaps more surprisingly, the Liberal Government in office since 1993 has also shown a willingness to accept a reduced national role. To some extent, the motivation is again one of hoping to placate the provinces (and especially Québec) by offering them greater jurisdiction in such areas as employment training, mines, forestry, tourism and recreation. In addition, however, the national government is now motivated by its desire to reduce its expenditures and bring its deficit and debt load under control. As mentioned earlier, much of the national expenditure has been on the exercise of the federal spending power, which has been criticized as allowing too much federal encroachment into areas of provincial jurisdiction. Ottawa's position almost seems to be:

"Since our support for these programs isn't wanted, and we can't afford it anyway, we'll withdraw that support."

Passing the Buck:
Changes in Federal-Provincial Financial Relations

From the time of Confederation, there has seldom been a very good balance between the expenditure commitments of a level of government and the revenues available to it. Because it was believed that the national government had been given all of the important powers, it also received unlimited taxing powers, whereas the provinces were limited to direct taxation.[4] As the provinces gradually expanded their responsibilities, their expenditures inevitably increased beyond the level which had been anticipated. This change became particularly apparent during the 1920s, when provincial and municipal expenditures increased at more than five times the national rate annually.

By this time, the national government was providing various subsidies to the provinces, including some conditional grants which had first been introduced in 1912. It was also providing special subsidies to the Maritime provinces in recognition of the economic disparities in this region. By this time as well, both the national and provincial governments were levying corporate and income taxes, with the national government having imposed the latter tax in 1917 **as a temporary measure** to finance the First World War.

This problems with this "double taxation" became particularly apparent when the Great Depression hit in the following decade. One response, first introduced during World War II, was a series of *five year agreements* covering how the national and provincial government would share the fields of corporate tax, income tax and succession duties. However, as the provinces (and municipalities) increased

---

[4]The distinction is that a direct tax is levied upon the person expected to pay it, whereas an indirect tax is levied with the expectation that it will be passed on to a third party. A good example of an indirect tax is a wholesale tax which is absorbed and becomes part of the final price for a product paid by the consumer.

Tax Sharing
Agreements

their expenditures in response to the rapid urbanization following the war, there was continued pressure on the national government to increase the provincial share, to give the provinces more tax room.

By the late 1970s, the tax sharing and coordination effectively ended. The national government indicated that in setting its own rates it would "take account of" provincial rates. But the provinces became responsible for setting their own rates to meet their expenditure needs. In effect, the national government told the provinces that they should increase their tax levels (and accept the political responsibility for so doing) rather than expect the national level to forego its revenues by levying less tax to make more room for the provinces.

Throughout this postwar period, a number of national government grants to the provinces had also developed. These can be briefly summarized as follows:

a) Federal payments to share in the costs of hospital care.

b) Federal payments to share in the cost of physicians' services.

c) Federal payments in support of post-secondary education.

d) The Canada Assistance Program (*CAP*) to support the cost of, and bring more standardization to, widely varied provincial social programs.

e) Equalization payments provided to the provinces with weaker tax bases so that they could provide services at an adequate level without imposing excessively high levels of taxation.

In 1977 the national government replaced the first three grant programs with something called *EPF* or Established Program Financing. The latter was a block grant which was essentially unconditional in nature — except that there were requirements relating to access in health care (which later became a major issue) and to non-discrimination in education.

The new arrangements were less satisfactory than the national government had hoped. Its financial commitment continued to grow, but provinces took advantage of the relatively unconditional nature of the payments and used some of the money for priorities other than health and education. In response, the national government passed the Canada Health Act in 1984, with its financial penalty for provinces allowing extra-billing or user charges by hospitals — as discussed in Chapter 11.

The following year saw the first in what has become an ongoing series of cuts in federal transfers to the provinces as part of the national deficit reduction efforts. By 1990-1991 a two year freeze on payments under EPF was introduced, and then extended through to the end of 1994-95.[5] A similar pattern occurred with the Canada Assistance Plan. A 5% "cap" on the growth of Canada Assistance Plan payments to the "have" provinces of Ontario, British Columbia and Alberta was introduced in 1990-91 and then extended through 1994-95. With this cap in place, payments to those three provinces did not keep pace with the increase in welfare costs associated with the prolonged recession in the early 1990s. While the national government had been paying 50% of the Canada Assistance Plan costs, the result of the cap is that this proportion fell to 47% for Alberta, 37% for British Columbia and 28% for Ontario.

Further major changes have been introduced by the federal Liberals since they assumed office in October 1993. Both EPF and the Canada Assistance Plan have been replaced, effective the 1996-97 fiscal year, with a new Canada Health and Social Transfer (*CHST*). It is a block fund, like the EPF which it replaces. It will also be substantially reduced in amount, by some $7 billion over the period from 1996-98.

---

[5]The Ontario Government estimated that the total revenue loss to all provinces resulting from the changes to the EPF formula amounted to $33.6 billion, according to Paul Hobson, "Current Issues in Federal-Provincial Fiscal Relations," in Ronald Watts and Doug Brown (eds.), *Canada: The State of the Federation, 1993,* Queen's University, 1993, p. 181.

Leaks in the "Watertight Compartments"

Underlying the shifts in the balance of power between the federal and provincial levels, there has also been a growing overlap in activities, a growing encroachment by one level into the sphere of the other. This has happened in spite of the best intentions of the framers of the constitution who thought that they had so clearly divided the responsibilities of government that they were sealed in watertight compartments. Instead, a great deal of seepage has occurred over the years.

According to Stevenson, the only areas of exclusive federal jurisdiction appear to be military defence, veterans' affairs, Indian affairs and monetary policy; and provinces only have exclusive jurisdiction for municipal institutions, elementary and secondary education, and some areas of law related to property and to non-criminal matters.[6]

The provincial governments claim that the overlapping of government activity has occurred because of federal encroachment into their fields, and in this regard we have already noted the use of the federal spending power with respect to social programs. But it should also be recognized that provinces have intruded into a number of areas of federal jurisdiction.[7] Most larger provinces are active in the field of international trade and commerce, have departments dedicated to that field and have trade missions in foreign capitals. The larger provinces also assert their right to deal directly with foreign governments on a variety of issues. Provinces such as Newfoundland and British Columbia have been active in fisheries, which is an area of federal jurisdiction. Western provinces and Québec have moved into the federal jurisdiction over "Indians and land reserved for Indians." Ontario and Québec are actively involved in television broadcasting, for which they claim jurisdiction because of the educational nature of the

---

[6]Garth Stevenson, "Federalism and Intergovernmental Relations," in Michael Whittington and Glen Williams (eds.), *Canadian Politics in the 1990s*, 4th edition, Toronto, Nelson Canada, 1995, p. 410.

[7]The examples which follow are from Garth Stevenson, "The Division of Powers," in R. D. Olling and M. M. Westmacott (eds.), *Perspectives on Canadian Federalism*, Scarborough, Prentice-Hall Canada Inc., 1988, p. 44.

programs, even though broadcasting was placed under federal jurisdiction by court ruling in 1932.

We should also be careful not to assume that areas of overlap are
automatically problem areas. Overlap, in which two governments are
involved in the same field, is not necessarily the same as duplication,
in which two governments are doing the same thing in the same field.
Overlap also does not necessarily mean conflict. It can lead to beneficial collaboration and coordination. Indeed, it can be argued that
overlap is preferable to watertight compartments (completely separate
jurisdictions) as a way to govern because it provides some flexibility,
encourages a variety of approaches through comparison and competition and avoids a monopoly situation.

Draining the Watertight Compartments: Which Way Will the Water Flow?

Even those who might agree with the desirability of reducing overlap
and clarifying the division of responsibilities between the federal and
provincial governments worry about the end result of any such redefi-
nition. The prevailing forces in the country appear to favour decentralization as the means of reducing overlap. Shifting powers from the
federal level to the provinces would appear to meet the federal objective of reducing its financial obligations and the provincial objective
(especially of provinces like Québec) of gaining increased jurisdiction.

◆ *Something to Think About*

But what are the implications for Canada of such a shift? What are
the arguments for reasserting a strong role for the federal government
versus strengthening the provincial level?

The Case for a Strong National Government

One of the most forceful and best known proponents of a strong
national government is former Prime Minister Pierre Trudeau. At a
Montreal news conference in March 1990, he offered this challenge:

"Canadians have to make up their minds. Do they want a loose confederation of provinces, that exists courtesy of the provincial governments — or do they want a real country with a real government?"

Advocates of a strong national government believe that it is the only institution capable of asserting and protecting the national interest.[8] They reject the notion that the sum total of the various separate provincial interests can somehow be added up and combined to form a national interest. They contend that Canada is a national community defined by the Charter, not a variety of distinct communities and cultures with their own collective rights which clash with the individual rights guaranteed to all Canadians by the Charter.

Proponents of a strong national government also see it as an essential vehicle for ensuring minimum standards of service in areas which help to define us as Canadians. They point to the marked disparities in economic health and income levels among the regions of Canada and argue that only a strong national government is in a position to tax the wealth wherever it may be concentrated in Canada, and then to redistribute it to where it is most needed. They reject the notion that desired national standards could somehow be achieved through interprovincial cooperation, pointing to the failure of the provinces even to eliminate the costly internal trade barriers which currently inhibit the free movement of goods and services in Canada.

Those backing a strong national government concede that it must do a better job of articulating and accommodating provincial and regional interests. They acknowledge the need for reform of national institutions like the Senate, which was originally designed precisely for the purpose of representing and protecting regional interests within the new country of Canada. They even acknowledge that flexibility is needed to respond to the different needs of different provinces and concede that, to allow these arrangements, *asymmetrical federalism*

---

[8]The arguments which follow are partly based on M. M. Westmacott, "Conflicting Constitutional Visions: Is There a Case for a Strong National Government?" in Mark Charlton and Paul Barker (eds.), *Crosscurrents: Contemporary Political Issues*, 2nd edition, Toronto, Nelson Canada, 1994, pp. 117-123.

may be necessary.[9] But they insist that the federal government should retain an over-riding constitutional authority to assert the national interest and that there should be no limits placed on the use of the federal spending power in support of such interests.

The Case for Strong Provinces

Defenders of the role of the provinces start by noting that the reference to "levels" of government (such as is found throughout this Guide) improperly implies some sort of superior-subordinate relationship. Instead, they argue that what we have is two "orders" of government, each with its own constitutional sphere of authority.[10] They contend that the national interest should not be defined and/or imposed by the federal government; rather, it should emerge as a result of intergovernmental negotiations. They claim that provinces have shown themselves able to work together effectively. To those critical of provincial trade barriers, for example, they point to the June 1994 agreement to reform government procurement practices, to introduce a code of conduct to prevent provinces "poaching" investment from each other, and to increase labour mobility between provinces.[11]

Provinces should play a prominent role, it is argued, because they have demonstrated a great deal of innovation and creativity, often stimulating the adoption of their approaches in other jurisdictions. Examples include the introduction of Medicare in Saskatchewan, the Québec Pension Plan, New Brunswick's introduction of the Ombudsman, the first condominium legislation from British Columbia and the

---

[9]This cumbersome term is used to describe a federal system which would not have an identical relationship between the federal government and every province. Instead of that "symmetry," bilateral agreements would give some provinces different arrangements (such as greater decentralization of powers) than others — resulting in an asymmetrical federalism.

[10]The arguments in this section are partly based on R. A. Young, "What is Good About Provincial Governments," in Charlton and Barker, *op. cit.*, pp. 124-136.

[11]Christopher Dunn, *Canadian Political Debates*, Toronto, McClelland & Stewart Inc., 1995, p. 136.

first law protecting historic sites in Québec.[12] Having a strong level of provincial governments, proponents claim, provides more outlets for experimentation and innovation, for comparisons and competitive pressures — all forces which contribute to better government. Moreover, if there are mistakes made, their impact is more limited in a provincial laboratory than had the flawed program been Canada-wide.

It is conceded that competition amongst the provinces can also become harmful and destructive, that it can lead to a "race to the bottom," in which — for example — provinces keep reducing environmental regulations or "rights of workers" legislation in an attempt to make their jurisdiction more attractive to business. But those favouring strong provinces point out that a dominant federal government which promotes centralized conformity to the lowest common denominator is also harmful. Such an arrangement results in the imposition of central standards which are unlikely to match the varying needs and preferences of different parts of the country.

Even those supporting strong provinces see a continued important role for the federal government. It must provide those public goods which provincial governments have little incentive to provide and those goods for which economies of scale are possible from delivery over the whole country. It must bring together and accommodate regional interests on truly national questions and it must act as a referee in cases of destructive interprovincial competition. It must "build the fundamental commonalities of Canadian citizenship."[13] But it should learn to play a more modest, limited role. It should gather and disseminate information as a way of promoting better public policy rather than trying to dictate policy on its terms. For example, comparative information on the standards and levels of service which exist in the various provinces would alert citizens to resist efforts by a province trying to downgrade services.

Both points of view have merit and deserve careful study. If we are facing a diminished role by government within our lives, it may still be important which level of government carries out that reduced

---

[12]*Ibid.*, p. 128.

[13]*Ibid.*, p. 130.

role. The implications of this choice will become more evident when we examine particular policy fields in later chapters.

Municipalities in the Canadian Federation

Intergovernmental relations in Canada involve more than the federal-provincial relationship. There have also been shifts and pendulum swings in the relationship between municipalities and the senior levels of government. There are, however, some fundamental differences in the nature of these relationships which should be noted at the outset.

Notwithstanding the best efforts of Sir John A. to establish a dominant national level, the relationship between the federal and provincial governments is essentially one between two equals. Each level of government has a guaranteed right to exist under the constitution of Canada, and each has a number of responsibilities specifically assigned to it. Neither level can abolish the other. In contrast, the relationship between municipal and provincial governments is completely different in law. The two levels are not equal; municipalities are in a distinctly subordinate position. Their existence is not guaranteed by the constitution. Nor are they given any specific powers under the constitution. They are only mentioned in the constitution as one of the powers given to the provinces. As a result, they only exist and have structures, functions and finances to the extent that provincial governments see fit to provide for them. Legally, a provincial government could pass a law abolishing all of the municipalities within its jurisdiction — although there are solid practical and political reasons why it would not do so.

Parallels in Provincial-Local Relations

In spite of these very significant differences, the way in which the provincial-municipal relationship has evolved offers some striking similarities to the federal-provincial relationship.

◆ Just as the provinces were expected to play a minor role in the new country of Canada, municipalities were expected to provide only a limited range of local services, mostly related to property.

◆ Just as the provinces were not expected to need significant revenue sources, it was assumed that the tax on real property would be adequate to meet municipal revenue needs.

◆ Just as the responsibilities given to the provinces became increasingly important in the 20th century, so too did the responsibilities given to municipalities — especially by the time of the rapid urbanization following the Second World War.

◆ Just as the national government responded to the provincial revenue shortfall with a number of conditional grants and shared cost programs (under the umbrella of the federal spending power discussed earlier), the provinces responded to municipal revenue needs by offering a variety of conditional grants. As a result, municipalities found themselves intertwined with provincial administrations, and correspondingly limited in their freedom to set local priorities. Provinces turned a deaf ear to these municipal concerns, even as they made exactly the same complaints to the national level about the way federal conditional grants were limiting provincial operating freedom.

The parallels have continued throughout the 1990s. As we have seen, financial restraint efforts of the federal government have led to cuts in the transfer payments made to the provinces. To "soften the blow," the payments are being made unconditional — as with the new Canada Health and Social Transfer — so that the provinces will at least have more freedom as to how they spend less money. In exactly the same fashion, provinces are responding to their financial problems by cutting grants to municipalities but offering them the reduced funds on an unconditional basis. The Klein Government in Alberta, for example, introduced in 1994 a new unconditional grant and rolled into it a number of the existing conditional grant programs (relating to areas such as parks, public transit, policing and family support services). It projected that the unconditional payments would decrease from $166 million in 1994/95 to $126 million the next year and to

$88 million in 1996/97.[14] In a strikingly similar move, the Harris Government in Ontario announced in late 1995 that the existing roads grant would be lumped with other existing unconditional grants into a new block fund, the Ontario Municipal Support Grant (*MSG*), and that it would be reduced in amount by 47% over the next two years. A number of other grants to municipalities and local boards were also cut or phased out.[15]

For a time in the 1980s, it appeared that the provinces would also follow the example of the national government and try to deal with some of their financial problems by downloading responsibilities and costs on municipalities. Examples of this trend cited by municipalities in Ontario included recycling and "blue box" programs, court-room security, and new initiatives on transit for the disabled.[16]

Is Disentanglement the Answer?

In recent years, however, more attention has been paid to the concept of "*disentanglement.*" It addresses the extensive overlap of provincial and municipal responsibilities and activities and seeks to reduce that overlap. On the surface, it seems similar to federal-provincial efforts to drain the flooded watertight compartments found at those levels. But there are also some important differences.

The idea, in oversimplified terms, is that municipalities should retain responsibility for local functions and the province should have responsibility for matters of province-wide concern or matters which are income-redistributive such as health and social services. Since the functions retained by municipalities will be local in nature, there will be less need for provincial intervention on the grounds of protecting

---

[14]Alberta Municipal Affairs, *News Release*, February 24, 1994.

[15]See Association of Municipal Clerks and Treasurers, *Municipal Administration Program*, Mississauga, AMCTO, Unit Three, Revised 1996, Lesson 3.

[16]These and other examples were given by the Association of Municipalities of Ontario and reported in *Municipal World*, St. Thomas, July 1990, p.3.

some provincial interest. Proponents of disentanglement contend that it will result in a simpler and more streamlined system, leading to cost-savings and a more understandable and accountable arrangement for the public.

◆ Something to Think About

Given their desire to avoid tax increases, many municipal councillors have responded positively to past disentanglement initiatives. Some have seen the process as an opportunity to get rid of what are regarded as troublesome responsibilities like welfare.

The general public also find appealing the prospect of a simplified division of powers, less overlap and improved accountability.

But is disentanglement really beneficial for municipalities or their citizens?

Andrew Sancton has pointed out that this process inevitably means a narrower range of municipal functions. He is critical of the underlying rationale that municipal governments should focus on those matters which are inherently local. In his words:

> To base municipal government's existence on a mission to concern itself with inherently local issues is to insure its quick death. Does anyone believe that there are *any* issues which are still inherently local?[17]

Too much of the discussion about disentanglement seems over-preoccupied with administrative tidiness. The focus on who should deliver what services tends to overlook the fact that municipalities are more than a vehicle for service delivery.[18] They are a political mechanism through which local citizens in a defined area can express their collective concerns and objectives. Because that is, or should be, the

[17]Andrew Sancton, "Provincial-Municipal Disentanglement in Ontario: A Dissent," in *Municipal World*, July 1992, p. 23.

[18]The discussion which follows is from C. Richard Tindal and Susan Nobes Tindal, *Local Government in Canada*, 4th edition, Whitby, McGraw-Hill Ryerson Limited, p. 207.

case, it is important that municipalities be involved in as many areas as possible that are of interest and concern to the local community. This means expanding, not reducing, their sphere of influence. It means becoming or staying involved in areas in which municipalities cannot expect to be free of some provincial overlap or interference. As Sancton points out: "If municipal politicians are not interested in *all* government policies that affect their community, they can hardly complain if many in the community are not interested in municipal government."[19]

Studies to reallocate responsibilities between the provincial and local level have been carried out in a number of provinces over the past three decades, but the only substantial action until recently has been in New Brunswick. In 1967 the New Brunswick government took over responsibility for the administration of justice, welfare and public health, and also financial responsibility for the provision of education. Property assessment and municipal tax collection also became provincial responsibilities. While these changes addressed some pressing servicing problems, they also raised doubts about the future strength and viability of municipal government.[20]

These concerns have been a recurring feature of other disentanglement exercises as well. The end result usually involves some loss of powers from the municipal level to the province.

♦ Reforms in Québec centred on greatly increased provincial funding of the costs of education.

♦ A Nova Scotia discussion paper released at the end of 1993 called for the province to assume complete responsibility from local governments with respect to social assistance and the work of local boards of health. In return, municipalities would be given responsibility for defined local roads and local police services.

♦ Rather similar changes were pursued as part of a disentanglement

---

[19]Sancton, *op. cit.*, p. 24.

[20]Tindal and Tindal, *op. cit.*, p. 205. The New Brunswick reforms are discussed in Chapter 5 and 7 of this text, along with a more general analysis of disentanglement.

exercise conducted by Ontario in the early 1990s. The province offered to take over the municipal share of the cost of general welfare assistance. In return, to maintain the "fiscal neutrality" which was to characterize the exercise, municipalities were to assume responsibility for some provincial highways and to pay for the property assessment services provided by the province. A draft agreement was reached, but then abandoned, in early 1993.

At the beginning of 1997 the Ontario Government introduced a new disentanglement initiative of extraordinary breadth and complexity. It followed from the work of a *Who Does What* panel, chaired by David Crombie, although the Government's proposals did not follow the panel's recommendations in several instances. Leading the list of announced changes will be provincial assumption of greater responsibility for elementary and secondary education, along with the more than $5 billion in education financing which has been borne locally by residential property taxes. To offset these costs, municipalities will be responsible for providing services worth more than $5 billion annually for welfare, public health, care for the elderly, child care and public housing.[21]

Since municipalities also have to assume greater responsibility and financing (in some cases complete financing) with respect to services such as roads and public transit, sewer and water systems, libraries and policing, there are understandable concerns about the ultimate financial impact of these changes. Questions are also being raised about the appropriateness of shifting various social programs to the municipal level. The downloading of costs for social assistance is particularly troubling in this regard, and seems motivated more by the Government's need to offset its assumption of education costs than by any underlying rationale. It goes against the trend [22] which has

---

[21]Martin Mittelstaedt, "Municipalities get social services tab," *Globe and Mail*, January 15, 1997.

[22]Brian Wharf, "Social Services," in Richard A. Loreto and Trevor Price (eds.), *Urban Policy Issues: Canadian Perspectives*, Toronto, McClelland & Stewart Inc., 1990, p. 176.

seen this responsibility fully assumed by the provincial level in most provinces, including Saskatchewan, B.C. and Alberta in recent years. It also goes against the recommendations of a number of Ontario studies, including those of the *Who Does What* panel.

Initial indications are that the Ontario Government will also be retaining or increasing its supervision and control over many of these transferred services. If so, the result may be more one of re-entanglement than disentanglement, and a situation in which municipalities are faced with more pay but not more say. It is uncertainties such as these which suggest municipalities should approach with extreme caution the superficial attraction of disentanglement.

Searching for a new Balance

As Canada nears the 21st century, some fundamental changes have taken place in the distribution of powers and financial resources in its federal system. The long period of national domination is clearly over, and has been for some time. Even the financial superiority of the national level is long gone! Most provincial governments have made significant strides in bringing their financial houses back in order, and a number of them have registered balanced budgets in the past couple of years. Alberta even announced a $1 billion budget surplus in the spring of 1996. In contrast, the federal government has been operating with a deficit budget for more than 20 years.

With the use of the federal spending power sharply curtailed, it is unlikely that the federal government will launch major new national programs underwritten by substantial funding — even though the Liberals have been talking about a new program to combat child poverty as 1997 begins. With major cutbacks in federal payments to provinces, there are concerns that national standards in existing programs may not even be maintained. With widespread suggestions that federalism be "fixed" by shifting more powers to the provinces, it seems probable that the role and importance of the national government may be further diminished.

♦ *Something to Think About*

To the critics of the national government and of "big government" in general, all of these developments may seem desirable. But they certainly represent a vastly different federal system than Sir John A. had intended.

How do you feel about the declining role of the national government? If provinces step in to fill the vacuum created at the centre, how do you feel about having a country of even stronger provinces? Can the national interest of Canada be identified by taking the sum total of the various separate provincial interests, or do we still need that identification provided by a national government?

What if the provinces don't step into the vacuum, a distinct possibility since many of them seem preoccupied with the same cutback and downsizing mentality that has gripped the national government? If both of the senior levels continue to "pass the buck" downward — both literally and figuratively — what does this mean for municipalities? Will the level of government which has usually been regarded as the least important (if regarded at all) emerge as the most important level of government for the 21st century? The pendulum is unlikely to swing that far, but the re-allocation of responsibilities currently underway in Ontario, for example, certainly suggests that municipalities will become more prominent — if they can survive the functional and financial load being thrust upon them. Under the circumstances, it would seem wise for the 6 voters in 10 who typically do not vote in municipal elections to start paying more attention to those chosen to govern at this level.

Rightly or wrongly, Canadian efforts to improve intergovernmental relations always seem to revolve around major, and ill-fated, efforts at constitutional reform. The next chapter of the Guide will examine why constitutional matters loom so large in Canada and how the constitution affects the operations of our governments.

The Last Word

Definition of Terms and Concepts

Asymmetrical Federalism:
A term to describe the fact that Canada's federal system does not involve identical relationships (perfect symmetry) between the federal government and all provinces.

CAP:
Canada Assistance Program, under which the federal government paid 50% of certain provincial social assistance programs.

CHST:
Canada Health and Social Transfer, a new block grant from the federal government, replacing CAP and EPF.

Cooperative Federalism:
A term given to describe the era of enhanced consultation and cooperation in federal-provincial relations which was particularly associated with the period when Lester Pearson was Prime Minister in the mid-1960s.

Disallowance:
Power of the federal government (now fallen into disuse) to disallow or quash any provincial act up to one year after its passage.

Disentanglement:
A process designed to redistribute responsibilities between levels of government, so that there is less overlap. The objective is to simplify the allocation of responsibilities so that citizens can more easily see which level of government is responsible for what, and enforce accountability better.

EPF:
Established Program Funding (or Financing), a block grant introduced in 1977 to replace three conditional grants for hospitals, physicians' services and post-secondary education.

Federal Spending Power:
The power of the federal government to spend money in areas in which it does not necessarily have the power to legislate. Used to underwrite and promote national standards in a variety of programs, especially social programs.

Five Year Agreements: [See tax rental and tax sharing]

Keynesian Economics:
Derived from the writings of British economist John Maynard Keynes, and based on the notion that government could — and should — accept responsibility for the performance of the economy by pursuing various monetary and fiscal policies.

MSG:
Not something you don't want in your food, but a Municipal Support Grant introduced in Ontario in 1995 in place of existing unconditional grants and road grants.

Reservation:
The power of the Lieutenant-Governor to reserve any provincial bill for review by the federal government, presumably at federal request. Like disallowance, this power has fallen into disuse.

Residual Powers:
All powers left over and not otherwise specifically assigned to a level of government.

Tax Rental and Tax Sharing:
Process through which the federal and provincial governments, through a series of five year agreements, coordinated their joint occupancy of key tax fields, especially income and corporate tax.

Tax Room:
When there were tax rental and tax sharing agreements to avoid double taxation within the fields of income and corporate tax, the amount of tax room referred to the portion of the tax field available to one level of government without intruding on the portion reserved to the other. (Also known as tax points or tax credits.)

Watertight Compartments:
Term to describe the complete separation of federal and provincial responsibilities, in such a way as to avoid any overlap.

Points to Ponder

1. It appears likely that use of the "federal spending power" will be sharply curtailed in the future. What is your view of this prospect? Are there any new initiatives that you can think of that could benefit from the use of the federal spending power.

2. American President Harry Truman was famous for his saying "the buck stops here," by which he accepted responsibility for actions taken by his government. In Canada's federal system in recent years, municipalities might wish to adopt that saying since it is at their level that the downward passing of the buck finally stops. You should keep that situation in mind the next time you are criticizing your municipal council for raising the property tax.

3. Discussions to disentangle provincial-municipal responsibilities usually give special attention to the handling of education and social services. Which level of government do you think should look after these areas, and why? [Chapter 5 will provide some further consideration of the possible impact of the changes in educational jurisdiction announced for Ontario.]

4. This chapter has raised a number of concerns about the vacuum being created at the centre. Has this discussion caused you to re-think your views about whether Canada should continue to decentralize its government operations?

For Further Reading

Among the many texts which examine intergovernmental relations are:

Mark Charlton and Paul Barker (eds.), *Crosscurrents: Contemporary Political Issues*, 2nd edition, Scarborough, Nelson Canada, 1994, explores the merits of strong national/ provincial governments.

Paul Fox and Graham White, *Politics Canada*, 8th edition, Whitby, McGraw-Hill Inc., 1995, has sections on federalism, regionalism and Québec.

Robert Jackson and Doreen Jackson, *Politics in Canada*, 3rd edition, 1994, Scarborough, Prentice-Hall Canada Inc., Chapter 6, discusses federalism including the financial relationships. The same two authors also have a more condensed text, *Canadian Government in Transition*, 1996, from the same publisher. It includes a similar chapter on federalism.

C. Richard Tindal and Susan Nobes Tindal, *Local Government in Canada*, 4th edition, Whitby, McGraw-Hill Ryerson Limited, 1995, Chapter 7, explores provincial-municipal relations, including the issue of disentanglement.

Michael Whittington and Richard Van Loon, *Canadian Government and Politics*, Whitby, McGraw-Hill Ryerson Limited, 1996, Part Three, contains four chapters dealing with federalism.

Chapter 4

The Constitution, Charter and Courts

Objectives and Highlights

♦ To explain the continuing conflict surrounding Canada's constitution.

♦ To recognize the significance and limitations of the Charter and its impact on the operations of government.

♦ To appreciate the special roles played by the courts in our system of government.

For more than 100 years after Canada became a country, the central document of its constitution, the British North America Act, remained a statute passed by a foreign legislature (that of Britain). The constitution was finally brought home in 1982, only to have a new constitutional saga begin because of the refusal of the Québec government, then or since, to sign the agreement. This chapter provides a brief examination of Canada's continuing constitutional adventures.

Also examined is the Charter of Rights and Freedoms that was added to the constitution of Canada in 1982, and the impact that the Charter is having on intergovernmental relations and on the balance of power within our government system. Part of that impact, of course, has been to elevate the status and influence of the courts, which are called upon to interpret government actions in light of the Charter. Accordingly, the chapter includes a brief examination of the courts and the administration of justice, both of which also reflect the intergovernmental nature of Canada. Special attention is given to the Supreme Court of Canada and the important roles that it plays in our system of government.

Introduction: Once More into the Meech

Tennyson penned "once more into the breach" in his epic poem *The Charge of the Light Brigade*, but those soldiers doing battle in the Crimean War were scarcely more brave (or foolhardy?) than the Canadian politicians who have engaged in constitutional battles over the past half century. In our case, it has been "once more into the Meech," an adventure which has haunted us for a decade now.

Meech Lake is a pleasant body of water near the Prime Minister's summer residence in the Gatineau Hills. It was at this location that a major amendment to the Canadian constitution was developed in 1987, one which failed to receive approval from all ten provincial legislatures within the three year time limit specified. The *Meech Lake Accord* was not the first unsuccessful attempt to amend the *constitution* of Canada, nor — as we will see — was it the last.

♦ *Something to Think About*

Why have Canadian politicians expended so much time and energy in a futile effort to amend the constitution of the country?

What is a constitution and why are we so concerned about ours? Why should individual Canadians care about a constitution, and how can it affect them?

What Is a Constitution?

A constitution is a legal document setting out the fundamental "rules of the game" concerning a governmental system and its operations. A country does not absolutely have to have a constitution in order to exist and to function. However, a country which is a federation (like Canada) needs some type of written document outlining how powers are divided between the national and intermediate governments.

The country of Canada was created by the British North America Act, an 1867 statute passed by the British Parliament. Important as that statute was to Canada, it aroused little interest among the British politicians. According to Donald Creighton, the mention of things "colonial" was enough to clear the House of Commons, and the opening statements of the Colonial Secretary (in introducing the BNA Act) were lost in the noise of members departing "for the more intellectual atmosphere of the lobbies or neighbouring chophouses." The few members who remained could scarcely conceal their boredom. After the ordeal was over, "they turned with lively zeal and manifest relief to the great national problem of the tax on dogs."[1]

The BNA Act and its amendments over the years formed the central core of Canada's constitution. It provided for the machinery and operation of government at both the national and provincial levels, as well as for the distribution of governing powers between the two levels. But, as an Act of the British Parliament, the BNA Act could only be amended by Britain. As the decades went by, it became increasingly embarrassing for Canada to have to ask another country to pass legislation whenever it wanted to amend its own constitution!

The British Parliament would gladly have given up this task. In fact, it passed the Statute of Westminster in 1931, declaring that it would only legislate for Canada in response to a request from Canada. At that time, Canadians were urged to take over responsibility for any future amendments to the BNA Act. As the decades went by, however, national and provincial politicians in Canada were unable to agree on how they would bring home or "*patriate*" the constitution — and especially what amending formula they would use to change it as needed once it was brought home.

Unsuccessful initiatives in this regard were launched on several occasions over a period of 50 years. We came tantalizingly close to an agreement twice, with the Fulton-Favreau formula of 1964 and the Victoria Charter of 1971. The details of the long constitutional saga

---

[1]Donald Creighton, *Toward the Discovery of Canada*, Toronto, Macmillan, 1972, quoted in Jack McLeod (ed.), *The Oxford Book of Canadian Political Anecdotes*, Toronto, Oxford University Press, 1988, p. 23.

are well documented elsewhere, including in some of the readings cited at the end of this chapter.

Where Were You in '82?

Patriation was finally achieved in 1982, following determined efforts by Pierre Trudeau, who had been re-elected Prime Minister in 1980. A Constitution Act was passed by the Canadian Parliament. Incorporated within it was the BNA Act. An amending formula was included, which for most purposes requires the approval of the federal government and 2/3 of the provinces containing at least 50% of the population of Canada. The provinces were given expanded powers over their natural resources, a response to the concerns of Western Canada and its reaction to the federal government's National Energy Program which had been launched at the beginning of the 1980s. The other very significant addition was a *Charter of Rights and Freedoms*, discussed in more detail in a later section of this chapter..

Most of the initial attention given to the patriation process centred on the fact that one province — Québec — did not sign the agreement to bring home the constitution. Given the tremendous amount of time and effort which had been needed to reach agreement between the federal government and nine provinces, the decision was taken to proceed even without Québec. Since the Québec Government at that time was controlled by the Parti Québécois, headed by René Lévesque, it is reasonable to assume that it would not have signed **any** constitutional agreement, no matter how worded. Nonetheless, there were criticisms that Quebec had been betrayed or humiliated by the decision to proceed without its approval.

This interpretation of events was advanced strongly by Brian Mulroney once he became Prime Minister. It became his objective to undo this betrayal of Québec and to reach agreement on new arrangements which would allow Québec to return to the constitutional family. Strictly speaking, of course, Québec had never left the constitutional family. It might have refused to sign the patriation agreement, but it remained part of Canada and under its constitution.

The Meech Lake Accord

The Meech Lake Accord was to be Brian Mulroney's great triumph in statesmanship. It incorporated the conditions which Québec felt were a necessary prerequisite to signing the constitution. These were:

1. The recognition of Québec as a distinct society.
2. Increased powers in immigration.
3. The appointment of three Supreme Court judges from the Québec bench.
4. Containment of the "federal spending power."
5. A Québec veto on any future constitutional changes.

Agreement was reached on amendments to the constitution following a day-long meeting between the Prime Minister and the ten provincial Premiers at Meech Lake in April 1987. The agreement was presented as a *fait accompli*, something which had to be accepted without change. Any rejection of Meech, warned Prime Minister Mulroney, would be a rejection of Québec. This was a very dangerous, high-risk strategy, as well as being an unfair characterization of the situation.

It is true that some of the opposition to Meech was based on anti-Québec or anti-French sentiment. But it is equally true that much of the opposition was based on very real concerns by Canadians about the kind of country they wanted and how that might be changed if Meech were passed. A central issue (**never** fully explained or resolved) was how the inclusion of the *distinct society* clause might affect the provisions of the Charter. Would the Supreme Court be obliged to weigh any Charter challenges against actions taken by a future Québec Government in light of Meech's declaration that the role of the Québec Government was to "preserve and promote the distinct identity of Québec?" Were important distinctions involved, or just sloppy draftmanship, in the use of the phrase "distinct society" in some sections and "distinct identity" in others?" It didn't help public concern when the politicians involved issued totally contradictory and incom-

Distinct Society Clause
Anything but Distinct

patible statements concerning the distinct society provisions — telling English Canadians that the provisions were just symbolic, a recognition that Québec was different, while telling French Canadians that the provisions were fundamental and of great significance in protecting their interests.

There were also concerns about whether or not the Charter rights of other groups might be adversely affected by Meech. Shortly after the agreement was first announced, a clause was added to ensure that nothing in the Accord would affect the clauses in the 1982 Constitution Act that dealt with multiculturalism or aboriginal peoples. That prompted a demand that women's rights be given similar protection through specific wording. Much of the opposition to Meech came from "the fears of feminist groups, aboriginals, visible minorities, social policy activists and the disabled, that Meech Lake threatened their existing status or future goals."[2] Groups like these were also reacting to the secrecy surrounding the Meech Lake deliberations in contrast to the open process which had led to the patriation of the constitution in 1982.

A major problem faced by the Meech Lake Accord was the fact that a three year period was stipulated, within which all eleven governments must ratify the agreement. Over such a long time period, a number of the key players changed because of elections in several provinces. When the time limit expired (in June 1990), approval had still not been received from two provinces (Manitoba and Newfoundland).

| A Tale of Two Provinces | That's right! **Two** provinces failed to ratify Meech. The Mulroney Conservatives found it convenient to lay all of the blame on the Liberal Premier of Newfoundland, Clyde Wells, a version of events which has been repeated to |

this day. The facts are, however, that after experiencing a number of delays at the hands of one of its MLAs, Elijah Harper, who expressed various concerns of native groups across Canada, the Manitoba Legis-

---

[2]Alan C. Cairns, *Disruptions*, (edited by Douglas Williams), Toronto, McClelland and Stewart, 1991, p. 244.

lature adjourned on that final day of the three year time frame — without even beginning the public hearings at which some 3 000 delegations were listed to speak.

The Charlottetown Accord

As long and fruitless as the Meech Lake experience was, it is far from our last foray into constitutional battles. Spurred on by Québec plans for a separation referendum in 1992, the federal government launched a new drive for constitutional reform which culminated in the *Charlottetown Accord*. If the Meech Lake Accord had been seen by many as a "Québec round" of constitutional talks, the much more comprehensive (and complex) Charlottetown Accord had something for everyone. There was Senate reform for the West, aboriginal rights, native self-government — even a Canada clause to counterbalance the recognition of Québec's distinct society.

Charlottetown also differed from Meech in one other important respect. All Canadians would be involved in its ratification, in a vote scheduled for October 1992. As the time for the vote drew near, all political parties and much of the "intelligentsia" strongly supported the Charlottetown Accord. There was extensive advertising and a concerted national campaign to persuade Canadians of the wisdom of voting yes. Instead Canadians in six of the ten provinces voted no. One of the four provinces to vote yes was Ontario, but only by the narrowest of margins.

By this time, most Canadians were suffering from constitutional fatigue. While some in Québec saw the twin defeats as further evidence that separation must be pursued, many Canadians (including many Québecers) were just tired of hearing about what seemed to be a pretty abstract subject, compared to their real concerns about jobs, health care, the environment and so on. Those still paying attention to this subject began to appreciate the following definitions:

Meechified: Overcome by constitutional debate. (stupefied)

Son of a Meech: Offspring of parties to constitutional debates.

To Meechorize: To mesmerize, reduce to semi-comatose state. (See meechified, above.)

Meech ado about nothing: Common view of the whole process.

"Meechified" or not, it appears as 1997 unfolds that Canadians may once again not be far from a new round of constitutional discussions. Many Canadians may not understand the motivation of Québecers; many may argue that federalism has been good for Québec. The fact remains that almost 50% in Québec voted for separation in a provincial referendum held on October 30, 1995. Those numbers demand a response and, rightly or wrongly, it has become accepted that the response should be constitutional in nature. We may have a temporary reprieve, while Premier Bouchard and his government concentrate on dealing with Québec's economic and fiscal problems. But before this decade is out, we are likely to find ourselves "once more into the Meech."

Prime Minister Chrétien acknowledged the seriousness of the renewed threat to Canadian sovereignty in his January 1996 Cabinet shuffle. Reaching back thirty years, he followed then Prime Minister Lester Pearson's example of drafting the "three wise men" from Québec. This was the name given to three high profile Québecers Pearson persuaded to join his federal Cabinet as a way of demonstrating the kind of influence which French-Canadians wielded within the federal government and, by inference, why separation was unwise and unnecessary. Those three wise men were Jean Marchand, a fiery labour leader, Gérard Pelletier, a publisher, and a then relatively unknown intellectual and university professor named Pierre Trudeau.

Chrétien's Québec strategy differs from Pearson's in two key respects. He has only come up with two wise men: a trade consultant and foreign policy expert named Pierre Pettigrew and Stéphane Dion, a university professor. Dion is widely known in academic circles for his writings on constitutional matters, but the similarity with Pierre Trudeau ends there. In fact, Dion represents the complete opposite of the Trudeau position, which had always called for no special status for Québec. In a rather dramatic gesture, Dion released a manifesto the day he was sworn into the Cabinet, in which he called for the recognition in the constitution of Québec's distinct society status.

Brian Mulroney had hoped to have the last word on this subject of constitutional reform, so we will give it to him. In this instance, his "last word" was among the first words he had to say on the subject; it is a pity he didn't remember this observation after gaining power.

> We have developed our own peculiar cottage industry — highly paid and unproductive — in the field of constitutional reform. Imagine what might have been accomplished in, say, the field of medical research if the same amount of time and energy, talent and money, had been available as in the field of federal-provincial relations.[3]

Is Further Decentralization the Answer?

While there is much talk about "fixing" the federal system, there are few suggestions beyond the rather vague notion that more powers should be transferred to the provinces. As mentioned in the previous chapter, decentralization is superficially attractive. To those concerned about the size and debt of the federal government, it suggests a way of reducing both. Those who prefer moving decisions closer to the people also support decentralization.

♦ Something to Think About

But what, specifically, should be shifted to provincial jurisdiction and what, specifically, will be the impact on Canada of any significant reduction of the role of the federal government? How well will the provinces be able to handle additional responsibilities, given the wide disparities in their financial base and ability to raise revenue?

There is little evidence of any serious analysis of these important questions. Too many people have embraced decentralization as some magic solution which will placate the provinces and restore stability

---

[3]Brian Mulroney, *Where I Stand*, Toronto, McClelland and Stewart, 1983, p. 57.

to Canada's federal system. Yet, as discussed in Chapter 3, Canadians have also become accustomed to a country in which the federal government has used its "spending power" to underwrite the provision of key services and programs at something approaching a national standard. The current emphasis on decentralization includes within it a presumed curtailment of the federal spending power. Yet the negative reaction of Canadians to any perceived threat to such national programs as medicare suggests that they have not fully thought through the implications of the decentralization thrust which they claim to support. Never silent too long on the sidelines, former Prime Minister Pierre Trudeau warned in November 1995:

> "If we decide to decentralize any further, the rich provinces will get good services because they have a larger tax base, the poor provinces won't....And that will break up the country more surely than any separation."[4]

The Importance of the Charter

One of the reasons that the Meech and Charlottetown Accords were rejected is that something else very significant besides Québec's isolation happened when the constitution was repatriated in 1982. Added to the constitution of Canada was a Charter of Rights and Freedoms. Canadians had always enjoyed a long list of rights and freedoms as part of common law. To a large extent, these rights might be considered part of the unwritten portion of our constitution — that portion referred to as custom or convention. Such things as freedom of speech, of the press, of assembly, of worship, freedom from discrimination and from censorship, and right to the due process of law — all of these and more have always been considered part of one's heritage as a Canadian citizen.

However, one of Prime Minister Trudeau's main objectives in bringing home the constitution was to enshrine a charter of rights.

---

[4]Quoted in Joan Bryden, "Carving Up Ottawa's Clout," *Edmonton Journal,* November 11, 1995.

This had the effect of codifying, in constitutional law, what had hitherto existed in less well defined fashion as part of the customs of the
country. The specific rights provided in the Charter are listed in **Appendix A** of this chapter. While the list is impressive, there are two
qualifiers with great potential significance for the operations of the
Charter.

Limitations on the Charter

The first qualifier is the statement that the rights in the Charter are
subject to "such reasonable limits prescribed by law as can be demonstrably justified in a free and democratic society." This means that
Charter rights can be ignored or overridden where such an infringe-
ment can be justified as a reasonable limitation. For example, anti-
smoking legislation might be challenged as limiting freedom of
assembly and movement — given all of the restrictions on where one
is allowed to smoke. These restrictions, however, would presumably
meet the test of a reasonable limitation for a free and democratic society, because of what is known about the health hazards of tobacco
and about the dangers of second-hand smoke.

The second qualifier, the *notwithstanding clause*, is the "Achilles'
heel" of the Charter. It authorizes the federal government or any province to declare that one of its statutes shall operate notwithstanding
a provision in section 2 or sections 7 to 15 of the Charter. In other
words, this clause allows a senior government to "opt out of" the
Charter and carry on with legislation which is contrary to the Charter
— by the simple expedient of passing legislation declaring that it is
doing so. Any such action is limited to a five year period, after which
the legislation must be re-enacted to continue the override.

How could such an escape clause be included in the Charter and
in the constitution of Canada? Most provincial governments were
strongly opposed to the Charter. Apparently the only way that Prime
Minister Trudeau could achieve the inclusion of the Charter, which
he so fervently wanted, was to accept the inclusion of the notwithstanding clause. Presumably, the general feeling was that having this
escape clause would be sufficient to placate provincial politicians,
while at the same time public support for the Charter would be suffi-

ciently strong to deter provincial politicians from using — or at least from abusing — the notwithstanding clause.[5] Some supporters of this clause also argue that it makes the Charter more democratic by leaving final authority over these matters to elected representatives rather than judges.

Significance of the Charter

Even with these limitations, the addition of the Charter had significant implications for Canadian society.

1. It added a feature with which most Canadians were familiar as part of the American system of government. We had long been accustomed to hearing about the U.S. constitution's declaration of the right to life, liberty and the pursuit of happiness.

2. It altered the balance of power in our system of government. Before the Charter, Parliament was supreme — as it has always been in Britain. After the Charter, every action of Parliament became subject to the Charter. This meant that power shifted, from Parliament to the courts — whose role it is to interpret the Charter.

3. It emphasized that certain rights were enjoyed by all Canadians, regardless of their origins or their territorial location. On the positive side, the Charter gave many Canadians a feeling of empowerment, a feeling that they had equality under the constitution. On the negative side, this viewpoint was obviously contrary to the territorial claims being made by those French Canadians who wanted recognition of one geographic area — Québec — as a distinct society.[6]

---

[5]Ironically, it was Premier Bourassa's use of the notwithstanding clause, to support the continuation of the Québec Government's French-only sign legislation, which undermined the sympathy of many supporters in English Canada and contributed markedly to the defeat of the Meech Lake Accord.

[6]This discussion is largely based on Cairns, *op. cit.*, Chapter 10.

Canadians Love
the Charter

With hindsight, it appears that "the powers that be" had failed to recognize or understand the extent to which many Canadians had embraced the Charter and had come to value it as a protector of their rights. In the decade and a half since the Charter appeared, many groups which previously felt that they had little influence over a government system dominated by Parliament, and the political parties which controlled Parliament, have gained a great deal of influence through Charter challenges. We have seen the development of what some have termed a "court party," defined as "a loose alliance of judges, bureaucrats, lawyers, activists (who may also be bureaucrats and/or lawyers), academics and media personalities." They use the courts as "a new playing field for the pursuit of politics."[7]

LEAF, the feminist Legal Education and Action Fund, is a prime example of the new players and their strategies. By the early 1990s, it had become the most frequent non-government intervenor in Charter cases before the Supreme Court. It funded these challenges, in large part, through taxpayers' money provided through the Secretary of State and through the Court Challenges Program.[8] Other members of the court party include the Canadian Disability Rights Council, the Charter Committee on Poverty Issues, the Canadian Prisoners' Rights Network, the Advocacy Group for the Environmentally Sensitive, the Equality Rights Committee of the Canadian Ethno-Cultural Council, and EGALE (Equality for Gays and Lesbians Everywhere).[9]

Whether or not you approve of this apparent shift of power in our society largely depends, presumably, on whether you were previously one of the "ins" or the "outs." What is clear, however, is that the bal-

---

[7] Al Strachan, "The Hidden Opposition," *The Globe and Mail*, January 11, 1992, p. D3, reprinted in Gregory Mahler and Roman March (eds.), *Annual Editions, Canadian Politics*, Third Edition, Guilford, Dushkin Publishing Group, 1993, p. 46.

[8] *Ibid.*, p. 47.

[9] *Ibid.*, p. 46.

ance of power has shifted. One consequence is an enhanced role for the courts, and especially the Supreme Court of Canada, so it is time to take a closer look at this "third branch of government."

The Courts

Under the constitution of Canada, the provinces are responsible for the administration of justice. Each province has a superior or supreme court, usually divided into trial and appeal divisions. Some also have county or district courts with both civil and criminal jurisdiction. In addition, all provinces have courts presided over by judges appointed by the provinces to deal with lesser criminal and other matters. These include magistrates' courts and family and juvenile courts. In addition to the various provincial courts, there are two courts established by the Government of Canada — the Federal Court and the *Supreme Court of Canada.*

Most of us equate the courts with the sort of dramatic criminal trials which hit the headlines or are popularized in television shows and movies. *Criminal law* deals with the relationship between the individual and the state. The national government is responsible for criminal law, which deals with such matters as murder, theft and assault. In contrast, *civil law* involves actions between or among individuals and corporations. It falls under provincial jurisdiction and includes such matters as wills, family law and torts (legal liability). For most Canadians, any encounter with the courts will revolve around such relatively minor matters as fighting a speeding ticket or suing a neighbour over a fence which supposedly encroaches on one's property.

The subject of law enforcement is an important one, which could easily merit a separate chapter of its own. Canadians often hold very strong views about the appropriateness of existing or pending legislation, or how rigorously it should be enforced — as is evident, for example, with respect to the federal "gun control" and "anti-smoking" legislation. Controversy also surrounds the cost and effectiveness of our criminal justice system. In 1992, Canadian taxpayers paid more than $9.5 billion to hunt down lawbreakers, prosecute and keep them locked up.[10] It cost about $46 000 to keep an inmate in a federal prison in 1993 and $40 000 more than that to keep a young offender in a secure custody facility in Ontario.[11] Yet many Canadians seem to feel that what is needed is to "get tough with" lawbreakers and to keep them incarcerated longer. Others question the logic of supporting what is essentially a policy of increased spending on policing and prisons while governments are cutting expenditures on programs such as child care, social assistance and education. They see it as one more example of our tendency to focus on dealing with problems after they occur rather than trying to prevent them. They point to the research which estimates that $7 is saved in the costs of crime, welfare and education upgrading for every $1 spent on children when they are young.[12]

The administration of justice also illustrates well the intergovernmental nature of Canada. We have already noted the existence of both provincial and federal courts and judges. Policing is carried out by all three levels of government.[13] The Royal Canadian Mounted Police is responsible for enforcing all federal statutes and is also under contract to every province except Ontario and Québec and to over 100 municipalities to enforce criminal and provincial law. Ontario and Québec have their own provincial police forces, which may also contract to provide policing for municipalities. There are also many local police forces operated by municipalities, and there are local forces found in many native communities as well.

---

[10]Rob Tripp, "Dollars and Pain: The Economics of the Justice System," *Kingston Whig Standard*, November 25, 1996.

[11]*Ibid.*

[12]*Ibid.*

[13]This section is based on Robert Jackson and Doreen Jackson, *Canadian Government in Transition*, Scarborough, Prentice-Hall Canada Inc., 1996, pp. 207-208.

**Special Role of Courts
to Enforce Rule of Law**

There is, however, an entirely different role which the courts play as key institutions within our machinery of government. They exist to enforce the principle of the *rule of law*. Simply put, this principle states that all government actions must be authorized by law; that there must be specific legal authority for the actions taken by government. This principle is an essential part of our democratic system. It helps to ensure that no one, even the most senior government personnel, is above the law. It helps to protect us from arbitrary or capricious actions taken by government.

The courts are particularly concerned to ensure that government decisions affecting individuals meet certain tests.

♦   Did the government have the legal authority to make the decision?

♦   In the process of arriving at the decision, did the government give any affected individuals the equivalent of their "day in court"? In other words, were the affected individuals given advance notice about the decision to be taken, the opportunity to attend, the right to hear and be heard, and reasons for the decision taken?

♦   Is the decision consistent with the provisions of the Charter?

If the courts determine that government decisions do not measure up to these tests, they will be quashed as "ultra vires" or contrary to the "proceedings of natural justice." The net result is protection for the individual from any abuse of power by government.

The courts or judiciary represent a "third branch of government," and one which is central to our democratic system. In countries which are not democratic, the courts usually exist as an arm of the ruling group and are used to enforce their actions. In contrast, the courts and judges in Canada are separate and independent. Judges of the two federal courts (the Supreme Court of Canada and the Federal Court of Canada) and of the higher level courts in the provinces enjoy a very secure tenure and can only be removed from office by a vote of both Houses of Parliament.

The issue of tenure for judges came to the fore in mid-1996 as a result of comments made by Québec Superior Court Justice Jean Bienvenue concerning women and Jews. A Canadian Judicial Council inquiry committee recommended his removal from the bench, the first time in this century that a federally appointed judge has been the subject of such action. In fact, only five cases of judicial misconduct have made it to Parliament since 1867 and the judges involved either died or resigned before a final vote was taken on their fate.[14]

◆ Something to Think About

The disparaging remarks made by Judge Bienvenue were deeply offensive and most Canadians who followed the incident probably welcomed the recommendation for his dismissal. But it is important to remember why judges have been given such secure tenure, and why they should be removed from the bench only in the most extreme circumstances.[15]

Judges must be free to carry out their duties without any political interference. They must make decisions which often fly in the face of public opinion or anger powerful interest groups and lobbies. If we start holding judges responsible for remarks they make and opinions they have — however distasteful — we start down a very slippery slope. Would it not be even more dangerous and undesirable to have judges who think, but hide, unacceptable ideas? At least when judges reveal their true colours, a litigant can show an Appeal Court why unfair treatment occurred. It is noteworthy that the day after the recommendation to remove Judge Bienvenue, the Québec Justice Minister announced that he would introduce measures to make judges

---

[14]Lisa Fitterman, "Committee Wants Judge Removed from Bench," in *Kingston Whig Standard*, July 5, 1996. Bienvenue also chose to resign instead of awaiting a vote on the issue.

[15]The discussion which follows is based on Julius Grey, "Bienvenue Case May Undermine Judicial Independence," in *Kingston Whig Standard*, July 12, 1996.

"more accountable" in general. Any such action could undermine the independence of the judiciary and, ultimately, the protection of the rights of the public in a democracy. As a result, even those who found Bienvenue's words anything but "welcome," may want to reconsider defending his right to say them.

Supreme Court of Canada

As the highest court in the land, the Supreme Court's decisions are binding on all the lower courts. It deals mainly with cases that have been appealed at least once in the lower courts. It does not accept to hear all appeals. Rather, it is selective in its approach, allocating its limited time and resources to questions it regards as being of fundamental importance to Canadian society.[16]

Much of the work of the Supreme Court has centred around two very important types of case:

1. Those relating to the division of powers and the operations of Canadian federalism, and

2. Those dealing with Charter challenges.

The Courts and the Division of Powers

Wherever there is a federal system of government, there will be uncertainty and debate over who is responsible for what. This uncertainty can arise because of a possible lack of clarity in the wording of the original division of powers. It may also arise because roles for government develop which were not even contemplated or covered in the original division of powers. Both of these factors apply in the Canadian case. In addition, the long delay in agreeing on an amending formula and in bringing home the constitution meant that Canada had

---

[16]This discussion is based on Robert J. Jackson and Doreen Jackson, *Politics in Canada*, Third Edition, Scarborough, Prentice Hall Canada Inc., 1994, p. 180.

to rely even more heavily on the Supreme Court and to hope that its interpretations could provide sufficient flexibility to allow an act from 1867 to meet the greatly changed conditions of the 20th century.

 Imagine yourself as a Supreme Court judge. How would you respond to the following jurisdictional questions?

You Be the Judge

1. Under the constitution, provinces have ownership of mineral resources and the federal government controls navigable waters. Since technology now makes possible the "mining" of off-shore resources, which level of government has jurisdiction over resources under coastal waters?

2. The constitution does not directly deal with responsibility for management of the economy, since this was not a government function at the time of Confederation. Both the national and provincial levels have pursued a variety of economic policies over the past half century. The national government introduces wage and price controls and you are asked to rule if its action is constitutional and on what basis.

3. Canadians are concerned about a number of environmental issues, including the destruction of the ozone layer, clear-cutting of forests, and water pollution. Which level of government has jurisdiction to act?

And the Answer Is.... In the first instance, the Supreme Court did rule that the national government had jurisdiction over off-shore resources. In the second instance, there was a court challenge when the Liberal Government of Pierre Trudeau introduced wage and price controls after its re-election in 1974. The court held that the national government could take such action under its "Peace, Order and Good Government" clause, even though previous rulings had indicated that this blanket power was only to be exercised in a national emergency, which had been presumed to refer to matters such as war.

There is no one answer to the third instance posed above. Both the national and provincial governments have passed environmental legislation, although the national level has left most of the initiative in this area to the provinces. Control over forests was specifically assigned to the provinces in section 92 of the BNA Act (and is also specified in the section 92a amendment added in 1982 when the Constitution Act was passed). Control over air pollution and over other activities harmful to the ozone layer can be exercised by both the national and provincial governments. Both these levels, along with municipalities, are involved or can exercise responsibility with respect to water pollution — with municipalities often in the forefront.

This third example is all too typical. While the original division of powers was supposed to be based on "watertight compartments," Chapter 3 has noted the growing overlap in the activities of the various levels of government. Today, there are very few areas of policy that are the exclusive responsibility of one level. One result, as previously discussed, is that much of the time of governments in Canada is spent in jurisdictional squabbles.

The Courts and the Charter

The Supreme Court now spends close to one quarter of its time just dealing with Charter cases. It has made many important rulings dealing with such matters as Canada's abortion law, the federal immigration appeal process, and the issue of maternity leave provisions under the Unemployment Insurance Act. Three of its more widely publicized decisions in recent years have been:

1. The "Askov" decision regarding the right to a speedy trial, which resulted in the dismissal (for undue delay) of some 40 000 cases in Ontario alone;
2. The "drunkenness as a defence" decision, in which the Court accepted the defence argument that an accused was too drunk to know what he was doing and could not be held responsible for his actions; and
3. The Sue Rodriguez case in which the Court ruled against the doctor-assisted suicide being sought by Rodriguez.

If the Charter has shifted power from Parliament to the Supreme Court, who are the members of that court? They are nine judges, appointed by the federal government — really by the Prime Minister of the day. They serve until age 75. Three of the judges are appointed from Québec in recognition of its different system of civil law (based on the Napoleonic code, rather than on English common law). All are presumed to have distinguished legal careers, although not all have been on the bench in lower courts. For example, the late Bora Laskin, who became Chief Justice of the Supreme Court, was a law professor when appointed. A current member, John Sopinka, was a practising lawyer at the time of his appointment.

The Unknown Nine

While their legal credentials are solid, what about their beliefs and values? These are obviously of equal importance, and may significantly affect the kinds of decisions which are made by the court. The short answer is that we don't know![17] Canadians do not have anything like the American system of "advise and consent" in which the U.S. President's nominees for the Supreme Court are examined by Congress in highly publicized hearings, before being approved (or not). Perhaps we would not wish such a system, especially after the spectacle of the Judge Thomas hearings and the Anita Hill accusations of sexual harassment against Thomas. Without some type of hearing process, however, Canadians have no way of knowing anything about the nine people who have acquired such substantial decision-making power. It is reasonable to assume that a Prime Minister in power for a considerable period of time will have the opportunity to appoint several judges who share his philosophical or ideological bent. For example, there is some evidence[18] to support the notion that the appointments made by Brian

---

[17]The current members are Their Honours Cory, Gonthier, Iacobucci, L'Heureux-Dubé, La Forest, Lamer, McLachlin, Sopinka and Stevenson.

[18]Morton et al., "The Supreme Court's First Decade of Charter Decisions," in Paul Fox and Graham White (eds.), *Politics Canada*, Whitby, McGraw-Hill Ryerson Limited, 1995, Eighth Edition, p. 77.

Mulroney during his two terms in power have been more conservative and less supportive of Charter challenges. Indeed, all but one of the judges serving in 1996 were Mulroney appointments, and half of those had some connection with the Conservative party.[19]

Concluding Observations

These first four chapters of the Guide have laid the foundation for an understanding of our system of government, its importance and its changing nature. The country of Canada began with what was thought to be a clear division of powers (into watertight compartments) and a clearly superior and dominant national government. That neither of these arrangements survived the past 130 years should not be surprising, given the vast changes which have occurred in the nature of our economy and society. The watertight compartments have long since flooded back and forth, and the national dominance which seemed so overwhelming in the middle of the 20th century has been fading away over the past decade.

After spending half a century before finally reaching agreement on the patriation of our constitution, Canada's governments have spent the last 15 years wrestling with what amendments can be made to that constitution in an attempt to satisfy the one province (Québec) that did not agree to that patriation. We are also still coming to grips with the full implications of the Charter of Rights and Freedoms and the way it has altered the balance of power between governments and the courts.

Given this background, it is time to take a closer look at the structure and functioning of Canada's governments. This examination is the focus of the next two chapters of the Guide.

---

[19]Jackson and Jackson, *op. cit.*, p. 198.

Appendix A
What Are your Charter Rights?

1. Fundamental freedoms

♦ of conscience and religion
♦ of thought, belief, opinion and expression
   (including freedom of the press and other media)
♦ of peaceful assembly (note the qualifier — "peaceful")
♦ of association

2. Democratic rights

♦ to vote and to be a candidate for office
♦ five year limit on term of all legislatures, (except in an extreme emergency)
♦ one sitting of a legislature at least once every 12 months

3. Mobility rights

♦ Every citizen has the right to enter, remain in, and leave Canada
♦ Every citizen and permanent resident has the right to move to any province and to pursue a livelihood in any province
♦ Programs favouring existing provincial residents are permitted if the rate of unemployment is below the national average

4. Legal rights

♦ To life, liberty and security of person
♦ To be secure against unreasonable search or seizure
♦ Not to be arbitrarily detained or imprisoned
♦ On arrest or detention, everyone has the right:
   ● to be informed promptly of reasons
   ● to be informed of right to counsel, and to obtain counsel promptly
   ● to have validity of detention confirmed

- If charged with an offence, everyone has due process rights
- Not to be subjected to cruel and unusual punishment
- To protection against self-incrimination
- To an interpreter

5. *Equality rights*

- Every person is equal before and under the law, free from discrimination based on: race, national or ethnic origin, colour, religion, sex, age, mental or physical disability
- Affirmative action programs permitted

6. *Language rights*

- English and French are the official languages of Canada and have equality of status as to their usage in all institutions of the government of Canada
- English and French are the official languages of New Brunswick, with the same equality provisions
- Either English or French may be used before any court established by the federal or New Brunswick governments
- The public can communicate with the federal government in English or French, where there is a significant demand for such language
- Minority language educational rights guaranteed

The Last Word

Definition of Terms and Concepts

Charlottetown Accord:
The name given to the comprehensive constitutional reform package on which Canadians voted (negatively) in October 1992.

Charter:
The Charter of Rights and Freedoms was added to the Canadian constitution when it was patriated in 1982. It provides a consti-tutional guarantee of certain rights for Canadians, to which parlia-ment and the provincial legislatures must adhere.

Civil Law:
This body of law deals with actions between or among individuals and corporations. It covers such matters as wills and family law.

Constitution:
The "rules of the game" concerning a governmental system and its operation, usually found in a central document or documents and in various customs and conventions.

Criminal Law:
The body of law which deals with the relationship between individuals and the state (government), including such matters as murder and assault.

Distinct Society:
A phrase open to many interpretations. At one extreme is the suggestion that this phrase merely recognizes the fact that Québec is different. At the other extreme is the contention that this phrase could be used to justify government actions otherwise contrary to the Charter but directed toward protection and enhancement of

Québec's distinct society. In short, there is no specific, commonly accepted definition.

Meech Lake Accord:

The name given to the constitutional amendment package which was agreed to by the Prime Minister and Premiers in 1987 but which failed to receive ratification by all provinces within the three year time frame required.

Notwithstanding Clause:

The override clause which allows the federal government or any province to opt out of the Charter (section 2 and sections 7 to 15) by the simple expedient of passing a law which declares that it (that law) is exempt. Any such legislation is limited to a five year term, but can be re-enacted.

Patriation:

Refers to the process of "bringing home" the constitution from Britain. This was accomplished in 1982 when the Constitution Act was passed by the Parliament of Canada, incorporating within it the British North America Act which hitherto could only be amended by the British Parliament which had originally passed it in 1867.

Rule of Law:

Fundamental principle that all government actions must be authorized by law. This principle is enforced by the courts which stand ready to declare "ultra vires" any government action which is without proper legal foundation.

Supreme Court of Canada:

The final court of the law for Canada. It consists of nine judges appointed by the federal government and devotes most of its time to Charter challenges and issues relating to the division of powers.

Points to Ponder

1. Given all that has happened in the ten years since the Meech Lake Accord was introduced, do you think it should have been approved, and why or why not?

2. Before reading this chapter, what rights did you think you enjoyed as a Canadian, and how did they compare to the Charter rights as summarized in the Appendix to this chapter?

3. How do you feel about your constitutional rights being subject to a "notwithstanding" clause?

4. What do you think about the way the Charter has shifted the balance of power in Canadian society away from parliament and those who control parliament? Does the Charter empower more individuals and groups or does it mainly empower Supreme Court judges who are not elected by or accountable to anyone?

5. Does the important role which the courts play in protecting our rights and freedoms justify the kind of independence enjoyed by our judges? Should inappropriate comments and attitudes by judges be tolerated as the price to pay for judicial independence? Should the appointment of judges only be confirmed (as in the United States) after a public hearing which brings to light more about their backgrounds and values?

For Further Reading

Alan Cairns (edited by Douglas Williams), *Disruptions: Constitutional Struggles, from the Charter to Meech Lake*, Toronto, McClelland & Stewart Inc., 1991, provides an excellent analysis of the events during this period.

Paul Fox and Graham White, *Politics:Canada*, 8th edition, Whitby, McGraw-Hill Inc., 1995 has a number of readable articles in a section on the constitution and the Charter and also has a section on the judiciary.

Robert Jackson and Doreen Jackson, *Politics in Canada*, 3rd edition, Scarborough, Prentice Hall Canada Inc., 1994, Chapter 5 provides a detailed examination of the evolution and patriation of the Canadian constitution. *Canadian Government in Transition*, 1996, by the same authors and publisher, includes both a chapter on the constitution and one on the courts.

Garth Stevenson (ed.), *Federalism in Canada*, Toronto, McClelland & Stewart Inc., 1989, contains articles on a wide-range of constitutional and federal-provincial issues.

Michael Whittington and Richard Van Loon, *Canadian Government and Politics*, Whitby, McGraw-Hill Ryerson Limited, 1996, has four chapters dealing with the constitution and the judicial process.

Chapter 5

Local Governments: A Closer Look

Objectives and Highlights

♦ To describe categories of municipality and common governing structures.

♦ To evaluate the merits of the municipal amalgamations being pursued by several provincial governments.

♦ To examine the role and operation of local boards, especially school boards.

The level of government most taken for granted is also the level which would be most quickly missed were it to disappear. It is the services, facilities and regulations provided by local governments that largely shape the quality of our day-to-day lives. The existence of a large number of local governments provides decentralization, convenient access for public participation, differing responses to the varying needs of different localities, and opportunities for creativity and innovation. All of these strengths have been exhibited, to a greater or lesser extent, by Canada's municipalities.

Reform efforts underway in a number of provinces place at risk the "localness" of local government. Provincial policy makers are preoccupied with the creation of larger units of administration (whether for municipalities or local boards like school boards) which they feel will better handle the provision of services. They are not just ignoring the representative and political role of municipal governments but are, in provinces like Ontario, actively citing the elimination of local councillors as a positive benefit of the amalgamation process.

This chapter will attempt to give you an appreciation of the nature of local governments, how they govern, what they do, and why you should care about their survival.

Introduction

If Canadians know something about government, it is likely to be about their federal or provincial government. The senior levels receive most of the media attention and are considered to be involved in the more important and more "glamorous" activities. Local governments are apt to be dismissed as minor players. They are just people from the community, fussing over roads and sewers and other mundane topics.

Look again! Far from being insignificant, local governments may just be the most important level of government, especially in terms of the impact on our day-to-day lives. That paradox is but one of many which one encounters in any examination of local government. Consider these factors:

♦ Local governments include many of our oldest governing institutions, with many municipalities incorporated well before Confederation in 1867 brought us our national and provincial governments. **Yet** they also include many of our newest governments, since they continue to be established in response to population growth and to go through restructuring and reform initiatives.

♦ They are the level of government closest to the people, and are hailed by some as the foundations of democracy. **Yet** they can be secretive, remote and bureaucratic and are frequently criticized for serving the interests of the property development industry more than those of the general public.

♦ They are the weakest level of government, having no guaranteed right to exist in the constitution — unlike the national and provincial levels. **Yet** they may assume growing importance as the 21st century approaches. The federal and provincial governments are preoccupied with their deficit and debt problems. As discussed earlier in this Guide, part of their solution is to "pass the buck" (and more responsibilities) to the next level down. As the senior levels retrench, local governments will likely be called upon to fill the gap that is being created.

What are the local governments that face these future challenges and opportunities? As previewed in Chapter 2, they exist in great numbers and wide variety. Canada has one national government, ten provincial governments and two (soon to be three) territorial governments. But it has over 4000 municipalities and probably close to that many agencies, boards and commissions which also form part of what we know as local government. Our first task, therefore, is to provide a brief overview and some definitions. We begin with municipalities, since they are what most people think of when there is a reference to local government.

Municipalities

Municipalities are elected local governments. They have a defined geographic area and are distinguished from other local governments in having the power to levy taxes on the inhabitants and landowners within their boundaries. They are also corporations, limited to the powers given to them by the body which incorporates them, that is, the government of the province. These powers are exercised on behalf of all residents of the municipality by a council elected by those residents. This arrangement is somewhat similar to that found with a private corporation where the powers are exercised by a Board of Directors on behalf of the shareholders.

Depending on where you live in Canada, you may find yourself under a number of possible municipal government arrangements.

i) You may be governed by two levels of municipal government. This occurs when your local (*lower tier*) municipality is part of a two tier system, in which you receive some of your municipal services from the *upper tier* county, region or district municipality.

ii) You may be within a *single tier* municipality, which is not part of any two tier system, and from which you receive all of your municipal services.

iii) You may not be within a municipality at all. Much of the area of Canada (although only a small proportion of its population) is what is known as "unorganized territory." This means that it is not within any incorporated municipality. This is true, for example, of much of Northern Ontario, the vast majority of British Columbia and large stretches of the Northern territories. Inhabitants within unorganized territory may receive local services from a nearby municipality, from a provincial or territorial government, from a local board, or from various types of community organization.

Classifications of Municipality

Provincial legislation provides mainly for two broad categories of municipality, urban and rural, and may distinguish several types within each category. Nova Scotia, for example, has cities, towns and rural municipalities; while Manitoba provides for cities, towns, villages and rural municipalities. In the case of Alberta, cities, towns, villages and summer villages are considered urban municipalities, and municipal districts, counties, improvement districts and special areas are designated as rural municipalities.[1]

Ontario has one of the most elaborate municipal structures, originally designed for the mid-19th century, when urban and rural differences were quite pronounced. The provincial Municipal Act provides for a rural municipality known as a township, three urban municipalities known as villages, towns and cities (in ascending order of size) and an upper tier municipality known as a county or region. Counties date from the original Municipal Act of 1849 and provide a limited range of services on behalf of all townships, villages and towns within their geographic area. Cities do not form part of this two tier system, but operate as single tier, "stand-alone" municipalities — a reflection of the fact that cities were quite distinct from surrounding rural areas when this structure was first created. In contrast, cities do come under the jurisdiction of regional municipalities, which also differ from counties in having more responsibilities. The two structures are depicted in the chart which follows.

---

[1]Jack Masson with Edward Lesage Jr., *Alberta's Local Governments*, Edmonton, University of Alberta Press, 1994, p. 69.

Chart 1
County and Regional Two-Tier Systems

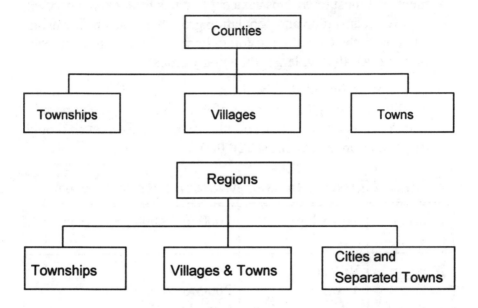

A further difference is that county councils are "*indirectly elected*" in that they consist of members who were initially elected as reeves and deputy reeves of the lower tier township, village and town councils. While most regional councils started out with that kind of composition, an increasing number have moved to direct election of their members.

Ontario's municipal classifications also include boroughs, which are essentially cities and are now found in only one municipality (East York), and separated towns, which are towns which have left the county system and essentially operate like cities. There are also specialized municipal units created for the small and scattered population found in Northern Ontario, notably improvement districts and local roads area boards and local services boards. The basic classifications are summarized in tabular form below. The population ranges specified are only guidelines, however, since it is a municipality's option whether or not it applies to be reclassified as a "higher" municipal unit when its population reaches the appropriate level.

Two examples will suffice to show the deviations from the pattern.

1. Townships were originally created to be rural units of government. Yet most townships adjacent to cities have experienced extensive urbanization and population growth. Kingston Township, adjacent to the City of Kingston in Eastern Ontario, has a population of over 40 000, larger than many cities.

2. Towns were intended to be the middle category of urban municipality, changing to city status after reaching 15 000 in population. Yet Oakville, west of Toronto, remains a town even though its population is now about 120 000.

Main Classifications of Municipality in Ontario

1 Rural	Township	1000 to 25 000 population
2 Urban	Village Town City Separated Town Borough	500 to 2000 2000 to 15 000 Over 15 000 Town not in county system A city (East York only)
3 Upper Tier	County Regional	Townships, villages and towns are part of county system All municipalities, including cities, are part of regions

How Are Municipalities Governed?

As noted in Chapter 2, the basic governing structure of municipalities is quite simple, compared to the senior levels of government with their separate executive and legislative branches. The basic municipal model simply consists of the council and the municipal staff — with the latter organized into a number of separate departments reflecting the major responsibilities of the municipality.

While simple in appearance, this model may contribute to a rather fragmented approach to municipal operations, especially in larger municipalities with a dozen or more separate municipal departments. Each department tends to be preoccupied with the needs of its particular service area and rather inward looking when it comes to the broader issues which cut across the jurisdiction of several departments. The same tendency is evident in provincial and federal departments as well. The big difference is that each of these senior level departments is headed by a minister, with all ministers belonging to the same political party and sitting together in the Cabinet. Coordination of departments is reinforced by the twin forces of Cabinet solidarity and party loyalty. There is nothing like these arrangements at the municipal level, with the result that coordination of departments can be much more difficult.

Standing Committee System

This difficulty is not helped by the *standing committee system* which is also found in many municipal governing structures. These committees normally consist entirely of councillors, although citizen members can be appointed to them and sometimes are. They are established by council, mostly at council's discretion. They usually have two main responsibilities: **(1)** to oversee the operations of one or more municipal departments and **(2)** to investigate and report to council on any policy matters referred to them.

▬▬▬▬▬▬▬▬▬▬

Pros and Cons

▬▬▬▬▬▬▬▬▬▬

Councillors are able to specialize and to focus their attention on the particular departments which especially interest them and which fall under the jurisdiction of their committees. This specialized perspective, however, tends to perpetuate and even to accentuate the divisions inherent in the departmental structure. If councillors are preoccupied with the needs of "their" departments, who, it might be asked, is worrying about the needs of the municipality as a whole?

On the other hand, standing committees can be a positive feature from the point of view of public participation in municipal government. First of all, the fact that most issues are referred by council to a standing committee for an investigation and report means that there is a built-in delay before council makes a decision on the matter. This delay gives citizens who may be interested in a particular matter more opportunity to be aware of its presence on the council agenda and to make their response. Second, committee meetings tend to be much more informal than council meetings, especially council meetings held in larger municipalities. Here again, citizens may benefit from the more relaxed atmosphere in making presentations and interacting with councillors. In contrast, those unaccustomed to speaking in public can be intimidated by an appearance before full council, with the bright lights from the local cable T.V. coverage of the meeting reflecting off the chains of office of the Mayor!

CAO System

Another variation of governing structure increasingly found in municipalities is that of the *Chief Administrative Officer* (CAO) system. This involves the appointment of a senior official responsible for leading and coordinating the administrative activities of the municipality within the policy guidelines laid down by council. The introduction of this position has often coincided with the abolition of standing committees, as a two-pronged effort by council to overcome fragmentation and improve coordination instead. Perhaps surprisingly, however, standing committees are often combined with the CAO model, as depicted in the chart below.

At its best, a CAO structure can significantly improve the coordination of municipal operations — both in terms of the development of municipal policies and the implementation of these policies. A smoothly functioning CAO system can allow councillors to concenrate on their primary roles of representing the public and determining priorities for action.

At its worst, however, the CAO system can become very bureaucratic. Councillors may feel rather cut off from the day-to-day operations of the municipality since all staff report to council through, and receive directions from, the CAO. Department heads may become resentful, unless the CAO is skilled in developing a sense of teamwork and in demonstrating the benefits of working together. If the CAO becomes too prominent, there may be friction with the head of council or other councillors. To a considerable extent, the difficulties that can arise relate to the age-old problem of how to keep the expert (the CAO) "on tap, but not on top."

Chart 2
CAO System

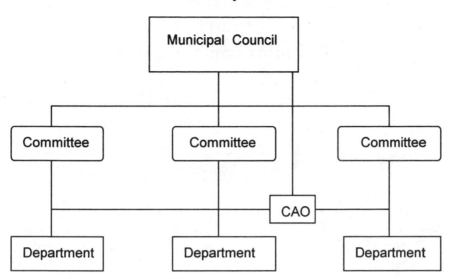

Executive Committee System

While CAOs may provide strong administrative leadership, other internal structures have been introduced in an attempt to provide stronger political leadership. Essentially, these involve the establishment of some form of executive committee of council. One of the most common versions of this system is to have an executive committee chaired by the head of council and comprising the chairs of the major standing committees of council. This arrangement, which is illustrated below, is supposed to approximate the cabinet structure found at the senior levels — but it lacks the twin cohesive forces of collective responsibility and party solidarity.

The executive committee in this model is normally given responsibility for spending decisions and often for personnel, and there may be a further provision that reports of standing committees go through it to council. However, the effectiveness of these arrangements obviously depends on the personalities involved, their willingness to work together, and the ability of the head of council or other dominant members to forge a team approach. Unfortunately, such cooperative action is not always forthcoming, and executive committees have not been as successful in providing political leadership as CAO systems have in providing administrative leadership.

Chart 3
Executive Committee System

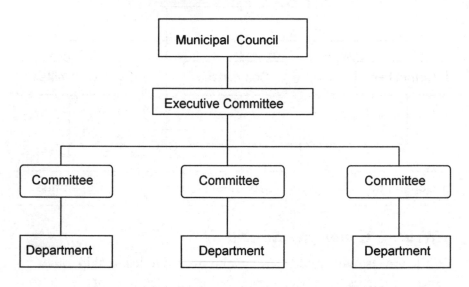

Are Political Parties the "Missing Link?"

Those seeking stronger political leadership sometimes advocate the introduction of organized political parties at the local level — on the assumption that a council organized on party lines would better approximate the parliamentary model of the senior levels.[2] By this reasoning, which clearly is most applicable to the very large municipalities, the position of any executive committee and head of council would be strengthened by the backing of a solid block of party votes. On the assumption that more than one party would contest the seats on council, there would also be an official opposition group

---

[2]The following discussion of pros and cons is based on C. Richard Tindal and Susan Nobes Tindal, *Local Government in Canada*, 4th edition, Whitby, McGraw-Hill Ryerson Limited, 1995, pp. 274-278.

providing a "watchdog" function. These arrangements would provide a much clearer focus of accountability than is normally found on council, with everybody responsible for everything and no one really responsible for anything. Other alleged benefits from introducing political parties into local government include the fact that parties would subsidize the increasingly high cost of election campaigns and that party debate would stimulate more interest and increased voting.

Opponents of political parties at the local level rebut a number of the alleged advantages. They point out that much would depend on the nature of the political parties involved. Proponents assume a balanced situation with two or more parties which would alternate in power. If one party is very dominant and controls council over a period of years however, then there is undoubtedly more likelihood of insensitivity to public opinion and other abuses — traits exhibited by the provincial and federal governments in the same situation. Those opposed to local parties often point to the long period of domination in Montreal by Jean Drapeau and his Civic Party to illustrate their concerns.

Opponents of parties at the local level also wonder whether the parties which might become involved would be local parties focused on local issues, or just branches of the existing national parties. In the latter case, the concern is that the parties would likely neglect local issues and become essentially a grass roots organization for the senior level party. There is also the danger that local election results would reflect the popularity or unpopularity of the "parent" parties rather than the positions taken by the parties on local matters. This pattern has been noted in Britain, where many municipal council elections are contested by the national Labour and Conservative parties.

One of the main arguments against the introduction of parties is that they would bring division where none exists or should exist. "There is no political way to build a road," claim proponents of this viewpoint that reflects the lingering notion that local government activities are administrative not political in nature. Yet, if the actual construction of a road is a matter of engineering not politics, the decision on where to locate a particular road is certainly political. The decision on whether the traffic problem in question should be solved through building a road or providing an alternative form of public transportation is also clearly political. The decision on whether the scarce financial resources of the municipality should be used on transportation or some other pressing need is again political. Indeed, if the municipal council is concerned with establishing priorities in relation to conflicting public needs and demands, its role must be political. If the council is not to be charged with this task, one may well question the value of a separate level of local government.

> ... politics like sex, cannot be abolished ... because it is the nature of man to disagree and contend.... The fact is that even in a society of altruists or angels there would be politics, for some would conceive the common good one way and some in another....[3]

It must be acknowledged, however, that parties tend to exaggerate differences and to criticize excessively for purely partisan purposes. These traits have been all too evident in the actions of the parties operating at the senior levels of government, and it is understandable that many do not want to see such a divisive, confrontational style dominate council discussions.

Ultimately, it doesn't really matter how soundly based are the arguments against the introduction of local political parties. If people **feel** that they are a bad idea, then they won't receive support, whatever might be their objective merits. To date in Canada, the vast majority of citizens appear to see more drawbacks than advantages to the party politics in local government.

What Do Municipalities Do and Why Should We Care?

The most obvious purpose served by municipalities is that they provide a wide range of services and facilities which affect the quality of our day-to-day lives. The rather fanciful adventures of our student Frank N. Earnest, found in Chapter 2, illustrated this fact.

---

[3]Edward C. Banfield and James Q. Wilson, *City Politics*, Cambridge, Harvard University Press, 1963, pp. 20-21.

The importance of municipal services in the everyday life of Canadians cannot be overemphasized. To suggest that "the city council's services mean the difference between savagery and civilization" is scarcely an exaggeration — even though this observation was made 150 years ago![4] If anything, the observation rings more true today.

Look around you. You drive on municipal roads, walk on municipal sidewalks and, increasingly, cycle on municipal bike paths. Any land you own can only be developed in conformity with planning policies and regulations established by your municipality. That land is serviced by municipal water and sewer lines or, in most rural areas, by a well and septic tank system inspected by local health officials. Your property is protected by a municipal fire department, perhaps made up of volunteers from the community. You enjoy recreational and library facilities provided by the municipality and attend cultural events in facilities provided or supported by the municipality. Your garbage is collected by the municipality — whether directly by municipal staff or indirectly through the hiring of a private contractor. Depending on your circumstances, you may make use of day care centres, homes for the aged, public housing, or public health programs — all provided or financially supported by municipalities.

Providing Services is NOT the Primary Role

While these servicing considerations are important, they are not — or should not be seen as — the main role of municipal government.[5] Municipalities are not just a vehicle for service delivery. They are much more; they are a separate, elected level of government. As such, they have a representative and political role which is the primary reason for their existence. The real value of municipalities is that they provide a political mechanism through which a local community can express its collective concerns. At their

---

[4]By Sir Ernest Simon, about British local government, as quoted in K. G. Crawford, *Canadian Municipal Government*, Toronto, University of Toronto Press, 1954, p. 4.

[5]The discussion which follows is largely based on Tindal and Tindal, *op. cit.*, especially Chapter 1.

best, they exist as an extension of the community, as the community governing itself. Municipalities have this potential because they are the government closest to the people (certainly in the physical and geographic sense), most aware of local conditions, concerns and needs, and most responsive (usually) to such local knowledge.

At a time when the public has become increasingly disillusioned with governments and critical of their remoteness and lack of response, it is municipalities which are regarded as the most sensitive and the most accessible. While no level of government may be rated as highly as private organizations in terms of "customer satisfaction," municipalities consistently rate best among the levels of governments. One can argue that customer satisfaction is a private sector concept which is unfairly applied to governments — which deal with taxpayers or citizens, rather than customers. Even if that contention is valid, the fact remains that when all governments are compared in this way, municipalities fare much better than the senior levels.[6]

Impression of Service Provided	
Grocery Stores	68%
Banks	53%
Airlines	41%
Municipal Government	38%
Provincial Government	26%
Federal Government	24%

A rating of 38% is hardly a cause for celebration in municipal circles, but it is fully one-third better than the rating given the senior levels.

---

[6]1992 survey by Insight Canada Research, reflecting the proportion of respondents rating service as excellent or good, cited in F. Leslie Seidle, *Rethinking the Delivery of Public Services to Citizens*, Montreal, Institute for Research on Public Policy, 1995, p. 77.

Is Bigger Better?

As the 21st century approaches, however, there is strong pressure on municipalities to consolidate. Most provinces have a large number of municipalities, many containing very small populations. For example, Québec has over 1400 municipalities, three-quarters of them rural and under 2000 population. Ontario, even after substantial consolidations over the past three decades, still has close to 800 municipalities, two-thirds of them with populations under 5000. The conventional wisdom is that most of these small municipalities have insufficient resources to handle the responsibilities they face. According to this viewpoint, conditions will only worsen as the senior levels of government cut transfer payments and shift costs and responsibilities downward in an effort to deal with their own deficit and debt problems. In response, it is argued, municipalities must *amalgamate* to reduce duplication and to achieve economies of scale and greater efficiency.

Municipal Amalgamations Again to the Fore

As a result, recent years have seen a revival of the kind of municipal restructuring initiatives which were prevalent in the 1960s in several provinces. The Atlantic Provinces have been quite active in this regard with substantial amalgamations in the Saint John's area of Newfoundland, in the Charlottetown and Summerside areas of Prince Edward Island, in the Miramichi area of New Brunswick and in the Cape Breton and Halifax areas of Nova Scotia.[7]

There were some relatively modest restructurings in Ontario at the beginning of the 1990s involving the city of London and also municipalities in Lambton and Simcoe counties. However, these were apparently just "warm-ups" for the massive amalgamations which have been aggressively pursued by the Harris Government since its election in mid-1995. Some of these involve relatively small and rural municipalities, such as those affected by amalgamations which have

---

[7]For a general discussion of these and other reform initiatives, see Tindal and Tindal, *op. cit.*, Chapter 5.

been agreed to in three separate restructurings in the counties of Frontenac, Lennox & Addington, and Prince Edward, all in Eastern Ontario. Others, however, involve much larger municipalities. The Province has declared its intention of merging the six municipalities in the Hamilton-Wentworth area to create one city of half a million people. There have been suggestions that it favours a similar "supercity" for the Ottawa-Carleton area. Most dramatic of all, however, has been the introduction of legislation to eliminate the municipality of Metropolitan Toronto and to amalgamate the six municipalities in the Metro area to create a "megacity" of 2.3 million people.

♦ *Something to Think About*

Do these amalgamations make sense to you? On the surface, it sounds logical that having fewer governments should mean less duplication and less cost. But even if that were the case, are you comfortable with **local** governments that become this large?

In some situations, amalgamations may indeed make sense. Municipal boundaries often reflect historical patterns that bear little relation to the population movement of today and may divide natural "communities of interest." Divided jurisdictions within one socio-economic area may also inhibit desirable cooperation or may produce inequities in the sharing of costs for services which are accessed across municipal boundaries. One should be wary, however, of the two main "benefits" currently being promoted as the rationale for amalgamation in the province of Ontario: **(1)** that it will save money and help municipalities to cope with cuts in Provincial transfers and **(2)** that it will reduce the number of municipalities and municipal politicians, which is somehow presented as a self-evident boon to society.

The first argument flies in the face of the overwhelming evidence that amalgamations increase costs rather than reduce them.[8] Some

---

[8]Much of this evidence has been very effectively summarized and analyzed by Andrew Sancton, "Reducing Costs by Consolidating Munici-

important cautionary comments in this regard were provided by the recent Task Force on the *GTA* (Greater Toronto Area) which noted that the benefits of amalgamation are often overstated. Whatever savings may be achieved from eliminating administrative duplication are often lost because of the upward pressure on wages and service standards that occurs when different wage and service structures are combined. The Task Force also pointed out that amalgamation means fewer municipalities against which to compare efficiency and performance and less pressure to keep costs down.[9] This absence of choice and competitive pressure is, of course, why we fear monopolies in the private sector. Experience has shown that they usually result in higher prices and lower quality. It is strange that we should advocate through municipal amalgamation the creation of the same monopoly situation we seek to avoid in the private sector.

Experience to date with the recent amalgamation of four municipalities in the Halifax area also casts doubt on the notion that savings will result. Proponents of the scheme did concede that transition costs would reach $10 million, but that this amount would be recouped within five years and that savings would then accumulate. Since the new city commenced operations on April 1, 1996 however, costs have already increased by $25 million and the payback period has been extended to ten years.[10]

The second widely cited argument in support of amalgamation is both dangerous and inherently anti-democratic. Proponents play on the widespread public disillusionment with government and politicians in praising the fewer municipalities and municipal politicians which will result. **Let us be very clear**. Amalgamation doesn't give us less government; it gives us bigger government, farther removed

---

palities: New Brunswick, Nova Scotia and Ontario," in *Canadian Public Administration*, Fall 1996, which, contrary to its title, demonstrates that cost reductions do not occur.

[9]Report of the GTA Task Force, *Greater Toronto*, Toronto, Publications Ontario, January 1996, pp. 212-213.

[10]Tim Harper, "Halifax shows us how not to amalgamate," *Toronto Star*, December 8, 1996.

from the people it is meant to represent and to serve. It gives us more bureaucratic government, in which the personal touch which citizens enjoyed in small municipalities is replaced with the touch tone phone and the computerized list of numbers to push to listen to recorded messages while searching vainly for a human voice. It results in increased workloads for councillors, which often makes the job full time and thus unavailable to a wide cross-section of citizens. The fact that campaigning over large areas is also more expensive, further reduces the pool of potential candidates.

You should ask yourself what benefits are gained when the number of municipal councillors in an area is reduced by half or two-thirds. What is beneficial about reducing the number of representatives who are elected by, and on behalf of, the local community? There isn't even any significant savings in taking this action, in part because of the very low salaries paid to councillors in most municipalities. Moreover, those salaries inevitably go up because of the increased workload associated with amalgamation. The Halifax example is again instructive. The number of councillors has been reduced from 60 to 23, but at a salary which has more than doubled.[11] Experience in Winnipeg also demonstrates that as the number of councillors has been reduced over the years, the salary for Mayor and councillors has increased substantially and has, since 1992, extended to an allowance of $35 000 per councillor to hire political staff to assist with constituency work.[12]

Perhaps you aren't overly impressed with your particular municipal councillors, but they are all you have in support of local democracy — "a poor thing, but your own." Whatever the faults of your municipality, it is **your** municipality. Don't give it up without careful consideration if you find yourself in the midst of an amalgamation exercise.

---

[11]Remarks by Gloria McCluskey (former Mayor of Dartmouth) on *Commentary*, CBC Radio, November 14, 1996.

[12]Jae Eadie (Deputy Mayor, City of Winnipeg) in *Municipal World*, November 1996, p. 25.

Local Boards and Commissions

While they are numerous and diverse enough, municipalities are not the only form of local government found in Canada. There are also a wide variety of special purpose bodies, often referred to as agencies, boards and commissions or *ABCs*. Their prevalence varies by province, with Ontario having the largest concentration of these bodies and providing the examples used in this section. Probably the best known example is that of school boards, which in Ontario spend more of the local tax dollars raised than municipalities do. Other bodies with which you are likely familiar are public utilities commissions, health units, community centre boards, conservation authorities, library boards and police services boards.

By their very nature, these boards operate outside of the municipal structure. They usually have only one or a very limited range of functions, as implied by the term "special purpose" body. Some boards finance at least part of their operations from *user charges, such as the bus fares charged by a municipal transit system and the ice rental and concession charges of a community centre*. While some boards operate within the boundaries of the municipality, many are intermunicipal in nature and take in two or more (often many more) municipalities.

A local government structure which includes many of these separate boards is often criticized for being fragmented and lacking in overall priority setting. Concerns are also raised about accountability, since most of these boards — with the notable exception of school boards and public utilities commissions — are not elected but appointed, and their sheer numbers make it easy to "pass the buck" and evade responsibility for problems that arise.

On the other hand, it is possible that more of these boards will be established in the future, as a vehicle for administering and coordinating new partnerships which are being promoted amongst municipalities and between municipalities and the private sector. In part, this reflects the growing recognition that municipalities can be "*service arrangers*" rather than necessarily direct service providers. This involves a council working with the local community to identify what services are needed and then making whatever arrangements are most cost-effective for the delivery of those services.[13] In response to the Ontario Government's objective of streamlining municipal government, a number of areas are discussing the replacement of existing upper tier governments with some form of joint servicing board. This board would arrange for the delivery of a limited number of cross-boundary services over whatever combination of municipalities produce the greatest economies of scale.[14] This flexible structure is essentially a variation of the regional district model which has operated in British Columbia for more than thirty years.

School Boards

Among local boards, the school board merits special attention, given the importance of its responsibilities and the size of its claim on financial resources. It is also the board which comes closest to being like a municipality.

School boards are comprised of elected trustees, making the governing body somewhat comparable to a municipal council. There are two main exceptions to this arrangement. The first is found in Alberta where, in thirty of the school systems, the control of education is in the hands of county governments. Instead of a school board, there is a committee made up of county councillors and representatives from the towns and villages within each area.[15] The second exception is in New Brunswick, where parent councils have replaced school trustees.

---

[13]This important distinction was popularized as the difference between steering (setting direction and determining needs) and rowing (providing services) in David Osborne and Ted Gaebler, *Reinventing Government*, New York, Penguin Books, 1993.

[14]This type of joint board for cross-boundary services has been proposed or is under active consideration in such areas as Hamilton-Wentworth, Ottawa-Carleton and the Greater Toronto Area.

[15]Robert Carney and Frank Peters, "Governing Education: The Myth of Local Control," in James Lightbody (ed.), *Canadian Metropolitics*, Toronto, Copp Clark Ltd., 1995, p. 254.

School boards look after a number of services and facilities which are linked (or should be linked) to responsibilities of the municipality. For example, in provinces like Ontario:

♦ schools have libraries and so do municipalities;

♦ schools have playgrounds and recreational facilities and so do municipalities;

♦ schools have buses and so do many municipalities; and

♦ schools have meeting rooms and so do municipalities (and many libraries).

It is clear that there is great potential for collaboration and joint ventures between school boards and the municipalities in their area. Traditionally, however, contact and communication was very limited, mainly arising at budget time when councillors complained about the cost of the school board operations.

The school board is also like the municipality in its dependence on the property tax[16] and provincial transfers to finance its operations. This pattern is changing, however, because of prolonged criticism of the inappropriateness of financing education from the property tax. Most provinces fund all or the bulk of the costs of elementary and secondary education, and Ontario is now moving in that direction. The Ontario Government introduced plans in January 1997 for assuming the portion of the education costs generated by the residential property tax (currently about $5.4 billion). Commercial and industrial property taxes will remain, and will still be collected by municipalities, but the Province will determine the tax rate and the distribution of these funds to school boards.

Another similarity is that school boards have also gone through restructuring and amalgamation, in fact earlier and to a greater degree than municipalities. The proliferation of small school districts made

---

[16]This is a tax levied upon real property (that is, land and buildings) within the boundaries of the municipality. For further details on this tax, see Appendix A.

such changes inevitable.[17] In Alberta, for example, where the first major consolidations occurred, there were in 1935 almost 4000 distinct school districts. Each of these had its own school board and most boards were responsible for single-room schools. Many of the tiny rural districts lacked an adequate financial base and consolidation was seen as a way of spreading the cost of schooling over a broader economic base and enhancing the quality of programs available. As a result, the number of school boards was reduced to under 200 by 1995 and then to 66.

Similar programs of consolidation have occurred in the other provinces.[18] For example, following a study in 1945, B.C. regrouped its 650 school boards into 75 boards, which are to be further reduced to 59. Québec reforms in the 1970s regrouped some 1800 local school authorities into fewer than 200 and there is a current proposal to reduce them further to 100. In Ontario by 1950, 3465 small rural districts had been consolidated into 536 township boards. There was a major restructuring at the end of the 1960s to create some 166 county school boards (public, separate and Francophone). These will be further reduced to only 66 (29 public boards, 26 separate boards and 11 French boards) as a result of plans announced in early 1997. This restructuring is part of a series of changes which will increase Provincial control over education. As already noted, even more drastic changes have occurred in New Brunswick, where all school boards and elected trustees have been abolished and replaced with parent councils. The Province retains final approval for hiring teachers and principals and all non-teaching school employees have become provincial civil servants — prompting critics of the change to label the new system of parental participation a "shell game" designed to conceal increased centralization of power in the province.[19]

---

[17]The examples which follow are from Carney and Peters, *op. cit.*, pp. 249-250.

[18]The figures which follow are from Brett Lodge, "Management and financing of schools across the country," *Toronto Star*, January 14, 1997.

[19]Susan Kastner, "New era in NB: Schools without trustees," *Toronto Star*, September 29, 1996.

♦ *Something to Think About*

Are we on the right track? Should education become a provincial responsibility, so that it can be funded from sources other than the property tax and so that province-wide standards can be ensured?

This is certainly where we have been heading, in a number of provinces. If current trends continue in provinces like Ontario, we will see fewer and much larger school boards, increasingly funded from provincial revenue sources. The first reaction of municipal tax-payers is to welcome any change which will shift such an expensive burden off the property tax. It is important to recognize, however, that such changes also mean an increasingly centralized and bureaucratized educational administration. They take decisions about education farther away from the local community. Granted, New Brunswick has set up parent councils and Ontario is setting up school councils composed primarily of parents and including school principals, teachers and community representatives. But, it remains to be seen how long enthusiasm for, and commitment to, these essentially advisory bodies can be sustained if decision making becomes increasingly centralized at the provincial level.

It must be remembered that education isn't just a cost; it is a vital social program which has been shown to have the potential to make a very positive impact on the development of young Canadians. The same parents who currently complain to their school board about the high cost of education today, may have a new cause for concern if such spending decisions become centralized in provincial administrations preoccupied with deficit and debt reduction. Two years ago, the Alberta government took away the right of school boards in that province to levy taxes — an action which is currently the subject of a lawsuit mounted by the boards.[20] Much the same arrangement will prevail in Ontario, since only commercial and industrial property taxes will continue to fund education and the Province will decide the

[20]Brian Laghi, "School boards pursuing lawsuit against Alberta," *Globe and Mail*, November 16, 1996.

standard tax rate to be levied. The *Who Does What* panel [21] had recommended that school boards retain the discretion to charge up to 5% of their annual expenditures on the residential property tax (for local enrichment programs), but the Province ignored this proposal.

Currently, local citizens have the discretion, through their elected school boards, to give as high a priority to education as they are prepared to finance. It is appreciated that the result of this local discretion has been a considerable variation in the standard of education across Ontario. The proposed new arrangements will bring greater standardization, which many welcome — but standardization at what level? Given its record to date, and its frequent pronouncements about reducing expenditures on education, there are reasonable grounds for concern that the Harris Government would use its new powers to force down spending on education by dictating modest taxes on business properties. If so, local citizens will be helpless to prevent this action and may actually find themselves missing those "spendthrift" school boards that they used to decry.

Concluding Observations

Municipalities have usually been the most neglected level of government in Canada — not only in terms of their limited resources and lack of constitutional recognition, but also with respect to the degree of apparent public interest in their activities. As this chapter has attempted to show, however, municipalities play (or should play) a fundamental representative and political role, providing a vehicle through which local communities can identify and address their collective concerns. Municipalities and other local governing bodies also provide a wide range of services, facilities and regulations which help to define the nature of the local community and its quality of life.

---

[21]Chaired by former Toronto Mayor David Crombie, the panel was established in mid-1996 "to ensure the very best service delivery by reducing waste, duplication and the overall cost of government at the provincial and local government levels."

How well municipalities will play their political and service delivery roles in the future is a matter of debate at present. As the lowest level in Canada's complex intergovernmental system, municipalities find themselves bearing the brunt of the downsizing and other debt and deficit reduction strategies being pursued by the senior levels of government. They continue to face heavy, even increasing, demands for services, while the resources available to them are sharply curtailed through cutbacks in provincial transfer payments. International pressures, many relating to the globalization of the economy, also place constraints on municipal actions. Perhaps most of all, municipalities are threatened by the anti-government sentiment prevalent in society today, sentiment which allows some provincial governments to present forced amalgamations as an inherently beneficial step because the result is fewer municipal politicians.

Now, as perhaps never before, it is essential that citizens give far more attention to that level of government they have too often taken for granted in the past. To ignore it, is to run the risk of losing it, and to end up with local governments which are no longer "local," either in terms of the area served or the capacity to make decisions which reflect local rather than provincial priorities.

Appendix A
The Real Property Tax

While most Canadians are somewhat familiar with the taxes they pay at the provincial and federal levels, including sales tax and income tax, there is usually considerably more confusion about the property tax and how it is determined. For those interested, this appendix provides a brief explanation.

As with all taxes, the property tax has two components: a tax base and a tax rate. For example, in the case of the personal income tax, the tax base is your total taxable income (that is, after all deductions) and the tax rate is expressed in percentage terms. As you move into higher income levels, a higher percentage of tax must be paid.

In contrast, the tax base for the property tax is "real property," essentially defined as all land and buildings on land. A dollar value or assessment is placed on all of this real property, usually by provincial staff as is the case in Ontario. The tax rate is expressed in mills, with one mill being 1/10 of a cent. This means that one mill would raise $1.00 if levied upon $1000 of assessment. To determine the amount of property tax it will impose, therefore, a municipality starts with the total amount of assessment it has available to tax and then calculates how large a mill rate it will need to impose in order to generate the funds it requires for the coming year's operations.

A simplified formula for this calculation is as follows:

$$\frac{\text{Amount to be raised from taxation}}{\text{Total taxable assessment}} * \text{(multiplied by) } 1000$$

The amount to be raised from taxation is determined as part of the municipality's annual budget process. It is the amount of money that will be required to run the municipality **less** the amount of money that can be raised from sources other than the property tax. [The two other sources are transfer payments from the senior levels of government (which are being sharply reduced) and miscellaneous local revenues such as license fees, development charges, and various user fees on such activities as garbage pick-up or disposal, public transit and rental of ice at the community centre.] This amount is divided by total **taxable** assessment because not all land can be taxed. Government buildings, churches, cemeteries, schools, and public hospitals are examples of tax-exempt properties on which municipalities receive payments-in-lieu (of taxes) instead. The resulting figure is then multiplied by 1000 because a mill is only 1/10 of a cent. This produces a mill rate, essentially a ratio which, when applied against the taxable assessmen,t will produce the amount of money needed.

Let's take a simple example and work it through. What if a municipality determines that it will need $15 000 000 for the coming year and can only expect to raise $5 000 000 from sources other than the property tax. What mill rate will the municipality have to levy if it has $200 000 000 of taxable assessment? Apply the simple formula:

$$\frac{\text{Amount to be raised} = \$10\ 000\ 000\ (\$15\ M - \$5\ M)}{\text{Taxable assessment} = \$200\ 000\ 000} * 1000 = 50\ \text{mills}$$

This calculation shows that 50 mills is required. If we levy a tax rate of 50 mills against an assessment base of $200 000 000, it will yield the $10 000 000 required by the municipality.

What happens if the municipality has twice as much assessment?

$$\frac{\text{Amount to be raised} = \$10\ 000\ 000}{\text{Taxable assessment} = \$400\ 000\ 000} * 1000 = 25\ \text{mills}$$

When the assessment is doubled, it only takes half as large a mill rate to generate the same amount of money. It is the amount of taxable assessment which is the key to a municipality's financial health. The mill rate is simply whatever ratio is needed to generate the required funds. Still not convinced? Follow it through to the level of an individual home — your home! Let's say that in the first example, one part of that $200 000 000 in taxable assessment is your home, assessed at $10 000.[22] Your tax bill of 50 mills means that you will owe $500. In

---

[22]This low amount reflects the fact that assessed values often lag far behind market values (which has certainly been the case in Ontario).

the second example, all properties have doubled in value, so your home is now assessed at $20 000. But, since your tax rate is now only 25 mills, the taxes you owe are unchanged at $500.

Appearances (assessments) Can Be Deceiving!

As should be clear by now, having a low assessment doesn't mean that you will have low taxes. It just means that the municipality will have to levy a higher mill rate to generate the funds it needs. A low assessment also doesn't mean that you are "beating the system." Your neighbour's property may be even more underassessed (in relation to its real value) than yours — in which case you are still paying an excessive share when the municipal mill rate is levied upon the two properties.

An effective and fair system of property taxation, therefore, requires that the assessment base be regularly updated and that comparable properties have comparable values. The responsibility for carrying out the assessment of properties has gradually shifted to the provincial level in most provinces. This shift occurred in Ontario more than 25 years ago, and was to ensure the introduction of an equitable system known as market value assessment. It appears that the Ontario Government has finally decided that action is needed. The Minister of Municipal Affairs announced in July 1996 that a new province-wide system known as actual value assessment (AVA) will be introduced beginning on January 1, 1998.

The Last Word

Definition of Terms and Concepts

ABCs:
> Agencies, boards and commissions — a term used to described the variety of separate bodies (such as school boards and utility commissions) which form part of the local government system.

Amalgamate:
> To join together two or more complete municipalities to form only one. This contrasts with the process of annexation in which part of one municipality is joined to another, leaving the two separate municipalities, one now larger and one smaller.

Assessment:
> The dollar value placed upon the real property (land and buildings) within a municipality to determine its tax base on which the property tax is levied.

CAO (Chief Administrative Officer):
> Coordinating officer appointed by council to lead and direct the other employees of the municipality, to provide cohesive policy advice to council and to coordinate the implementation of council's decisions.

Executive Committee:
> Senior coordinating committee of council, usually composed of the chairs of the various standing committees and headed by the Mayor. This committee is expected to provide leadership and executive direction, especially in relation to setting priorities and allocating finances.

GTA (Greater Toronto Area):
Term to describe the area covered by the Municipality of Metropolitan Toronto and the four surrounding regional municipalities
of Durham, Halton, Peel and York.

Indirectly Elected:
Refers to situations in which members of a municipal council
hold their position by virtue of their prior election to another
governing body. For example, reeves and deputy reeves elected
to Ontario township, village and town councils automatically become members of, and are considered indirectly elected to, county
councils.

Lower Tier: (See two tier system.)

Municipalities:
Elected local governments which exercise assigned responsibilities, including the power to levy the property tax, within a
defined geographic area.

Property Tax:
Tax expressed in mills which is levied upon the assessed value of
real property (land and buildings on land) found within a municipality.

Real Property: (See property tax.)

Service Arranger:
Term to describe the fact that municipalities need not be direct
service providers, but can deliver services through partnership
arrangements with other public bodies or with the private sector.

Single Tier:
Term to describe municipalities which are not part of a two tier
system. Only Ontario, Québec and BC have two tier systems, and
in Ontario single tier municipalities are still found in the North
and in the case of cities separate from the county system.

Two tier System:
Municipal government systems which comprise a lower tier of cities, towns, townships and other municipalities, and an upper tier of counties, regions or districts.

Upper Tier: (See two tier system.)

Points to Ponder

1. How old is your municipality? Was it incorporated before Canada became a country? Has it gone through any boundary changes or other restructuring in recent years?

2. Is your municipality part of a two tier system? If so, do you know which tier is responsible for what services?

3. Do you know what local boards operate in your area? Try preparing a list of these boards, along the lines of the *Guide to Government Directory* in Chapter 2.

4. Look at your last municipal tax bill. It will identify the portion of taxes related to municipal services and (if applicable) education and upper tier expenditures. Where is your property tax money going, and how satisfied are you with what you are getting in return?

5. On what basis is property assessed in your municipality? Does the assessed value which has been placed on your property seem fair and reasonable? Remember that a very low assessment may not be advantageous. It is easiest to make sense of your assessment if it is based on market value or some variation of that system, since most people have a good idea of the selling price of the property.

For Further Reading

For a good introduction to various aspects of local government across Canada, see C. Richard Tindal and Susan Nobes Tindal, *Local Government in Canada*, 4th edition, Whitby, McGraw-Hill Ryerson Limited, 1995.

Other books with a general or Canada-wide perspective include James Lightbody (ed.), *Canadian Metropolitics*, Toronto, Copp Clark Ltd., 1995 and Richard Loreto and Trevor Price (eds.), *Urban Policy Issues*, Toronto, McClelland & Stewart Inc., 1990.

There are also a number of books which focus on the local government system in individual provinces. Examples include:

Kell Antoft (ed.), *A Guide to Local Government in Nova Scotia*, 3rd edition, Halifax, Dalhousie University, 1992.

Robert Bish, *Local Government in British Columbia*, 2nd edition, Victoria, University of Victoria, 1991.

Jack Masson, *Alberta's Local Governments: Politics and Democracy*, Edmonton, University of Alberta Press, 1994.

Ontario Municipal Management Institute, *You and Your Local Government*, 3rd edition, Whitby, 1993.

Various articles on local government developments, and information on legislative changes affecting the local level, are found in the magazine, *Municipal World*, St. Thomas, monthly.

Chapter 6

Federal and Provincial Governments: A Closer Look

Objectives and Highlights

♦ To explain the roles of the Cabinet and why it, and the Prime Minister, have become so dominant.

♦ To examine the roles and effectiveness of the House of Commons and Senate.

♦ To assess the demands on MPs by examining their various roles.

Every four years or so, Canadians have an opportunity to elect members to the House of Commons (and to the legislative assembly in their province). How significant is this democratic exercise, and how important are the roles played by these elected representatives?

This chapter examines the organization and functioning of the parliamentary system of government found at the senior levels. It discusses the reasons why the public service, the Cabinet and the Prime Minister have all gained in power and influence throughout the 20th century. It explores the nature and effectiveness of the representative, lawmaking and watchdog roles of the House of Commons, and it explains the key roles the Senate was expected to play and why its importance and legitimacy have declined over the years.

Our parliamentary system is certainly not without its problems and weaknesses. But it also has the potential to enforce a healthy degree of accountability — of the executive branch to the elected members and of the elected members to the public. By examining these links, this chapter helps you to understand how your government works and how you can most effectively participate in it.

Introduction

B oth the federal and provincial governments are organized on the parliamentary model. According to this model, Parliament is supreme and Prime Ministers or Premiers and their Cabinets only govern as long as they are supported by a majority of the elected members in the House of Commons or the Provincial Legislative Assemblies. From at least the beginning of the 20th century, however, power began shifting from the legislative branch to the executive branch. By the middle of this century the only question for debate was **where** in the executive branch the power was concentrated: in the Cabinet or in the senior civil service.

Over the past thirty years a number of reforms have been introduced to strengthen the legislative branch and to restore a greater balance in the executive-legislative relationship. While only partially successful, these reforms are important to you. Since your main direct involvement is to elect a government every four years or so (assuming that you vote), the rest of the time you depend upon the elected members in the legislative branch (especially the opposition members) to keep an eye on the government for you between elections. How well they exercise that role has a lot to do with how well you are governed.

These shifting patterns in the focus of power in our governmental system will become apparent in this chapter, as we take a closer look at the governing machinery and how it operates. While the main focus will be on the national government, the provinces operate in essentially the same manner.

The Cabinet and its Growing Dominance

Historically, the Cabinet was a group of advisors to the Monarch (or the Governor in the case of the colony of Canada), without any real power of its own. Its official title was, and is, the *Privy Council* — reflecting its role as 'private' advisors.

The full Privy Council consists of all past and present Cabinet members, past and present chief justices of the Supreme Court, past and present Speakers of the Senate and Commons, and other distinguished persons whom the government wishes to honour. Once appointed to the Privy Council, a person is entitled to be referred to as "The Honourable," a title which is kept for life. (A Prime Minister receives the title of "Right Honourable.") The full Privy Council does not meet except in very exceptional circumstances, such as the ascension to the throne of a new monarch. Our focus in this section is the active part of the Privy Council — that is, the Cabinet of whatever government is in power at the time.

With the introduction of the principle of responsible government in the 1840s, it became established that the Governor of the Colony (the forerunner of the Governor General) could only appoint as advisors people who would be supported by a majority of the elected members to the colonial assembly (and since Confederation in 1867, to the provincial and federal legislatures).

To this day, the Governor General officially appoints the members of the Privy Council. With the rise of disciplined political parties, however, support from the Assembly has become translated into support from the political party which controls the majority of seats in the Assembly. This, in turn, means that a Governor Governor really has no choice but to call upon the leader of the party which wins the most seats in an election to form a government. The leader of that winning party becomes the Prime Minister and decides which of his or her colleagues will be appointed to serve in the Cabinet. In practice, then, it is the Prime Minister who decides on the appointments to the Cabinet, even though they are officially and legally made by the Governor General.

The federal election in the fall of 1993 was fought with Kim Campbell as Prime Minister and the Progressive Conservative party in power in Ottawa. The election results reduced the governing Conservatives to two seats and gave the Liberal party 178 of the 295 seats in the House of Commons. Officially, it was the Governor General's responsibility to appoint the new government. In practice, the voters had left no doubt about the choice — as is appropriate for a democracy.

Choosing the Cabinet Members

On what basis does a Prime Minister select those who will be appointed by the Governor General to serve in the Cabinet? The recruitment process followed for most positions might suggest a search for the best qualified people among all Canadian adults. Instead, however, the talent pool to be drawn upon is dramatically more limited. One of the customs or conventions of our system of government is that those appointed to the Cabinet must have a seat in the House of Commons (or must secure such a seat within a short time of their appointment). The latter situation arose, for example, when Prime Minister Chrétien decided to strengthen his Cabinet representation from Québec following the very close vote on separation in late 1995. As outlined in Chapter 4, he appointed a trade consultant and foreign policy expert named Pierre Pettigrew and a university professor named Stéphane Dion. Both of these appointees then had to win election to the House of Commons (which they did) in order to retain their Cabinet positions.

Other Factors

There are also several other factors that a Prime Minister must consider when forming a Cabinet, including:

1. Geographic balance, since all areas of Canada expect representation in this important body.
2. Appropriate diversity, since Cabinets are expected to reflect the population of Canada by including women (in sufficient numbers), Francophones, new Canadians and other segments of society.
3. Prior government experience, since Cabinet members will assume many challenging responsibilities.
4. Background of education and experience appropriate for assuming a Cabinet post and heading a government department.
5. Past relationship with the Prime Minister, since, "all things being equal," Prime Ministers will tend to select those who have been long-standing acquaintances or supporters over those who may have supported rivals of the Prime Minister within the party.

Reasons for Cabinet Dominance

The growing domination of the Cabinet in the 20th century came about because of several factors, notably:

♦ The fact that the Cabinet is usually backed by a majority of members in the House of Commons from the same political party, as discussed above;

♦ The growing volume and complexity of government activities in the 20th century, and the corresponding "knowledge gap" in the House of Commons, where opposition members had little in the way of staff or expertise to help in carrying out their watchdog role; and

♦ The change in the nature of the lawmaking process. Statutes or Acts must be passed by Parliament (comprising both the House of Commons and the Senate). However, statute laws have become increasingly general in nature. They no longer attempt to encompass the total law on a subject. This change has occurred mainly because Parliament (and its members) lack the time and the technical knowledge to elaborate the law in all of the detail required. Moreover, often the government is introducing law into new areas of economic or social activity, and needs the flexibility to adapt the law quickly as conditions change.

As a result, most statutes passed over the past several decades set out the general purpose of the law and delegate the authority to some part of the executive branch to elaborate the law in detail over time. The growth in this *administrative law* (also known as *delegated legislation* or *subordinate legislation*) has meant a reduction in the power and importance of Parliament and a further expansion of the power of the Cabinet (and civil service, who actually make the detailed laws).

To illustrate administrative law and to show the helpful but potentially worrisome role it can play in our government system, consider the example which follows. It actually relates to a provincial law, but provides what will be a familiar example for most people.

Getting a "Lift" out of Lawmaking

Take a look at the wall in front on you in the next elevator in which you ride. You will see a notice which indicates that the elevator has been licensed to carry a certain number of people. It tells you that the elevator has been inspected by government officials to ensure its safe operation.

Try to imagine what it was like the first time a government tried to pass a law dealing with elevator safety. This is a very technical subject, concerned with things like thickness of cable, tensile strength, pneumatics and hydraulics. It does not lend itself to debate among political parties; nor is there a discernable difference between the Liberals, Conservatives, NDP or any other party concerning hydraulics!

As a result, the Elevator Safety Act itself is a brief and general statute, mainly establishing that there will be elevator safety standards and providing a mechanism for enforcing them. The Act then delegates to the executive branch the authority to establish the actual safety standards. These standards are equally the law of the land, arguably the most important part of the law. But they were not passed by the legislative branch in a statute. They were enacted later, gradually over time, by the executive branch. This kind of arrangement is logical for dealing with such technical matters. But as it is repeated over a wide range of government activities, you can see the effect it has on shifting power from the legislative branch to the executive branch.

The Power of the Prime Minister

As much as the Cabinet has gained in power and influence over the 20th century, it has been surpassed by the increasing concentration of power in the position of Prime Minister (and Provincial Premier). This development illustrates well the contrast between law and practice which is often found in the operations of the Canadian system of government. There is virtually no mention of the position of Prime Minister in the constitution of Canada; yet the occupant of that office is the undisputed leader and his or her dominance is reflected in the way governments are personalized as the Chrétien Government, the

Mulroney Government, the Klein Government in Alberta or the Harris Government in Ontario.

Part of the Prime Minister's power, of course, comes from the fact that he[1] alone determines who will be chosen to sit in the Cabinet, what portfolio they will hold, and how long they will stay. There are some constraints on these choices, however, since powerful regional Ministers will expect, and will have to be given, Cabinet positions. The Prime Minister also chairs the Cabinet meetings and can exert influence over the decisions which are made — although he must obviously "pick his spots" and not try to force his view on every issue.

Much of the Prime Minister's power comes from being the head of a political party, especially when that party holds a majority of the seats in the House of Commons. There are a number of positive and negative inducements which ensure that members vote the party line. Party discipline is especially strong with respect to members of the governing party, since any defection by them could potentially bring down the government. An ultimate weapon, to be used very sparingly, that a Prime Minister has to keep rebellious *backbenchers* in line, is to threaten to dissolve parliament and bring on an election campaign.[2] Going back to the electorate is a risky and expensive proposition for members, and a judicious use of this threat can be effective.

The Prime Minister, either on his own or acting officially as part of the *Governor-in-Council*,[3] also has extensive appointment powers which add to his power and influence. In addition to the selection of

---

[1]To simplify references, the pronoun 'he' will be used throughout this section.

[2]As discussed elsewhere in the Guide, dissolution is actually carried out by the Governor General on a request from the Prime Minister but, except in very unusual circumstances, this request will automatically be granted.

[3]Since the Cabinet per se is not mentioned in the constitution of Canada, when it wishes to speak legally it does so as the Privy Council in conjunction with the Governor General, or what is known as the Governor-in-Council. In practice, appointments made by this body are the choice of, or at least have the blessing of, the Prime Minister.

Cabinet Ministers, already mentioned, the Prime Minister appoints Senators, Supreme Court judges, ambassadors and a variety of other government positions. When Jean Chrétien came to power in 1993, for example, there were more than 2000 positions on the appointment list to be filled by his office. [4]

The Importance of Image

Above all else, however, a Prime Minister has great power if he is "a winner," if the party feels that he is the key to victory, if individual candidates believe that they owe their seats to the Prime Minister's personal popularity, that they have gone to Ottawa "on his coattails." In the age of television, "winnability" is largely determined by the image one is able to project and this enhances the value of party leaders who can be packaged and marketed effectively.

This is not a new development. Forty years ago, John Diefenbaker scored a stunning upset victory for the Progressive Conservatives after they had spent a generation in the political wilderness, then won again by a landslide the following year (1958). Many PC candidates rode to Ottawa on Diefenbaker's coattails that year, and they remained fiercely loyal to "The Chief" long after he had been deposed as party leader. The famous Nixon-Kennedy television debate was held almost forty years ago (1959), as a result of which the underdog but much more photogenic Kennedy went on to defeat his rival. Robert Stanfield fought three unsuccessful election campaigns against Pierre Trudeau between 1968 and 1974, hampered by an unflattering public image, especially when contrasted with that of Trudeau. Whatever the substantive policy issues, what Canadians "saw" was the image of Stanfield fumbling the football at a pre-game ceremony for the Grey Cup game versus Trudeau sliding down bannisters, racing around in a sportscar and dating Barbra Streisand. It doesn't matter whether either image accurately portrayed the individuals involved. Perception is reality, and nowhere more than in politics. Mulroney clearly demolished a rusty John Turner during the television debates

---

[4]Robert Jackson and Doreen Jackson, *Canadian Government in Transition*, Scarborough, Prentice-Hall Canada Inc., 1996, p. 128.

preceding the 1984 election, while a better coached and better prepared John Turner solidly outperformed Mulroney in the 1988 debates. Kim Campbell was chosen by the Progressive Conservative party to replace Brian Mulroney and the party's popularity climbed impressively for a few months on the strength of little more than her lively image and irreverent style.

The point of all these examples is that when Prime Ministers have a very popular public image, and especially when they are clearly more popular than their party, they have great influence. The party knows that it can win with them, but it is not sure that it can win without them. The Liberal party is still doing well in the polls, but it scores well below the approval rating which Jean Chrétien continues to enjoy and which clearly augments his power. On the other hand, Prime Ministers who are less popular than their party may find themselves in a weak position, no matter what are supposed to be the strengths of the office. There is no better example than that of Joe Clark at the end of the 1970s. The Progressive Conservatives seemed to feel that they had won in spite of Clark, not because of him, and the pressure continued to build until he resigned as leader and was replaced by Mulroney. Ironically, once deposed, Clark's public image steadily improved and he eventually became the most respected member of the Mulroney Government.

The Prime Minister and the President

The popular image of the office of U.S. President is that it is all-powerful. The incumbent exercises various powers, including Commander-in-Chief of the Armed Forces. He operates independently of Congress, can veto bills passed by Congress (although the veto can be over-ridden by a two-thirds majority in both Houses of Congress), and can negotiate treaties with foreign countries (although they must be approved by the Senate). Perhaps above all, the President holds office for a fixed, four year term — whether or not he is supported by Congress (which he often is not). In contrast, Canadian Prime Ministers have virtually no specific powers of their own and must answer at all times to the House of Commons, ultimately by seeking a new mandate in an election if the Commons withholds its support.

◆ ***Something to Think About***

The reality of the Prime Minister–President comparison is rather different.[5] The position of Prime Minister can be at least as powerful and some observers wonder if there are adequate safeguards to protect against abuse of power by a Prime Minister.

A Canadian Prime Minister backed by a majority government has a very impressive power base, especially when compared to a U.S. President facing a Congress dominated by members of the opposite political party. Actually, Presidents may have enough trouble when facing a Congress comprised of a majority of members of their own party! Voting patterns are not nearly as disciplined in the United States, partly because there is no such thing as "defeating a government" since the President is in office for a fixed four year term. Members of Congress often act and vote very independently, forcing Presidents to give careful attention to building support within their own party.

As already discussed, the media focus on the style and personality of the party leader can add greatly to the power and influence of a Prime Minister with a popular public image. The result has been the development of what has been termed "leadership politics." Even veteran Conservative Dalton Camp observed that "elements of the imperial prime ministership crept in" during the Mulroney era, as evidenced by the ever-expanding entourage of aides, guards, courtiers and equipment that accompanied the Prime Minister on his travels.[6] Denis Smith concludes that "as long as Canada has party pollsters to guide the leaders, its own television networks to display them, and parliamentary elections to legitimize them, nothing much is likely to change in the dominance of the Prime Minister."He argues that the

---

[5]The ensuing discussion is based on Denis Smith, "Is the Prime Minister Too Powerful? - Yes" and Joseph Wearing, "Is the Prime Minister Too Powerful? - No," in Mark Charlton and Paul Barker, *Crosscurrents: Contemporary Political Issues*, Scarborough, Nelson Canada, 1994, pp. 154-166.

[6]Quoted in Smith, *op. cit.*, p. 156.

Prime Minister enjoys the powers of the President without the constraints imposed by an independent Congress.[7]

Joseph Wearing disagrees with this assessment,[8] and suggests that if there are problems or concerns, they arise from the ineffectiveness of such bodies as political parties, Parliament, the electorate and the media in monitoring the exercise of Prime Ministerial power. He argues that Prime Ministers need to rely on strong regional ministers and other leading members of their Cabinet, many of whom have important power bases in their own right. Members of the President's Cabinet have no such power base and are more easily replaced. Prime Ministers are also held to a greater accountability (precisely because they enjoy a solid block of support in Parliament) than Presidents, who can always blame an obstructionist Congress for their difficulties.

The Influence of the Civil Service

As noted in Chapter 2, the day-to-day work of governing is carried out by full time employees known as civil servants or public servants. The majority of these employees work for departments headed by Cabinet Ministers. Others work for various boards and commissions such as the Atomic Energy Commission, the CBC and the Bank of Canada. They are still part of the executive branch of the government of Canada. These bodies are the counterpart of the ABCs which are prevalent within local government, except that the federal (and provincial) governments are free to create, alter or abolish their boards as they see fit. In contrast, local boards such as school boards have a mandated existence and are beyond the control of municipal councils.

With the increasing complexity of government activities in the 20th century, the full time experts in the civil service became more and more influential as advisors to the temporary amateur politicians

---

[7]*Ibid.*, p. 158.

[8]Wearing, *op. cit.*, p. 162.

supposedly in charge of the departments. The growing influence of the civil service was compounded by the long period of one party domination in Ottawa. A whole generation of civil servants worked only with Liberal politicians (who governed between 1935 and 1957) and a very close relationship developed. That closeness was shattered by the election of the Progressive Conservatives under Diefenbaker in 1957. It did not reappear with the return of the Liberals in 1963, largely because they had only minority governments during Pearson's two terms of office in the 1960s. As a result, they were more sensitive to the views of their members of Parliament (in fact, all members of Parliament) not just to the whispered asides of senior civil servants.

PMO and PCO Expanded as Policy Advisors

A majority Liberal government reappeared in 1968, but the new leader was Pierre Trudeau, and life would never again be the same for the civil service! Trudeau liked to question established ways of doing things, and doubted that the regular civil service would be very imaginative or creative in suggesting alternative approaches. His solution was to expand greatly the roles of two long-standing support offices — the Prime Minister's Office (*PMO*) and the Privy Council or Cabinet Office (the *PCO*) — especially with respect to their policy advisory role. By so doing, Trudeau deliberately created alternative sources of policy advice from that of the regular civil service. If this new system gave the Cabinet a variety of viewpoints, it presumably assisted in the decision-making process. If, as its numerous critics charged, it only substituted a new PMO monopoly on policy advice for that of the old civil service monopoly, then it was not an improvement at all.[9]

Whatever else it did, however, Trudeau's system reduced somewhat the civil service's former dominance. Many adjustments have been made in the years since, the details of which are beyond our purpose in this Guide. While senior civil servants remain extremely

---

[9]This was certainly the view of Walter Stewart in his critical and lively discussion of the "supergroup" then wielding power in Canada. See *Shrug: Trudeau in Power*, Toronto, New Press, 1971, Chapter 11.

influential, however, it is arguable that they have never regained the peak of power and influence that they enjoyed up until the late 1950s — when they were "the only game in town" as far as policy advice to the government.

What About the Governor General?

So far, discussion has centred on three parts of the executive branch, the Cabinet, the Prime Minister and the civil service. The story has been the same for all three — an increase in power and influence during the 20th century. But what about the other part of the executive branch, the position of Governor General? According to the constitution, the Queen is the Head of State for Canada and the Governor General acts as her representative in Canada. Here again, however, there is quite a contrast between law and practice; although the position of Governor General has not become obsolete or without value, as some Canadians seem to think.

Historically, Governors General were appointed from outside of Canada, presumably to ensure the necessary detachment for performing their duties. Beginning in 1952, however, the first Canadian Governor General was appointed, in the person of Vincent Massey. The current Governor General is Roméo Leblanc, an Acadian. The official term of office is six years, but appointees usually serve five.

The Governor General has many official duties, in Canada and abroad.[10] They include representing Canada at "non-political" international events, such as the opening of a world's fair or the coronation of a monarch. Other duties involve receiving dignitaries, heads of state and other important persons and awarding civilian or military medals recognizing the merits of citizens who have distinguished themselves. In addition, the Governor General provides a state presence at a variety of artistic, scientific and sports events, and makes many appointments. As discussed earlier, these appointments are on

---

[10]The summary which follows is based on John Fraser, *The House of Commons at Work*, Ottawa, House of Commons, 1993, pp. 8-9.

the advice of the Prime Minister and, indeed, the Prime Minister could carry out the other social and ceremonial duties of the Governor General — as the President or other Head of State has to do in countries which are republics. But the Prime Minister's workload is already substantial and, in any event, the Governor General is seen as a more neutral, non-partisan figure, better suited to representing all Canadians. This important distinction may be blurring, however, since such recent Governors General as Roméo Leblanc, Ramon Hnatyshyn, and Jeanne Sauvé were active in the Liberal or Progressive Conservative parties at the time of their appointments.

In addition to social and ceremonial duties, the Governor General also has a limited number of discretionary powers which are the remnants of the prerogative power of the Crown, reflecting the notion that the Queen/Governor General is to act as the guardian of the constitution and protector of the public interest. Chief among these are the Governor General's responsibility to ensure that we always have a Prime Minister in office and a Government in power and to receive and deal with any requests from Prime Ministers for dissolution of Parliament and the calling of an election. Usually the situation is quite straightforward and the Governor General has no real choice to make. But not always! Consider these examples:

♦ In October 1925 Mackenzie King's Liberal Government was defeated in an election, falling to only 101 seats, compared to 116 for the Conservatives. Yet King didn't resign, persuaded the Governor General that he should be allowed to meet the House of Commons and attempt to govern, and did so for six months. When King then asked the Governor General to call another election, Lord Byng refused and turned to the Conservatives to form a new government when King resigned in anger.

♦ The 1972 election was a cliff-hanger, with the lead changing hands several times during election night. The Liberal Government headed by Pierre Trudeau lost a large number of seats but still ended up with two more than the Conservatives. While there was some question of who had won or lost, Trudeau never considered stepping down. After serving for a year and a half, he lost a vote in the House, obtained dissolution and won a majority.

♦ **Something to Think About**

In 1979 Joe Clark formed a minority government. How long would he have to govern before he would be entitled to call another election? Would the Governor General have any say about this timing?

There is no "correct" answer. From the examples above, it would seem safe to assume that six months is not long enough to entitle one to an election call, while eighteen months is more than enough. As it happened, Joe Clark's government lasted nine months, after which his request for an election was granted. But instead of a precise time frame, Canadians essentially leave this kind of "loose end" to be resolved by the Governor General if necessary.

It may be argued that the Governor General can only come up with a decision which would have the support of the main political parties and, ultimately, of the Canadian people. That is quite true, and Governors General certainly prefer not to be placed in situations where the choices are not clear and where they may have to exercise some discretion. The fact remains that if Canada did not have a Governor General, we would need to set down some rules to deal with situations like how long a term of office needs to be before a party in power is entitled to seek re-election. We would also have to appoint someone to act as the "Grand National Host," since it is would still be necessary to meet and entertain foreign dignitaries. The office of Governor General handles these duties well, building as it does on centuries of tradition and pageantry. Those Canadians who regard the retention of the Governor General and the Monarchy as some kind of historical anachronism may wish to reconsider the practical value of these positions.

The House of Commons

If Canada has a democratic, accountable system of government, it must be centred on the House of Commons; this is the only body that we elect. As previously discussed, the House of Commons is composed of 295 members, elected from 295 geographic areas (known as *ridings* or *constituencies*) into which Canada is divided. The composition of the House and the boundaries of individual ridings are reviewed after each census (compiled every ten years), so that adjustments can be made to reflect the changing population patterns. In fact, the number of members will increase to 301 for the next federal election, expected in 1997. The geographic allocation of ridings is outlined in the table which follows, with the increased numbers for 1997 in brackets. It illustrates the domination of the Commons by the two very populous provinces of Central Canada, which together hold 60% of the seats.

Province/Territory	# of Commons Seats
Alberta	26
British Columbia	32 (increasing to 34)
Manitoba	14
New Brunswick	10
Newfoundland	7
Northwest Territories	2
Nova Scotia	11
Ontario	**99** (increasing to 103)
Prince Edward Island	4
Québec	**75**
Saskatchewan	14
Yukon	1
Total	295 (increasing to 301)

The Layout of the House

The House is set up with two halves and a wide central aisle. This division reflects the fact that members are elected on party lines and that the House is organized into a 'Government' and one or more 'Opposition' parties. The aisle is slightly more than two sword lengths wide — a very practical consideration from a time in Britain when members wore their swords and scabbards in parliament. Even if members drew their swords in the heat of debate, they could not reach each other across the aisle. In today's Parliaments, members content themselves with making cutting remarks instead.

The Speaker

At the front of the House sits the Speaker's chair on a raised platform. The *Speaker* has an extremely important role to play in presiding over the deliberations of Parliament and enforcing the rules of procedure. He or she is expected to be neutral and to ensure that the rights of all members are respected and protected. The Speaker is to enforce the rules in such a way as to allow the opposition members to pursue their watchdog role while also allowing the Government to fulfil its mandate by governing. Achieving this delicate balance is no easy task, especially in a House filled with partisan debate and remarks more emotional than considered.

Until the mid-1980s, the Speaker was chosen by the Prime Minister, usually after consultation (as a courtesy) with the leader of the Opposition. Tradition called for each Speaker, upon being chosen, to be led very reluctantly to the front of the House, with the Prime Minister and Opposition leader literally dragging the person along by each arm. This ritual was more than just an expression of modesty on the part of the new Speaker, more than a reluctance to assume the serious responsibilities of the position. Instead, it reflected the historical experience of early Speakers in Britain. When the "House of Commoners" met back in the days when the King ruled supreme, it would appoint someone to carry grievances to the King and to act as Speaker on behalf of the concerns of the common folk. The King was not amused with these interferences with his divine right to rule. His response was to have early Speakers beheaded. Thus, modern day Speakers have a historical reason for feigning modesty. They don't want to lose their heads over their jobs!

Election of Speaker

Reforms introduced in the mid-1980s provide for the election of the Speaker from the House of Commons. Conservative MP John Fraser was chosen as the first elected Speaker in September 1986 after a marathon session with many candidates. The current speaker is Liberal Gilbert Parent, elected in January 1994. Given their numerical strength, it is likely that a candidate from the governing party will be successful in gaining election. Nonetheless, this change is seen as reinforcing the notion of the Speaker as an independent officer of the House, rather than a hand-picked choice of the Prime Minister.

The side of the House to the right of the Speaker holds the members of the governing party, with the Prime Minister and members of the Cabinet along the front row (and the second row as needed). The remaining members of the governing party sit further behind on the backbenches — giving rise to their popular name as "backbenchers."

On the other side of the House are the opposition parties. If the Government has a large enough majority, their members may spill over onto the opposite side as well. Directly across from the Prime Minister sits the leader of the *Official Opposition.* Around this leader sit other senior members of the Official Opposition, those who would likely form a Cabinet if their party were to win the next election. These senior opposition members are usually assigned specific Cabinet Ministers and departments to monitor and criticize as part of their watchdog role. It is common to refer to this "cabinet-in-waiting" as the *Shadow Cabinet.*

The Parliamentary Schedule

A "Parliament" lasts from one election until the next. The current Parliament (as of January 1997) is the 35th since Confederation and it began following the federal election in October 1993. A Parliament ends with dissolution (requested by the P.M. and usually granted automatically by the Governor General) which leads to an election.

Within a Parliament there will be several sessions, depending largely on the wishes of the government of the day. A session of Parliament begins with all members of both Houses gathering in the Senate to hear the Governor General read the *"Speech from the Throne."* While this once was really a speech from the Throne or ruling Monarch, today it is a speech from the Government setting out its plans and proposed legislation for that session. It ends with what is termed *prorogation.* All legislation not passed when the House is prorogued is dead, and must be reintroduced from the beginning.

There is much "pomp and ceremony" associated with the operations of Parliament, most of it representing historical traditions which remain important and are recognized and reinforced through the continuation of the ceremonial features. A good example is provided by the Mace, which is carried on the shoulder of the Sergeant-at-Arms when the Speaker travels from place to place. Without the Mace in the House, proceedings cannot begin. In the Middle Ages, the Mace was the weapon of the Sergeant-at-Arms, who was the bodyguard of the King. For another intriguing example, read on.[11]

"Black Rod" Comes Calling

A quaint, but historically significant, part in the opening of Parliament is played by the "Gentleman Usher of the Black Rod," surely one of the most curiously named personages to be found within a government. After the Governor General has taken a seat on the Throne in the Senate, Black Rod proceeds to the House of Commons to ask its members to come to the Senate to hear the Speech from the Throne. As he approaches, the door of the Commons is slammed in his face. Three knocks with his ebony staff bring the question, "Who is there?" Upon replying "Black Rod," he is admitted to the House, extends his invitation, and then departs. The members of the House follow him, led by the Speaker.

---

[11]This example is summarized from John Ricker and John Saywell, *How Are We Governed?*, Toronto, Clarke, Irwin and Company Limited, 1980, pp. 76-77.

While this process may seem strange or silly, it reflects an underlying fact of great significance. It draws attention to the independence of the House of Commons from the Monarch, a distinction members have made a point of emphasizing ever since Charles I entered the Commons in Great Britain to arrest some of its members. In fact, when members return to the Commons after hearing the Speech from the Throne, they emphasize their independence by deliberately introducing a subject of their own choosing for debate, rather than proceeding with any of the matters outlined in the Throne Speech.

Within any term of Parliament, there will be several "sessions," each one beginning with a Speech from the Throne. Reforms introduced in 1983 provided a regular schedule for sittings of Parliament and for vacation breaks in the fall, winter and spring terms. Changes were also made to the hours of the House. Previously, MPs used to be in meetings with constituents, committees or caucus (closed strategy meetings of each party) in the mornings and then in the Commons from 2 until 10:30 or more at night — a brutal schedule which almost ensured exhaustion and frequent absenteeism from the House. The new arrangements provided for the Commons to sit from 11 a.m. until 6:30 most days. Further changes introduced in 1991 lengthened the Christmas and summer recess periods and provided for an adjournment of the House every fifth week.

♦ **Something to Think About**

As you read this schedule, your first reaction is likely to be one of annoyance about all this "free" time that members of Parliament have. How can this be justified, you want to know.

Much depends on how that time is used. Canadians have often complained that their members lose touch with their roots, get too caught up in events in Ottawa, develop a "Central-Canadian" bias, or otherwise fail to represent properly those who sent them to Ottawa in the first place. Well, if you want your MP to be available in your riding, to stay in touch with local needs and concerns, you have to give him or her an opportunity to be there! This is a vast country and visits back to the riding represent a very long trip for many members. The main reason for providing for an adjournment every fifth week was to make it easier for members to stay in touch with their ridings.

The Roles of the House of Commons

As outlined in Chapter 2, the Commons has three main roles which will be examined a little more fully in this chapter: **(1)** representative role, **(2)** legislative role, and **(3)** watchdog role.

1. Representative Role

In theory, the 295 (soon to be 301) members of the Commons represent the views and concerns of the 30 million residents of Canada. In practice, there are several factors which make the Commons less than representative of the Canadian people. Chief among these are:

a) *With the exception of a very rare independent member, almost all MPs are members of political parties.*

Party discipline restricts the ability of MPs to represent the views of their constituents, especially in the case of Government backbenchers — who are constantly threatened that any desertion on their part could bring down the Government and force an election. Dissident members, sometimes called "mavericks," may face party sanctions for their lack of complete loyalty, including not being appointed to committees of their choice, not being supported by the party in fundraising efforts, or even not being approved as a candidate for the party in the next election.

Some recent examples illustrate the impact of this discipline. When Progressive Conservatives Alex Kindy and David Kilgour broke ranks and voted against their own party on the legislation introducing the GST, Mulroney expelled them from the party. In 1995, Warren Allmand, a long time Liberal member and former Cabinet Minister was strongly critical of what he saw as the Chrétien Government's abandonment of social programs in its preoccupation with the deficit and debt. His comments led to his removal as Chair of a Commons committee. In the spring of 1996, John Nunziata voted against his party because of its failure to live up to its promise to scrap the

GST. For this act of rebellion he was expelled from the party caucus. Both men remain members of Parliament, since only the voters can take that privilege away from them. However, while Allmand also remains a full (if less than happy) member of the Liberal party, Nunziata's future with the party is much less certain.

b)   *The composition of the Commons does not reflect the make-up of the population of Canada.*

If it did, it would have 148 female MPs, half would be under 35, under 10% would have university degrees, and the largest single group would be unskilled workers and homemakers.[12] Instead, the Commons is overwhelmingly male, middle-aged, and drawn from a privileged socio-economic background. The largest single group is made up of lawyers, usually about one-quarter of all MPs.

◆   *Something to Think About*

Is it reasonable to assume that MPs from a privileged background are unable to represent effectively Canadians from "other walks of life?"

To put it another way, if we could somehow produce a Commons which reflected accurately a cross-section of all Canadians, would all of their views be represented more effectively?

The short answer is "not necessarily." One should not assume that an MP from a privileged background is incapable of speaking out forcefully for the rights of the less fortunate. Nor should one assume that a "have-not" MP would be an eloquent and effective speaker on behalf of those he or she represents. Nonetheless, the **perception** is that the Commons isn't representative of ordinary Canadians and, as has been said before, perception is reality.

c)   *The electoral system causes serious distortions between the per-centage of popular vote and the percentage of seats won.*

This happens because a candidate doesn't have to win 50% plus

---

[12]W. L. White, R. H. Wagenberg and R. C. Nelson, *Canadian Politics and Government*, Sixth Edition, Toronto, Harcourt Brace, 1995, p. 202.

one to be elected, just more votes than any other candidate — a system often termed "first-past-the-post." With several candidates contesting each riding, rarely does the winning candidate have 50%.

To illustrate, consider the Mulroney landslide victory in 1984. The Progressive Conservatives won 75% of the seats with 50% of the vote. The Liberals won 14% of seats on 28% of the vote, and the NDP won 11% of the seats with 19% of the vote. If the number of seats had reflected the popular vote received, the standings would have been Conservatives 141, Liberals 79, NDP 54 and all others 8.

An even more dramatic example is provided by the results in the the 1993 federal election, as summarized below:

Federal Election Results, 1993

Party	% of Vote	% of Seats	# of Seats
Liberal	41	60	178
Reform	19	18	52
Conservative	16	01	02
Bloc	14	18	54
NDP	07	03	09

With only 41% of the vote, the Liberals won a substantial majority. They gained 60% of the seats in the Commons even though almost exactly that percentage of Canadian voters in the election did **not** support them. Perhaps even more dramatic was the positive result for the Bloc. Even though it was fourth in percentage of popular vote, with seats in only one province, the Bloc won the second largest number of seats in the Commons and became the Official Opposition. In contrast, the Progressive Conservative Party was nearly wiped out in the House of Commons, even though it retained significant support among the voters. With the Bloc votes concentrated in Québec and the Reform votes concentrated in the West, the Conservatives were squeezed out in their two traditional strongholds.

◆ **Something to Think About**

Should Canada introduce a system of *proportional representation*? In other words, should there be some formula which assigns political parties a number of seats that constitutes about the same percentage of total seats in the House as each party's votes are a percentage of all votes cast? Such a system is used in countries like Denmark, Ireland and Israel, and Australia uses it for senate elections.[13]

If the seats in the House of Commons had been allocated proportional to popular vote after the last federal election, the standings would have been very different, as illustrated in the table below.

Comparison of Actual and PR Seats

Party	# Seats Won	# Seats if P.R.
Liberals	178	121
Reform	52	56
Conservatives	02	47
Bloc	54	41
NDP	09	21
Other	0	09

These figures indicate that the Liberals would still have formed the government, but only with a minority. The Reform Party would

[13]For further details, see Paul Fox, "Should Canada Adopt Proportional Representation?" in Paul Fox and Graham White (eds.), *Politics Canada*, Seventh Edition, Whitby, McGraw-Hill Ryerson Limited, 1991, pp. 343-350. For arguments for and against this system, see John Hiemstra, "Getting What You Vote For" and Paul Barker, "Voting for Trouble" in Charlton and Barker, *op. cit.*, pp. 280-301.

have been the Official Opposition, the Bloc would have been in fourth place, and the NDP would have been a conspicuous presence with 21 seats instead of the 9 they got.

While the results under P.R. might be "fairer," they also highlight one of the main alleged drawbacks of this system — the failure to produce a majority government. Only a few times in the 20th century has a winning party won more than half of the popular vote in a federal election. As more parties contest elections, such results are likely to be even less in evidence. A system of proportional representation, therefore, would presumably mean frequent minority governments for Canada. How much of a drawback this is, of course, depends upon one's view of the merits of minority governments. Moreover, it is possible to minimize this problem by adopting a mixed system (such as found in New Zealand, Germany and Sweden), in which half the members are elected from constituencies as they are now and half are drawn from party lists according to the parties' share of the popular vote.[14]

d) *Rural areas are over-represented on the basis of their populations.*

This imbalance is unavoidable, given their small, scattered populations. Although the ideal arrangement is to have each MP representing roughly the same number of people, rural ridings would be much too large to cover if they were to encompass as many people as are found in compact urban areas. The result is that an MP from a city riding may represent 90,000 people, while an MP from a rural riding represents only 75,000. Every effort is made to ensure that population variations are never wider than 25%.

2. Lawmaking Role

Most legislation results from Government initiatives designed to carry out its election promises or otherwise fulfill the agenda of the party in power. However, legislation can result from **three** different kinds of bill. As will become clear from the brief summary below, these can

---

[14]Andrew Coyne, "First-past-the-post electoral system is broken," *Kingston Whig Standard*, October 17, 1996.

be distinguished on the basis of their sponsor, their scope and their fate.

1   Government Bill

It is sponsored by the Government, and introduced by the appropriate Minister. For example, a bill dealing with farming would be introduced by the Minister of Agriculture. Government bills are national in scope and they almost always pass. In the unlikely event that a Government bill is defeated, the result is usually interpreted as a loss of confidence and the Cabinet finds itself under strong pressure to resign or to seek a new mandate from the Canadian people by calling an election.

2   Private Members' Bill

This type of bill is equally national in scope, but has quite a different fate. It is sponsored by any private member (that is, anyone not in the Cabinet). Private members' bills are usually introduced by an opposition backbencher as a way of criticizing deficiencies in Government legislation, with the result that the Government — which controls the agenda — does not make time for them to be passed. Procedural reforms ensure discussion of a few private members' bills on a weekly basis, but their chances of passage remain slim.

An early "success" under these reforms was the passage of Bill C-204, the Non-Smoker's Health Act, in June of 1988. What is popularly known as the anti-smoking legislation was introduced as a private members' bill, randomly selected for further study, given second reading after five hours debate, reviewed and amended by a legislative committee, and finally passed by the House after a further two hours of debate provided under the new rules.[15] An important piece of legislation, affecting the health of all Canadians, this bill was initiated by a backbench MP, Lynn McDonald of the NDP. Unfortunately, these examples are all too rare.

---

[15]This summary is based on Nora Lever, "What's Happened Under The New Rules," *Canadian Parliamentary Review*, Ottawa, Autumn 1988, pp. 14-16.

3   Private Bill

Sponsored by a Senator, this bill is very limited in scope or jurisdiction and almost always passes. Examples would include a company charter or a bill authorizing the use of a professional designation
by a particular organization. These bills are introduced first, and receive their main examination, in the Senate.

The Bill Passing Process

How does a bill pass through Parliament, and what is meant by the
various "readings" which are given to a bill? For the purpose of this
very brief summary of the process, let us assume that we are dealing
with a Government bill, which has been introduced into the House of
Commons.

Step 1 First Reading

The bill is introduced by the appropriate Minister and copies are
distributed to all members. There isn't any debate or vote. The
significance of this stage is that the bill is now officially before
Parliament.

Step 2 Second Reading

After what may be a considerable interval, the bill returns for
second reading. This involves what may be extensive debate and
then a vote on the general principle(s) of the bill. If the bill is defeated at this stage, it is dead — and so might be the Government,
for reasons already discussed. If the bill passes this stage (as it
almost invariably does), then its principle cannot be changed
thereafter, only its details.

Step 3 Committee Stage

The bill is referred to the appropriate Commons committee for
detailed examination, clause-by-clause. These committees are
composed of members of Parliament, in proportion to party standing in the House. Through the use of these committees, members
are able to specialize in examining the same kinds of legislation
over and over, rather than the whole House trying to be experts on
everything by attempting detailed examination of every bill.

Step 4 Report Stage

The bill is reported back from committee to the full House. This stage is both debatable and amendable, in case the Commons wants to undo any changes made in committee. (Most of the time, however, the Commons defers to the expertise of those who have given the bill detailed examination in committee.)

Step 5 Third Reading

This stage is largely a formality. The bill has already been approved in principle at second reading and examined in detail at committee stage and report stage. But there is provision for further debate and a vote.

Step 6 Senate Approval

The bill then goes through essentially the same process in the Senate, although Senators give most of their attention to refining the details of the bill in committee. If the bill is defeated in the Senate (an extraordinarily rare occurrence), it is dead. The Government's life is not affected, however, since the Cabinet is responsible only to the Commons, not the Senate. If the bill is amended in the Senate, then it must return to the Commons and be passed again in its amended form. In other words, the same piece of legislation must pass through both Houses of Parliament. Further reference to the Senate's role in lawmaking is found later in this chapter.

Step 7 Royal Assent

This must be given by the Governor General. It is considered an automatic or rubber stamping duty of the Governor General, but until royal assent is given, a bill does not become a law.

3. *Watchdog Role*

The third major role of the Commons that we are examining is the watchdog role. Unlike the previous two, it is almost entirely carried out by the opposition members of the Commons — not by the whole House. The opposition members are supposed to keep an eye on the Government for Canadians, between elections. Through their close scrutiny, criticisms and suggestions, they are to ensure better legislation and wiser use of funds.

The watchdog role is important in at least two key respects. Through this role, the opposition parties act to protect our interests between elections. If we are to have responsible government, if the Cabinet (and civil service) really are to be held responsible to the legislative branch, there must be an effective watchdog role. Second, and perhaps paradoxically, a strong opposition is also good for the "Government," that is, for the party in power. Without an effective opposition, the governing party inevitably becomes complacent and arrogant, thereby sowing the seeds for its own potential downfall at the next election. Pushed by an effective opposition, the governing party is forced to extend itself, to perform better. There is much to the old saying that a good opposition produces a good government.

Questioning
Question Period

What are the main tools and techniques available to the opposition parties to carry out their watchdog role? Leading the list in familiarity is the daily *"Question Period,"* especially since its highlights have been a prominent feature on television in recent years. The saying that "familiarity breeds contempt," may well apply in this case, however, since the behaviour of members during Question Period has done little to enhance the image of our parliamentarians. Much of the time seems to be taken up with angry exchanges or good-natured banter, usually accompanied by desk-thumping and cries of "hear," "hear" or "shame," "shame" — depending on which side of the House is speaking or responding.

Question Period is held at the beginning of each day's sitting of Parliament, during which members can ask questions of any member of the Cabinet, including the Prime Minister. The questions are spontaneous, meaning that the Government does not know in advance who may be asked what. This is the key redeeming feature of Question Period. Since the Government sets the agenda (the "Orders of the Day"), it is usually in control. The opposition parties are largely restricted to reacting to what the Government presents. Not so during Question Period! The Government doesn't know what to expect. It can be (and often is) caught off guard. Even though most of the time in Question Period may be wasted on trivial or childish exchanges, it is arguably well worth preserving because of its ability to trip up the Government with well-timed, unexpected questions.

Any detailed examination of the other *watchdog tools* is beyond the scope of this Guide, but a brief summary of the main ones is found in **Appendix A** for those who are interested in learning more about them. Over the years, there have been a number of reforms which have strengthened the watchdog role — changes such as the provision of research funds for parties to close somewhat the "knowledge gap" in the House of Commons as compared to the expertise available to assist the governing party. Even the backbenchers of the governing party are not always as meek and obedient as their public demeanour would suggest. Behind the closed doors of weekly *caucus* meetings, they have an opportunity to raise concerns and to pressure the Government to respond to these concerns. A recent case in point involved the Government's amendments to the unemployment insurance plan, a great concern to the 31 Liberal MPs from Atlantic Canada. Repeated lobbying by them resulted in some softening of the provisions relating to seasonal workers.[16]

The Senate

As mentioned in Chapter 2, Senators are appointed not elected. They are appointed by the Governor General (officially), but on the advice of the Prime Minister — who actually makes the choices. Senators must be at least 30 years old, and must have real estate worth $4000 net, and total assets of at least $4000. These rather strange requirements date from the origins of the Senate, when it was expected to be made up of people of property and maturity, appointees who would bring a "sober second thought" to decisions of the elected House of Commons. A further requirement is that the Senators must reside in the province or territory for which they are appointed.

---

[16]Joan Bryden, "Backbench MPs are not powerless" in *Kingston Whig Standard*, December 9, 1996.

Originally, there were to be 24 Senators each from Ontario, Québec, the Maritime Provinces (10 each for New Brunswick and Nova Scotia and 4 for P.E.I.) and the West (6 for each of the four Western Provinces. When Newfoundland joined Confederation in 1949, it was given 6 Senators. Two more were added to represent the Yukon and Northwest Territories, for a total of 104.

The original idea was that the Senate would represent and protect the interests of each of the regions in the Parliament of Canada. Each region would have the same number of Senators to counter-balance the dominance that some regions held in the House of Commons, based on representation by population. However, as Western Canada has grown in population and economic importance over the past few decades, there has been growing dissatisfaction with the fact that the West is still limited to 24 Senators while Atlantic Canada (thanks to Newfoundland's late arrival) has 30 Senators. This imbalance underlies much of the push for Senate reform which has emanated from Western Canada in recent years.

Considerable attention was given to the composition and responsibilities of the Senate during the discussions leading up to the formation of the new country of Canada. It was expected to represent and protect provincial interests and it was given virtually equal lawmaking powers to those of the House of Commons. The only exception to this statement was the fact that legislation providing for the expenditure of public money or the imposition of taxes must be introduced in the House of Commons, even though it must still be passed by the Senate to become law.

Senate Decline

Given the important responsibilities with which it started, why has the Senate declined so much in influence and public perception? First of all, because the Senators are appointed and not elected, they were doomed to play a less and less influential role as the concept of a democratically elected and accountable government gained ground. They lack the legitimacy to block or overturn measures approved by the elected Commons; yet, if they simply rubber-stamp those measures they appear unnecessary.

Second, under the principle of responsible government, the Cabinet is responsible only to the House of Commons. A vote in the Senate can never defeat a government. As a result, all of the drama of our government system (and all of the media coverage) focuses on the House of Commons.

Even with these limitations, the Senate might have continued to play a useful role but for the shameful abuse of the appointing power by every Prime Minister since Confederation — a third and, arguably, the most significant cause of Senate decline. Rather than appointing leading Canadians from all walks of life, Prime Ministers have appointed party faithful, filling the Senate with (mostly) old politicians being rewarded for past service. As a result, the Senate has been dominated by appointees of whatever party formed the government for a period of years.

The pattern is very apparent in the table which follows, even with its incomplete figures.

Party Standings in the Senate

Period of Office of:	Conservatives	Liberals	Independent
Macdonald	63	10	
Laurier	17	57	
King and St. Laurent	05	78	
Mulroney	50	41	05
Chrétien	50	51	03

The figures show how the Senate was overwhelmingly Conservative in the 19th century, thanks to that party being in power so long (under Macdonald and his four successors). The Liberals dominated much of the 20th century and after 22 consecutive years in power (from 1935 to 1957) they had almost completely filled the Senate with Liberals by the end of the King/St. Laurent era. Diefenbaker redressed the balance somewhat during his time in office and Mulroney got the Conservatives back to a slight majority during his eight years in power. Not long after taking office, however, Chrétien had regained a slim majority position.

Still Life in the Senate?

During the Mulroney years, the Senate took a more active and confrontational role than usual on several occasions. With Liberals in the majority, the Senate attempted to block several government initiatives including the Canada-U.S. Free Trade Agreement and the imposition of the Goods and Services Tax (GST). The former issue was resolved by the 1988 election campaign, which reelected the Conservatives on a free trade platform. The GST deadlock was resolved when Mulroney appointed eight additional Senators in December 1990, under a section of the constitution that allowed such action in exceptional circumstances involving a serious conflict between the Senate and the House of Commons. This expanded Senate was temporary, however, since the constitution provides that the number must return to "normal" for each region and for the Senate as a whole before the Government appoints any additional Senators.

The Senate has continued its more active and aggressive role since the Liberals assumed office in October 1993, as the following examples illustrate.

◆ In late 1995, Conservatives in the Senate threatened to derail Liberal Justice Minister Allen Rock's controversial gun control legislation by making major amendments to it. Ultimately, however, the legislation did pass through the Senate without incident.

◆ In June 1996, the Senate defeated a bill which was intended to limit compensation to developers affected by the Chrétien government's cancellation of the Pearson airport privatization deal. The plan had been approved by the Conservatives in the dying days of the 1993 election campaign and cancelled by the Liberals shortly after their victory. The defeat of the bill means that it will be up to the courts to decide the amount of compensation to which those involved in the cancellation of the airport deal are entitled.

♦ The end of November, 1996, saw another Liberal bill defeated in the Senate, this time with 35 Liberal Senators among those who voted it down. The bill involves a constitutional amendment to end the church-run education system in Newfoundland, a matter which has generated considerable controversy.[17]

While these events serve to remind Canadians that the Senate exists, they don't necessarily generate any increase in support for it. Depending on the public view on an issue, any Senate opposition to actions of the Government of the day may be seen as an undemocratic intervention. As long as it remains an appointed body, the Senate lacks legitimacy in the eyes of many Canadians. Without legitimacy, it is hard for it to exert its views over those of the elected House of Commons. If it can't exercise an independent judgment on public affairs, why have it?

Senate Reform

There have been many suggestions for reform of the Senate over the years. One of the most persistent suggestions in recent years has been for a "Triple E" Senate — elected, equal and effective. According to proponents of this reform:

♦ **Election** is needed to give the Senate legitimacy and credibility, so that it can exert its powers without criticism.
♦ **Equality** is needed, precisely because some provinces are so much larger and more dominant than others. For constitutional purposes, a province is a province. This is something the U.S. has always recognized, with its provision for equal numbers of Senators from all states — Rhode Island and California included.
♦ **Effectiveness** would follow from the first two features.

The Triple E Senate has been strongly pushed by the Western Provinces, but any such significant change does not appear imminent. While almost everyone agrees that the West really should have more

---

[17]Susan Delacourt, "Senate vote returns Nfld. school plan to MPs' agenda," *Globe and Mail*, November 28, 1996.

Senate seats, Québec (especially) and the Atlantic Provinces won't consent to any substantial reduction in their proportions of Senate seats. Since the approval of 2/3 of the provinces with at least 50% of Canada's population is needed for such reform, it seems unlikely.

Summary:
Do MPs Earn Their Salary?

Given all of this background, we are now in a position to summarize the main roles of a member of Parliament, that much-maligned individual who is supposedly overpaid and underworked. These roles are:

1. Representing the interests, views and concerns of constituents.

2. Acting as an "ombudsman" or complaints investigator on behalf of constituents who have particular problems in their dealings with the government. This may be seen as an extension of the representative role, but it deserves separate billing. With the complexity of government today, the MP is a vital point of contact for citizens who have a problem (getting a passport, tracing a missing pension cheque, determining eligibility for some program) but don't know where to turn.

3. Acting as a "business agent" for the riding. This is also in some respects an extension of the representative role, but again one deserving of separate mention. While the specifics vary somewhat with the economic circumstances of each riding, members of Parliament are expected to make a contribution to the economic well-being of the riding. They are judged partly on how successful they are in attracting government grants, government buildings, the relocation of government offices, the start-up of new businesses, and any other initiatives which help to provide economic growth and employment in the riding. If carried to an extreme, this is little more than "pork-barrel politics." But it is an activity which MPs ignore at their peril, especially if their riding is suffering economically.

4. Acting on behalf of the party, not only in the actions taken in the House of Commons but in giving speeches, attending meetings and undertaking any other work which advances the cause of the party.

5. Being a member of the party caucus and attending its regular meetings. This is related to the fourth role, but deserves special mention as well. The effectiveness of any party, whether in government or in opposition, depends partly on how well developed its strategies are. Much of this work is done in caucus meetings, where individual MPs can make an important contribution.

6. Being a "parliamentarian," participating in Commons debates, taking an active part in Question Period and otherwise carrying out the responsibilities associated with being a member of Parliament.

7. Serving on standing (and occasionally special) committees of the Commons, working on the examination of departmental estimates and on the specifics of legislation.

8. Undertaking research on particular topics, whether as preparation for speeches, as background for reviewing legislation or departmental estimates, or as the basis for introducing a private members' bill.

This is by no means an exhaustive list — although it can easily be an exhausting one! It also deals only with the duties of a "backbench" MP. Members who are also appointed to the Cabinet have another full list of duties relating to work on Cabinet Committees, discussion of proposed legislation, strategy sessions on behalf of the party and overall responsibility for the operation of the particular departments for which they are Ministers. Members who take their responsibilities seriously have an enormous workload, one that can all too easily take its toll on their health or their family life.

In return, members of Parliament receive a salary of $64 800. In addition, they receive an expense allowance of $21 400, for which receipts are required, and are also provided with a travel allowance for trips back and forth to their ridings. MPs also receive what many

Canadians have regarded as an overly generous pension — available after five full years of service. What tends to be overlooked in the criticism of the pension is that members contribute 10% of their salaries toward it, and that many do not win the two elections which are needed to qualify for the pension. It is striking that 200 federal politicians retired or were defeated in the 1993 general election[18] — although that was an admittedly larger turnover than usual.

Not long after its election victory in 1993, the Liberal Government introduced some pension reforms, including rules to outlaw "*double-dipping*," an expression which describes a situation in which an MP retires, receives a pension, and then takes a government job and a second pay cheque. The Government also reduced a few of the "perks" enjoyed by MPs by removing free shoe shines and reducing the subsidies on meals in the parliamentary dining room.[19]

♦ Something to Think About

As in any group of close to 300 people, parliamentarians include some "bad apples." Those who want to be critical can always find members of Parliament who don't appear to earn their salary.

But what you have to ask yourself is whether you want to base the remuneration of MPs on the lowest common denominator, or whether you want to pay at a level which will attract the best qualified and most talented people within our society.

Concluding Observations

This lengthy chapter has barely scratched the surface of this complex topic, but it is hoped that it provides you with sufficient information

---

[18]Robert Jackson and Doreen Jackson, *Canadian Government in Transition*, Scarborough, Prenctice-Hall Canada Inc., 1996, p. 152.

[19]*Ibid.*

to improve your understanding of the machinery of government at the senior levels and how it operates.

As previously mentioned, the governing machinery at the provincial level is the same, except that there is a Lieutenant Governor instead of a Governor General, there is a Legislative Assembly instead of a House of Commons, and there isn't any upper chamber like the Senate. The operating principles are the same, as are the issues and challenges relating to the dominance of the executive branch and the need to strengthen the watchdog role of the opposition parties.[20]

For example, Fred Schindeler's landmark study of Ontario at the end of the 1960s concluded that the Legislative Assembly had become nothing more than "an ineffective appendage employed to make noises of approval or discontent."[21] Since then, a number of reforms, similar to those occurring at the federal level, have redressed the balance somewhat. However, concerns about executive domination continue to surface, and have come to the fore over the past year or so, since the election of the Conservative Government of Mike Harris. The new Government's attempt to secure quick passage, in December 1995, of an omnibus bill (Bill 26) covering amendments to some 47 statutes, provided a dramatic example of why we need watchdogs with teeth.

---

[20]For a recent examination of government structures and operations in various provinces, see Christopher Dunn (ed.), *Provinces: Canadian Provincial Politics*, Peterborough, Broadview Press, 1996.

[21]F. F. Schindeler, *Responsible Government in Ontario*, Toronto, University of Toronto Press, 1969, p. 261.

Appendix A
Watchdog Techniques

As discussed earlier in the chapter, these are the techniques available to the Opposition parties to question, criticize and hold accountable the Government for its actions. Chief among these techniques are:

1 Oral Question Period, discussed earlier, which can be foolish and embarrassing, but which also keeps the Government on its toes because of the spontaneity of the questions.

2 Written questions, which can be useful in obtaining information from the Government, but only after an interval — which may be extensive — and without any of the drama associated with Oral Question Period.

3 Debate on the Speech from the Throne (now limited to 6 days), during which members (especially from the opposition parties) respond to the Government's proposals for action during a session of Parliament.

4 Debate on the Budget (now limited to 4 days), during which members (again especially from the opposition) respond to the Budget statement from the Minister of Finance.

5 Specific motions of non-confidence. These are introduced as part of the debate on the Throne Speech and on the Budget, and may also be introduced at other times when the opposition is seeking to defeat a government. There is little chance that such motions will pass if there is a majority government, but debate on these motions can help to focus on alleged government shortcomings.

6 "Opposition days" (now 20), provided at intervals during each session of Parliament. On these days, the opposition parties chose the topics for debate.

7 Private members' bills which, as discussed above, can be used by opposition members to draw attention to alleged deficiencies in the Government's legislative program.

8   The lawmaking process, especially at second reading and at committee stage, where members get an opportunity to debate both the principle and then the detail of proposed legislation.

9   The estimates process (also known as "the power of the purse strings"), which involves parliamentary approval each year of the expenditures which will be incurred by the Government.

Estimates Versus Budget

There is often confusion about the estimates process and the budget process. In federal government parlance, estimates refers only to estimated **expenditures** for the coming fiscal year. These must be presented to the House by the end of February each year, are referred to the appropriate standing committees for detailed examination and must be reported back to the House by the end of May for final approval by the end of June.

A budget is a broader document containing not only the planned expenditures, but the methods of financing them, the net financial position of the government anticipated for the coming fiscal year, and various economic measures relating to issues facing the economy at the time. Budgets usually appear in February or March and are as much a political and economic document as a financial statement.

The Last Word

Definition of Terms and Concepts

Administrative Law:
(Also known as subordinate or delegated legislation)
> This is law made by the administration (that is, the executive branch of government) in contrast to statute law which is made by Parliament (or the provincial and territorial legislatures). Most statutes passed over the last fifty years or so authorize the executive branch to spell out the law in detail over time. It is this detailed law which is often referred to as administrative law.

Backbenchers:
> Members of Parliament who are not in the Cabinet or the "Shadow-Cabinet," and are so-named because they occupy the back-benches in the House of Commons.

Caucus:
> Closed meeting of party members in which strategies are discussed. In the case of the governing party, a primary purpose of the caucus meeting is to give backbench members a chance to voice any concerns about proposed government legislation before they are called upon to support it in public. Opposition party caucus meetings focus on how best to expose shortcomings in the Government's performance.

Closure:
> A procedural device used by the Government to force an end to discussion and voting on a particular stage of a bill.

Constituency: (Also known as riding)
> Geographic area into which Canada is divided for electing members to the federal House of Commons and provincial legislatures.

Dissolution of Parliament: (See also proroguing of Parliament.)
This ends the life of a Parliament and is followed by an election.
It differs from prorogation or proroguing of the House, in which
a session of parliament ends, but is followed by a new session and
a new Speech from the Throne.

Double Dipping:
Term to describe ex-politicians (and public servants) who retire
on a pension and then take another paying job with the government.

Official Opposition:
Title usually given to the party with the second largest number of
elected members, who act as a watchdog and offer themselves as
an alternative government.

PCO (Privy Council Office)
Not to be confused with the Privy Council or Cabinet, the PCO
consists of staff who provide secretarial and research support to
the Cabinet. These staff are civil servants on secondment (temporary reassignment) from regular departmental duties.

PMO (Prime Minister's Office)
This consists of staff who support the Prime Minister in carrying
out his or her responsibilities, not only as head of the Government but as leader of a political party. Its work parallels that of
the PCO, except that it is more partisan and political. Its staff are
mostly "outsiders" selected for their expertise and creativity with
respect to policy making.

Prerogative Power:
Remnants of discretionary power once exercised by the Crown.

Privy Council:
Essentially the legal name for the Cabinet, although it consists of
all those who were ever appointed to any Cabinet, as well as a
few honorary appointees. When the Cabinet of the day wishes to

act legally, it does so in the name of the Governor in Council, which means the Governor General and the Privy Council (the active part of it represented by the current Cabinet).

Proportional Representation:
System of election in which provisions are made to ensure that the number of seats awarded to a party is proportional to the percentage of popular vote it received in the election.

Proroguing of Parliament: (See also Dissolution of Parliament.) When Parliament is prorogued, it marks the end of that session, which had begun with the introduction of a Speech from the Throne a year or more earlier. [There is no set time for a session of Parliament. The Government decides when it has achieved the major portion of its legislative objectives and when it is time to announce new priorities through a new Speech from the Throne.]

Question Period:
Period at the beginning of each day's sitting of Parliament for spontaneous questions to be put to members of the Cabinet.

Shadow-Cabinet:
Group of leading members of the official opposition who act as a kind of "government-in-waiting."

Speaker:
Presiding officer in the House of Commons (and the Senate) who enforces the rules of debate.

Speech from the Throne:
Statement of Government's plans for the coming session of Parliament, read by the Governor General (or Monarch) on behalf of the Government.

Triple 'E' Senate:
Name for Senate reform proposal which calls for a Senate which would be elected, equal and effective.

Points to Ponder

1. Did you realize how limited is the "pool" from which Prime Ministers can choose members of the Cabinet? Do you find the various constraints on Cabinet selection appropriate?

2. What do you think about the merits of proportional representation? Did you realize how little relationship there could be between the percentage of popular vote for a party and the percentage of seats won by that party?

3. Have you reconsidered your view of the value of members of Parliament and whether or not they earn their salary? Are you at least willing to agree that good members, who take their varied roles seriously, have a demanding workload?

4. Should members of Parliament be free to represent the views of their constituents rather than being obliged to vote the party line? If you say yes, how will you hold any party accountable for its performance if its members are free to vote as they wish? Imagine Parliament as an enlarged version of a municipal council. Have you had much success trying to hold municipal councillors accountable?

5. It is clear that the Senate has flexed its political muscles rather more often in the past 15 years or so. Do you see value in having this upper chamber of Parliament to take a second look at legislation passed by the Commons? If the Senate is to remain, how would you amend it to make it more effective?

For Further Reading

There are many good texts providing detailed information on the structure and operations of government at the senior levels. For example, you could consult such works as:

Christopher Dunn (ed.) *Provinces: Canadian Provincial Politics*, Peterborough, Broadview Press, 1996.

Paul Fox and Graham White, *Politics: Canada*, 8th edition, Whitby, McGraw-Hill Ryerson Limited, 1995, which includes sections on the Cabinet, Civil Service, House of Commons and Senate.

John Fraser, *The House of Commons At Work*, Montréal, Les Éditions de la Chenelière inc., 1993, provides a very detailed look at the House of Commons.

James John Guy, *How We Are Governed*, Toronto, Harcourt Brace & Company Canada, 1995, covers the basics of government, including chapters on the provincial and municipal levels.

Robert Jackson and Doreen Jackson, *Politics in Canada*, 3rd edition, Scarborough, Prentice Hall Canada Inc., 1994, Chapters 7 and 8 especially. See also Chapters 6 and 7 of *Canadian Government in Transition*, 1996, from the same authors and publisher.

Graham White, *The Ontario Legislature*, Toronto, University of Toronto Press, 1989, is a good source of information on the operations of the Ontario Government, including the "watchdog" reforms introduced there over the past couple of decades.

Chapter 7

Political Parties

Objectives and Highlights

♦ To demonstrate the valuable roles played by political parties in our government.

♦ To distinguish among Canada's political parties and their place on the political spectrum.

♦ To examine the nature of pressure groups and to assess the roles they play.

The rather jaundiced view that Canadians tend to have towards most things governmental certainly extends to political parties. Those dubious about the motives of a politician are unlikely to feel any better when they contemplate a larger group of the same species.

Parties are criticized for indulging in mindless attacks and counter-attacks, playing out some ritual game without any particular regard for the real merits of the issue under debate. Worse still, they don't even maintain a consistent position, often shifting ground when it may gain them public favour. Parties demand rigid loyalty from their members, who, as a result, often seem quite unresponsive to the demands and preferences of those who elected them.

While these negative feelings are understandable, the fact remains that political parties are an indispensable part of the Canadian system of government, as this chapter will attempt to demonstrate. It also provides a brief introduction to the main political parties found at the national level in Canada and generally where they fit from left to right on the political spectrum. The chapter also discusses briefly the nature and role of pressure groups, often seen as rivals to parties, and assesses their value in our government system.

Purposes of Parties

E veryone who has ever seen "Question Period" — whether live or on late evening television — is likely to have a fairly negative view of the contribution of political parties to the Canadian system of government. What we see, all too often, is empty posturing, polarization, and insults hurled across the floor on the basis of little more than the fact that the other speaker sits on the opposite side of the House. Canadians could all too easily conclude that parties are a harmful addition to our government system, creating unnecessary division and angry debate.

What must be understood, however, is that political parties are an integral part of the government system at the provincial and federal levels of government. They are organizations devoted to fielding and electing candidates for office, with the objective of capturing the most seats and thereby forming the government. They serve a number of very practical purposes in our system of government.

1. They tell us who won the election and will form a "government." Imagine the chaos and confusion if 300 independent members turned up on Parliament Hill the morning after an election, attempting to decide who should govern.

2. They provide a watchdog and an alternative government in the form of the Official Opposition.

3. They provide a relatively clear focus of accountability. There is a governing group, usually with a majority of the elected members, and it will have to answer for its performance. Contrast the situation on most municipal councils, where all members sit as independents. There isn't any governing group or any official opposition. Everyone is responsible for everything, which also means that no one is really responsible for anything.

4. They allow for a smooth transition of power, since any new party which takes office has already formulated its plans about governing while serving on the opposition side. The amount of preparation may be less, of course, for a party that wasn't expecting

to win. But it will still be greater than would exist if a group of independent members with no common background or allegiance were suddenly asked to form a government.

5. Parties also simplify the election process, narrowing down the range of candidates and the choice of issues. Instead of just a list of names which may not mean much, the voter sees names *with party affiliations*, and the parties offer some more or less clear choices each election. Once again, the contrast with the municipal level is quite striking. Municipal voters face multiple ballots (for council positions, for head of council, for school board trustees, and — often — for public utility commissioners) which may add up to 30 or 40 names. Most of these individuals are unknown to the voter, and there isn't any party label to provide at least a basic identifier. Voting in such circumstances is a challenge and often a guessing game.

Parties also fulfil other more intangible, philosophical roles.[1]

6. They attempt to simplify the vast range of interests and choices available in society today and to organize public support around selected issues.

7. Parties help educate the public through debate on the issues of the day. Much of the public awareness and understanding of current issues, however superficial or imperfect, is derived from the party exchanges — as reported by the media. An example is the much wider public awareness of Canada's deficit and debt problems since a number of the political parties made this a key focus in recent years.

8. Parties are often described as "gatekeepers," because they allow certain public demands through to decision-makers, while they eliminate others or combine or modify them.

---

[1]The discussion which follows is largely based on Robert Jackson and Doreen Jackson, *Politics in Canada*, Third Edition, Scarborough, Prentice-Hall Canada Inc., 1994, pp. 414-416.

9. Partly because of their gatekeeper role, parties are central players in the formulation of public policy, as noted in earlier chapters.

10. Parties also **can be** important players in the process of political socialization. This refers to the need for parties to play special roles as "agencies for the creation of national symbols, experiences, memories, heroes, and villains."[2] The failure of Canadian parties to bind regional cleavages by building strong national bases of representation limits their effectiveness in this area.

Clearly, parties play a wide range of important roles. It is difficult to imagine our parliamentary system functioning without them.

A Two Party System?

Only two parties have ever held power at the national level. The Conservatives dominated the 19th century, largely because of the leadership of Sir John A. Macdonald. The Liberals have dominated much of the 20th century, notwithstanding the success of the Conservatives in the 1980s. Because of this pattern, Canada has historically been characterized as having a two party system — even though there are obviously other political parties which run candidates and enjoy some support across the country.[3]

What's in a Name? To avoid confusion, a brief explanation is in order concerning the name of the Conservative Party. It was officially changed to the Progressive Conservative Party in the 1930s as one of the conditions required by John Bracken, then the Premier of Manitoba, to accept the party leadership. While earlier references are quite properly to the Conservative Party, the correct name today is Progressive Conservatives or the P.C. Party.

---

[2]John Meisel, as quoted in *ibid.*, p. 426.

[3]For further information on parties, see Hugh Thorburn (ed.), *Party Politics in Canada*, 6th edition, Scarborough, Prentice-Hall, 1991.

The New Democratic Party (NDP) — and its forerunner, the Cooperative Commonwealth Federation (CCF) — has consistently elected federal members for over 60 years. The CCF/NDP has also enjoyed considerable success at the provincial level over the years, forming governments in British Columbia, Saskatchewan, Manitoba and Ontario.

A few other parties have also held power provincially, but in most cases their success was long ago and related to particular circumstances. For example, the United Farmers of Alberta held power for one term in the early years of the Depression[4] and the Union Nationale held power in Québec for several terms in the 1940s and 1950s, largely thanks to the leadership of Maurice Duplessis. The Social Credit Party enjoyed prolonged success in Alberta between 1935 and 1970 and has also formed governments in British Columbia on several occasions since the 1950s. As will be discussed, the Reform Party is, in some respects, a federal variation of the Social Credit Party.

Distinguishing Among the Parties

To party faithful, the merits of their particular party are self-evident, as are the deficiencies of opposing parties. To the average citizen, however, it is usually much less clear what a party stands for and why one should be supported over another. We begin with a brief summary of the only two parties ever to form a national government.[5]

The (Progressive) Conservatives

The first of these to emerge was the Conservative Party, which was formed by Sir John A. Macdonald out of a coalition of local interests

---

[4] A coalition of United Farmers parties from the Western Provinces and Ontario known as the Progressive Party enjoyed earlier, but very brief, success at the federal level, electing 65 MPs in 1921.

[5] The summary of the Conservative and Liberal Parties which follows is largely based on Jackson and Jackson, *op. cit.*, Chapter 10.

under the label the Liberal-Conservatives. This alliance of eastern commercial interests, conservative French Canadians and Ontario Tories was committed to bringing about Confederation and then developing the new country through constructing a national railway and promoting commerce behind tariff walls.[6]

Under the leadership of Sir John A., the Conservatives went on to dominate the national scene until almost the end of the 19th century. Macdonald was a very astute politician and a leader with a national vision which he pursued effectively. He remains one of Canada's best known Prime Ministers, not least because of the stories of his legendary drinking bouts.[7]

> One such occasion saw Macdonald attending a function where he was to speak against an opposition candidate in a Northern Ontario riding. Too much strong drink and a rough train ride on the way to the meeting caused him to throw up on the platform during his opponent's speech. Even Sir John's supporters were disgusted. When his turn came to speak, Macdonald began as follows: "Mr Chairman and gentlemen, I don't know how it is, but every time I hear Mr. Jones speak it turns my stomach." The audience dissolved in laughter and were back on side.

The pro-business stance of the Conservative Party did not endear it to Western farmers. Western disaffection was eventually reflected in the formation of the Progressive Party of the 1920s, one of many such Western protest parties, of which the present Reform Party is in some respects the latest. Nor were French Canadians supportive, because of the party's strong ties to Britain. The weak "French connection" was shattered when Conservative governments executed Riel[8]

---

[6]Tariffs are essentially taxes on imported goods, designed to raise their prices and, therefore, to encourage Canadians to purchase domestic products.

[7]The example below is from Jack McLeod, *The Oxford Book of Canadian Political Anecdotes*, Toronto, Oxford University Press, 1988, p. 28.

[8]Louis Riel was a Métis leader in Manitoba who led a rebellion protesting land losses and other grievances arising from an influx of English settlers.

in 1885 and imposed conscription in 1917. These factors combined to help ensure the electoral success of the Liberal Party throughout much of the 20th century.

Conservative fortunes improved, temporarily, under John Diefenbaker, who delivered strong support from his native Prairies and even picked up 50 seats from Québec in a sweeping 1958 election victory. Diefenbaker was in his own way as much a "character" as Sir John A., whom he greatly admired. He was a masterful story teller and excelled in the cut and thrust of parliamentary debate.[9]

> On one occasion an up-and-coming MP made the mistake of trying to interrupt Diefenbaker in full flight. Without breaking stride, "the Chief" snapped: "When a hunter is after big game, he doesn't stop for rabbit tracks." The member subsided, to lick this wounds.

The skills which made him an intimidating opposition leader, however, did not translate well into the role of leader of the Government. In the memorable words of Donaldson, "he had stormed the ramparts of power; now he didn't know how to work the drawbridge."[10]

Diefenbaker's forced departure created deep divisions which plagued his successor, Robert Stanfield, for years after. The succession to leadership of Joe Clark in 1976 further secured the party's support in Western Canada, but it continued to lose ground in most other areas of the country. Under Brian Mulroney, the party won its first election majority in more than a quarter century in 1984.[11] It scored a major breakthrough in his home province (Québec), and also received strong support across the country. This success was sub-

---

[9]The example which follows is from Thomas Van Dusen, *The Chief*, 1968, as quoted in McLeod, *op. cit.*, p. 174.

[10]Gordon Donaldson, *Fifteen Men*, Toronto, Doubleday Canada Limited, 1969, p. 192.

[11]Its last majority victory had been in 1958 under Diefenbaker. The party also won in 1962 and 1979 but only with short-lived minority governments.

stantially repeated in the election of 1988. By the spring of 1993, however, Mulroney's unpopularity was sufficient to prompt his resignation. He made much of the fact that he was the first Conservative leader to turn over the reins of power while still forming the Government. It didn't help. His successor, Kim Campbell, led the party to a crushing defeat in 1993, squeezed in the West by Reform, in Québec by the Bloc Québécois, and everywhere else by the resurgent Liberals.

The Liberals

Notwithstanding their ascendancy in the 20th century, the Liberal Party was much slower to develop on the national scene. While the party did win an election in 1873, its success was almost entirely due to the Pacific Scandal which engulfed Sir John A. Macdonald's administration. The party did not really take shape as a unified force until Laurier became leader in 1887. As Canada's first French-Canadian Prime Minister (from 1896 until 1911) Laurier solidified the party's position in Québec.

After Laurier's defeat, the Liberals were badly split by the conscription crisis of 1917 and emerged from the election of that year as largely a Québec "rump." However, the party soon rebuilt itself under the crafty but distinctly uncharismatic leadership of Mackenzie King. In an age before television and experts on make-up, dress and speaking skills, this short, balding undistinguished looking man who few claimed to like and even fewer admitted to voting for, managed to win more elections and serve longer in office than any Prime Minister in the British parliamentary system.[12] He did so partly by displaying, in an age before polling and sample survey techniques, an almost uncanny sense of what the Canadian people wanted or would accept and where he should take his party. While his shifts in policy and position were undeniably successful, they earned him (and the Liberals) the

---

[12]King won in 1921 and 1926, then was "lucky" enough to lose in 1930 and give the Conservatives the thankless task of governing during the Great Depression. He returned to power in 1935 and won two further elections before retiring and turning over the leadership of the Liberal Party to Louis St. Laurent in November 1948.

criticism of being without consistent principles. In the colourful words of John Diefenbaker: "The Liberals are the flying saucers of politics. No one can make head nor tail of them and they are never seen twice in the same place."[13]

The Liberals retained their power base in Québec throughout much of the 20th century — although there was (as already mentioned) a temporary defection to the Conservatives during the Diefenbaker landslide of 1958 and also a partial shift (largely in the form of a protest vote) to the Ralliement des Créditistes during the 1960s. However, the party steadily lost ground in Western Canada, to the point that there were frequent jokes about party meetings being held in phone booths. Trudeau's election victory in 1968 brought some upsurge in Western support, but only temporarily.

Just as Mulroney overstayed his welcome and left his party to face an overwhelming defeat, Trudeau experienced a somewhat similar fate ten years earlier. When John Turner replaced Trudeau in 1984, he almost immediately called an election. The result was a massive defeat for the Liberals who received their lowest support ever, at only 28% of the popular vote. Fortunes change quickly, however, and in 1993 the Liberals enjoyed one of their biggest victories, capturing 178 seats and receiving support from all areas of the country.

Tweedledum and Tweedledee: Trying to Differentiate the Parties

Tracing the party fortunes is a matter of historical record. Trying to explain party platforms, distinctions and differences is much more difficult. The traditional view has the Conservative Party stressing stability and respect for the established order, and the Liberals more readily embracing change and reform. But that doesn't get us very far; nor does it always jibe with past experience. The Conservatives attach great importance to the freedom of the individual, although still within a framework provided by government. The Liberals are equally concerned with the human condition, but often

---

[13]Diefenbaker in 1962, quoted in David Olive, *Canadian Political Babble*, Toronto, John Wiley & Sons, 1993, p. 114.

see the need for somewhat greater government intervention to ensure individual development and progress.

Part of the confusion for the public doubtless stems from the fact that the parties themselves shift in position or policy from time to time. Consider these rather striking examples:

♦ The Conservative Party introduced tariffs as part of Sir John A.'s "National Policy" of 1879, and defeated the Liberals under Wilfrid Laurier in 1911 by playing on fears that the Liberal proposal for reciprocity or free trade with the United States would undermine Canadian independence. In 1988, however, it was the P.C. Party which pursued and achieved free trade agreements, first with the United States and then with Mexico, while the Liberals vigorously opposed them.

♦ The Conservative Party was traditionally very pro-Britain and was not overly anxious to see closer ties between Canada and the U.S. (as in the free trade example already given). The Liberals were much more anxious to sever the ties with "the mother country" and to expand dealings with the Americans. It was Liberal governments which presided over the massive American investment in (critics would say buyout of) the Canadian economy in the post-war period. Yet it was also the Liberals in the 1970s who introduced the Foreign Investment Review Agency and other initiatives designed to limit foreign ownership of Canada's economy. Meanwhile, it was the Progressive Conservatives, especially under Brian Mulroney, who became preoccupied with fostering the closest possible ties with the U.S. — symbolized by the spectre of Mulroney and President Reagan warbling "When Irish Eyes Are Smiling" at the so-called Shamrock Summit meeting in Canada not long after Mulroney first became Prime Minister.

♦ Historically, the Liberals have been seen as a party which favours more government intervention in the economy and society than the Conservatives. But it was the Conservatives who set up the Bank of Canada and the CBC. It was a Progressive Conservative leader, Robert Stanfield, who proposed wage and price controls to deal with runaway inflation in the early 1970s. Moreover, it is the Liberals, since their victory in 1993, who are pursuing the downsizing of government in a much more forceful way than the preceding two Progressive Conservative administrations.

The Political Spectrum

The fact is that both the Liberals and the Progressive Conservatives are moderate, middle-of-the-road parties which have attempted to appeal to a broad cross-section of Canadians by avoiding extreme or overly specific policies. In terms of the political spectrum, it is common to characterize the Conservatives as centre-right and the Liberals as centre-left, but these distinctions are not very precise and still leave a large area of overlap in the middle. Moreover, within each party there are usually widely divergent opinions about the appropriate course of government action. "Red Tories" was a term heard often in the 1980s to depict Progressive Conservatives who were felt to be too progressive or liberal in their thinking. Conversely, the Liberal Party usually contains a number of influential members who are considered to hold right-wing and conservative views.

What is Left and Right Wing Anyway?

These are terms which have been associated over the years with certain attitudes about the role of government in our society. In greatly oversimplified terms:

♦   Those on the right prefer a distinctly limited role for government, and more individual freedom. Those on the left support a larger role for government, partly as a means of protecting individuals from economic uncertainty.

♦   A second distinguishing feature in recent years has been that those on the right take a tougher line on "law and order" issues and on the need for individuals to accept responsibility for their actions.

Historical Swing to the Left

From World War II until the 1980s, most Western nations supported a prolonged shift to the left on the political spectrum. In other words, there was a marked increase in the role and size of government, in the range of programs and services provided, and in the number of rules and regulations put into place. The federal government led the way in Canada.

♦ It gave a commitment to full employment, price stability and other economic goals even before the end of World War II. This marked the first time any Canadian government had ever accepted responsibility for our economic health, an obligation which has long since been taken for granted.

♦ It used the "federal spending power" to promote national standards in areas such as health, education and social services. This is the power of the federal government to spend money in areas in which it cannot legislate. During the first three decades following the Second World War, these federal initiatives shaped the modern welfare state.

♦ Partly through the support of federal transfers, most provinces also greatly expanded expenditures on such areas as highways, education and social programs. For example, close to 70% of the annual operating budget of the Ontario Government by the beginning of the 1990s was taken up by expenditures on just three areas: health, education and social services.

Throughout the postwar period, the whole political spectrum was shifting to the left. Governments of almost all Western nations accepted this expanded role in the economy and society. Government was increasingly viewed as having the answer to our problems. All too often, governments believed or even promoted this point of view. As governments grew in size and involvement, individual responsibility declined. As indicated in Chapter 1, *"Why doesn't the government do something about this or that"* became the standard public response to any problem, whatever its cause.

Recent Swing to the Right

Over the past decade or so, however, there has been a pronounced swing to the right. Politicians promising to "get governments off the back of people" have enjoyed success in countries like the United States (under Reagan) and Britain (under Thatcher). Deregulation, downsizing, and privatization have become "buzz words." Governments that were smaller and less obtrusive became the goal.

To some extent the call for less government was prompted by growing concerns about the size of annual deficits and accumulated public debt (an issue explored in Chapter 9). Another motivating factor was a feeling on the part of a substantial segment of society that government had become too large and invasive, took too much of our earnings in taxes, and provided social programs which encouraged dependency instead of self-reliance on the part of too many people.

The shift back to the right has been sufficiently pronounced that it has affected all political parties. Consider these three examples:

◆ The federal P.C. Party talked a lot about downsizing and deficit reduction during Mulroney's two terms in office, but it has been the federal Liberal Party, since taking office in October 1993, which has acted more "right wing" in terms of its attack on the deficit, its downsizing of the public service and its cuts in transfer payments for various social programs.

◆ The Ontario NDP Government began this decade with traditional left wing policies which included increased welfare payments and an expansionary budget designed to create jobs through various public works programs. As its term progressed, however, it became increasingly right wing in its policies in response to growing concerns about the Provincial debt. This shift was highlighted, in April 1993, by the introduction of a Social Contract and Expenditure Control Program which imposed cuts in transfers to schools, hospitals and municipalities.

◆ The Progressive Conservative Governments in power in Alberta and Ontario in the mid-1990s have pursued an agenda very much on the right side of the spectrum, introducing major spending cuts to social programs in order to reduce debt and to be able to offer tax cuts. For example, on November 29th, 1995, only a few months after taking office, the P.C. Government in Ontario announced expenditure cuts of some $6 billion over the next three years — the bulk of it coming from reduced transfer payments for education, hospitals, public transit, libraries, cultural organizations and municipal governments.[14] Part of the reason for the Ontario Government's tough actions in cutting expenditures is its continuing commitment to cut taxes by 30%.

It doesn't matter whether or not you agree with the actions which have been taken by the various governments cited. The fact is that these actions illustrate what are commonly described as left wing or (mostly) right wing positions.

Further insight into the shift to the right in Canadian politics was evident when the Progressive Conservative Party held a national convention in Winnipeg in August 1996. This was a vitally important gathering, designed to start the party back on the road to recovery from its devastating defeat in the 1993 federal election. There was strong pressure, especially from the youth wing of the party, for a commitment to substantial tax cuts. There were also calls for privatization of medicare, abolition of the Canada Pension Plan, the establishment of boot camps for young offenders and restoration of the death penalty.[15] Some of the right wing positions could be interpreted as positioning the P.C. Party to woo back disaffected supporters who had gone over to the Reform Party. But it is also evident from various comments made by delegates that many believe that government has become the enemy, that money should be shifted from government to private hands.

---

[14]See Ernie Eves, *1995 Fiscal and Economic Statement*, Ministry of Finance, November 1995.

[15]David Vienneau, "Hardliners, moderates staking out Tory ground," *Toronto Star*, August 24, 1996.

What About Third Parties?

Third parties have made some impact at the federal level. While they have never come close to forming a government, they have sometimes held the balance of power.

The New Democratic Party

By far the most prominent and enduring of these third parties has been the New Democratic Party (NDP). It was first formed in 1933 as the Cooperative Commonwealth Federation (CCF), which brought together an assortment of Fabian socialists, Marxists and farm and labour groups under the leadership of J. S. Wordsworth. The party's origins gave it a mainly Western rural support base which limited its electoral support (and its financial stability) over the almost 30 years of its existence.[16] In 1961 the CCF was dissolved and replaced by the New Democratic Party. This move was designed to embrace organized labour, thereby broadening the support base of the party, extending it more into urban Canada, and ensuring it of a more stable financial future based on union contributions.

As a party of moderate socialism, the NDP has wrestled over the years with how to maintain its founding principles and its commitment to extensive government intervention in the economy and society without being overly dogmatic and ideological and thereby losing possible electoral support. This internal tension triggered a split by the "Waffle" group in the late 1960s — an incongruous name, since their position was that the NDP must not waffle on its socialist principles. The party had popular and respected leaders in Tommy Douglas, David Lewis and, especially, Ed Broadbent, who in 1988 led the party to its best showing ever with 20% of the popular vote and 43 seats. However, his successor, Audrey McLaughlin, was only able to hold nine seats for the party against the Liberal landslide in 1993. This reduced standing meant that the party lost its official status

---

[16]The description of the CCF/NDP in this section is largely based on Jackson and Jackson, *op. cit.*, p. 432.

in the House and the research funds that went with it. McLaughlin's successor, Alexa McDonough, has yet to obtain a seat in the Commons or to establish much of a national presence. However, the NDP continues to enjoy some success provincially, and currently forms the government in both British Columbia and Saskatchewan.

The Bloc Québécois

One of the parties which replaced the Progressive Conservatives when they were reduced to two members in 1993 made a dramatic entry into national politics but that may be short-lived. That party is, of course, the Bloc Québécois, which succeeded in electing 54 MPs from the province of Québec on a platform of promoting separation from Canada. In the October 30th, 1995 referendum, they failed in this endeavour, although by the narrowest of margins. Their leader, Lucien Bouchard, has shifted to the provincial scene, accepting a "draft" to become leader of the Parti Québecois, and Premier of Québec. There was speculation that a number of Bloc members might leave federal politics without Bouchard at the helm. While this has not happened so far, it will be a tall order for the party to survive intact beyond the current term. Bouchard's replacement as Bloc leader, Michel Gauthier, announced in late 1996 that he was stepping down — largely in response to internal dissent.

The Reform Party

The future of the other new party is more difficult to predict and is intertwined with the fate of the Progressive Conservatives. That is because the Reform Party is essentially a more "right wing" version of the P.C. Party. A variation of this right wing party has been active at the provincial level for more than 50 years, primarily in Alberta and British Columbia, under the name of the Social Credit Party.[17] Indeed,

---

[17]The Social Credit Party elected a substantial number of members from Québec in the 1960s. But this result was not an endorsement of right wing views as much as it was a protest vote against the Liberals and Conservatives and a positive response to the charisma of fiery party leader Réal Caouette.

the Social Credit Party formed the government in Alberta from 1935 until 1970, for most of that time under the leadership of Ernest Manning. It is his son, Preston, who now heads the Reform Party.

On the surface, it might appear that the Reform Party with 52 seats in the Commons is much better placed to survive than the Progressive Conservative Party with its two seats. But, the P.C. Party should not be underestimated. It has almost a century and a half of proud tradition to call upon, unlike the neophyte Reform Party. It received almost as large a share of the popular vote as the Reform Party in the last election (16% as compared to 19% for Reform) and it still has active, grass roots riding associations in every riding in Canada.

Reform gained the large number of seats because its support was concentrated in the two most Western Provinces. That electoral advantage is also Reform's biggest drawback. It is a regional party, and may end up being nothing more than the latest in a long line of protest parties which have come out of Western Canada, made a brief appearance on the national scene and disappeared. The Progressive Conservative Party won only two seats because its popular vote was spread all across Canada. It is still more of a national party than Reform. It is still the second national party in the country, in spite of its current weakness in the House of Commons. Whether the Conservative Party will revive will depend, in large part, on how much it is able to win back those disaffected supporters who have switched their allegiance to Reform in recent years.

Support for the Reform Party has stalled or even declined during 1996, at least in part because of the rather extremist views expressed by some of its elected members. Several Reform MPs have indicated that they will not be running again, including two of the party's "brightest stars" and most high profile members, Jan Brown and Stephen Harper. There have also been questions raised about Preston Manning's leadership and his handling of some internal clashes involving statements made by some members. Reform's setbacks and perceived extremism provide an opportunity for the Progressive Conservatives to reclaim support as the only national alternative to the ruling Liberals.

The Parties and the Political Spectrum

From this admittedly very brief discussion, where do we place the main parties in Canada on the left-right political spectrum? The Bloc is omitted from the spectrum chart depicted below only because it does not fit a conventional left-right distinction. The Bloc includes members from all parts of the political spectrum, united mainly by their common objective of Québec independence.

LEFT	CENTRE	RIGHT
NDP (Liberals in a hurry)	Liberals and Conservatives	Reform (Ultra Conservatives)

The political spectrum can be useful in analyzing and under-standing political developments, especially if one bears in mind that the whole spectrum shifts to the left or right over time. In the past decade, as already discussed, there has been a pronounced swing to the right. The Liberals have positioned themselves very effectively by embracing many of the deficit and debt reduction strategies espoused but not followed very effectively by the Mulroney Conservatives. As a result, the Liberals now occupy most of the central ground in Cana-dian politics.

The Progressive Conservatives have been badly squeezed from both sides by the Liberals to their left and Reform to their right. This has not left them much room for manoeuvre. Staying near the centre makes them indistinguishable from the Liberals, who are currently — it might be argued —doing a better job of being Conservative than the Conservatives. If they move further to the right, they directly chal-lenge Reform and may even win back some supporters who had deserted to Reform in recent years. But they may also look so extreme that they alienate many other voters who prefer to stay in the centre, with the Liberals.

The NDP has faced this dilemma of positioning throughout its existence. If it moved more toward the centre, it became indistinguishable from the Liberals. Besides alienating its core supporters, such a move ran the risk that voters would decide to support moderate NDP-type policies indirectly and more safely by voting for the Liberals. This, in fact, was one of the keys to Mackenzie King's long success as Prime Minister. Whenever Canadians were ready to accept the kinds of policies being advocated by the CCF, he would shamelessly appropriate them for himself. By so doing, he kept the Liberal Party in the centre, wherever that centre might be. On the other hand, if the NDP moved sharply to the left, they provided a clear alternative, they consolidated their position with their core supporters, but they also ran the risk of alienating most other voters who tend to resist any form of extremism in Canadian politics.

The NDP's position is somewhat different today. With all other parties shifting to the right, the NDP represents the only choice for those who still support a significant role for government. Even by remaining fairly moderate in its stance and policies, the NDP of today can differentiate itself from the Liberals, Progressive Conservatives and Reform Party. That would seem to be its most appropriate course of action. Those supporting this strategy point to the recent success of the NDP in winning re-election in British Columbia on a fairly traditional platform which included a continuing strong role for government.

What About Pressure Groups?

If the emergence of a number of minor parties is one indication of declining support for Canada's traditional two party system, what are we to make of the proliferation of interest groups or pressure groups? John Meisel linked their growth to the decline of political parties and warned that "their numbers and means permit them to become rivals of political parties."[18] On the other hand, governments readily accept

---

[18]John Meisel, "Recent Changes in Canadian Parties," in Hugh Thorburn (ed.), *Political Parties in Canada*, Scarborough, Prentice-Hall, 1967, pp. 33-54.

and even encourage pressure groups, partly because they can provide policy makers with essential information.[19]

◆ *Something to Think About*

How should we view the existence of so many pressure groups interacting with government?

Does their proliferation undermine political parties and reflect a decline in the legitimacy of our existing political institutions? Or are these groups a positive development, providing increased access to government and decision making for Canadians?

Before we can attempt to answer these questions, some clarification of terminology is in order, since the terms interest group, pressure group and lobbyist are often used interchangeably.

Interest groups, as the name suggests, bring together people who share a common interest or concern. That interest may range from bird watching to preservation of world peace. Interest groups can be described as *pressure groups* when they attempt to exert pressure on government to do something or to refrain from doing something. Some groups rarely go beyond being interest groups. For them, political activity "is often a minor and unwelcome addition to the concerns that have brought them together."[20] For example, a group of bird watchers may meet regularly over many months or years for nothing more than the pure pleasure of searching out and enjoying their feathered friends. Then urban sprawl into a forested area, development encroaching on wetlands, or some other environmental threat to the habitat of birds, may transform them into a pressure group, seeking action from their governments to protect the environment. After fighting this battle, the members may again return to their original interest and resume their bird watching activities without paying much further attention to government.

---

[19]A. Paul Pross, *Group Politics and Public Policy*, 2nd edition, Toronto, Oxford University Press, 1992, p. 16.

[20]*Ibid.*, p. 5.

In contrast to groups which only occasionally and very temporarily indulge in political activity are those pressure groups whose main raision d'être is to attempt to influence government decisions. These are usually long-standing national organizations with ample resources and access to government. Examples would include the Canadian Manufacturing Association, Canadian Labour Congress, Canadian Petroleum Association, Canadian Bankers Association, Canadian Federation of Agriculture, and Canadian Medical Association. However, they may also include temporary or short term groups formed in response to a particular issue, and usually devoted to blocking something which is viewed as undesirable. Good examples would be citizen or neighbourhood groups formed to oppose the location of a high rise building or an expressway or a landfill site near their area. These latter groups are equally devoted to applying pressure on government, but they usually lack the resources available to the national organizations, and they rarely endure beyond the immediate crisis which brought them into existence.

While pressure groups "lobby" the government to advance their cause, the term *lobbyist* refers to individuals and organizations which specialize full time in the "art" of influencing government. These professional lobbyists are available for hire and their main value has been described — in a remark attributed to Senator Keith Davey — as helping clients "to tiptoe through the Ottawa tulips." This colourful phrasing refers to the fact that lobbyists are well plugged in to the policy process in Ottawa; they earn their money by keeping on top of what is breaking in government and whom to contact on a given item.

In fact, many lobbyists are retired public servants or former political advisors who retain an impressive network of contacts within government. Organizations concerned about policy developments which may affect them often decide that these interests can be better protected by purchasing the services of someone "on the scene" and well connected. Some large organizations hire their own full time lobbyists, but most work for public relations or government consulting firms and have a number of organizations as clients.

Since 1989, lobbyists have been required to register with the Ministry of Consumer and Corporate Affairs Canada, as a result of which we have information on some 1000 professionals who lobby on behalf of others and another 2000 who are employees of organizations and associations that lobby the government.[21] That information is very limited, however, and does not indicate the names of those who were lobbied or specifically what kind of lobbying activity took place. In addition, it is estimated that an unknown but sizeable number of those involved in lobbying have not registered.

Yet another variation is found in *social movements*, which bring together individuals and groups to press for greater government action on what are felt to be neglected or mishandled issues. Examples would include the feminist, animal rights, gay rights and environmental movements. The latter would include not only a large number of specific environmental groups but also others such as students, cottage owners, anglers and hunters, community groups and professional associations — both organized and unorganized.[22] These social movements can be distinguished from pressure groups by their structure, or lack thereof. They are not "organizations," but informal networks of interaction among a large number of often diverse individuals and groups who share a common cause. [23]

Pressure groups are by no means new to Canadian politics and Pross notes that even in pre-Confederation days it was common for groups to lobby authorities in Britain or France for public policy concessions that would advance their interests.[24] They have now become so prominent, however, that according to Jeffrey Simpson,[25] modern politics is interest group politics, "a giant bazaar where parties try with increasing desperation to satisfy interest groups which, by defi-

---

[21]James John Guy, *How We Are Governed*, Toronto, Harcourt Brace & Company Canada, Ltd., 1995, p. 304.

[22]Michael Whittington and Richard Van Loon, *Canadian Government and Politics: Institutions and Processes*, Whitby, McGraw-Hill Ryerson Limited, 1996, p. 442.

[23]*Ibid.*, p. 441.

[24]Pross, *op. cit.*, p. 20.

[25]Jeffrey Simpson, *Globe and Mail*, September 5, 1990, quoted in *ibid.*, p. 1.

nition, have a stake in being dissatisfied."

The diversity of Canadian society contributes to the proliferation of interest groups, and our federal system of government stimulates the organization of interest groups on various levels to apply pressure on several fronts. In addition, our parliamentary system of government provides multiple contact and pressure points, further encouraging the development of pressure groups.[26] Moreover, operating departments have often found it useful to forge alliances with outside interest groups (and even to encourage and foster their development). These links have provided helpful allies when the departments need to defend their programs and budgets, especially with the cutback mentality which has prevailed in recent years.

As discussed in the next chapter, these groups do provide another vehicle through which citizens can participate in public affairs. Many Canadians are disillusioned with political parties, which seem to avoid taking a clear stand on the issues that concern them, or reverse that stand when it suits their purpose. In contrast, interest groups — almost by definition — have clearly defined objectives which are pursued in a more consistent fashion. By joining groups which advocate positions similar to their own, individuals feel able to participate more effectively in society. Pross takes the view that the competition provided by pressure groups is not the problem; rather it is a symptom of the decline in the policy role of political parties and of our elected representatives.[27] This view would suggest directing efforts to improve our governing institutions rather than to restricting pressure groups.

The existence of widespread pressure groups is central to the pluralistic view of policy making, which sees government decisions essentially emerging as a result of the interaction of these groups and their demands. Not all Canadians belong to groups, however, and not all groups have equal resources or equal access to government. In particular, the poor and the less educated are much less likely to join

---

[26]These explanations for the prevalence of pressure groups are provided by Guy, *op. cit.*, p. 292.

[27]Pross, *op. cit.*, p. 16.

together in concerted efforts to influence government action. In the classic words of E. E. Schattschneider, "the flaw in the pluralist heaven is that the heavenly chorus sings with a strong upper-class accent...."[28]

Many believe that the front row of that chorus is occupied by business leaders and corporations. They certainly have the resources to promote their point of view, and they appear to have ready access to government as well. The fact that so much of the funding for the Liberal and Progressive Conservative Parties has come from business has certainly helped to ease that access. Chapter 9 explores the strong influence exerted by the business community over the economic policies and objectives pursued by our governments.

There are those who argue, however, that business groups don't have nearly as much decisive influence as is usually attributed to them. They face competition from other strong groups, representing the interests of labour, the environment, consumers and others. As Chapter 4 pointed out, the Charter has shifted some power in our system to interests and groups which had previously been relegated to the sidelines, but which now can use the courts to pursue their objectives. Competition between political parties and the need to appeal to the general public are also felt to prevent businesses from "having their way" with governments. The fact that some government policies are adopted over the strong objections of business is cited as further evidence that business influence has been overstated.[29]

Lobbyists at Work

Further insight into a number of issues discussed above can be seen from an examination of the activities of the tobacco lobby in response to government efforts to ban tobacco advertising. When legislation

---

[28]E. E. Schattschneider, *The Semi-Sovereign People*, New York, Holt, Rinehart and Winston, 1960, p. 35.

[29]For a very good discussion of both sides of this issue, see the articles by William Coleman and W. T. Stanbury in Charlton and Barker, *op. cit.*, pp. 336-363, on which the above summary is based.

was first introduced in 1987, the tobacco manufacturers hired a prominent lobbyist, Bill Neville, to work on their behalf, and mounted
a campaign of newspaper advertisements and direct mailings. Various
health groups, including the Canadian Medical Association and the
Canadian Cancer Society countered with their own campaigns, including black-edged postcards to MPs to symbolize the cancer-related
deaths in their ridings.[30] Rather than trying to kill the legislation, the
tobacco lobby concentrated, successfully, on delaying its passage for
a considerable time. Moreover, when the Tobacco Products Control
Act was passed in June 1988, opponents appealed to the Supreme
Court which ruled, in 1995, that the Act was unconstitutional because
its nearly total advertising ban violated the tobacco industry's right to
free speech.[31]

When the Liberal Government announced plans to introduce new
legislation to control tobacco advertising in the spring of 1996, those
in the tobacco industry employed several tactics.[32]

♦ They hired influential former civil servants, including chiefs of
  staff to two former Prime Ministers, for advice on how to make
  their case.
♦ They hired professional lobbyists with Liberal connections to
  lobby the public service and the office of the Minister of Health.
♦ They helped to establish and to fund an alliance of arts and sports
  groups, which had become dependent on millions in annual cigar-
  ette sponsorships for their events, to lobby politicians.
♦ They pointed out that economically depressed Montreal, home to
  the country's largest tobacco company and site of many cigarette-
  sponsored festivals, would be hard hit by the government's plans.

---

[30]This discussion is based on Robert Jackson and Doreen Jackson, *Canadian Government in Transition*, Scarborough, Prentice Hall Canada Inc.,
1996, p. 238.

[31]*Ibid.*

[32]The description of this round of lobbying is based on Mark Kennedy,
"Health issue entangled in issues of jobs and national unity," *Kingston Whig
Standard*, November 19, 1996.

◆ They even found a national unity link, reminding the government that the President of Imasco (Imperial Tobacco), one of Québec's leading companies, is a strong federalist voice in that province.

The tobacco industry also relied upon the close political ties it had built up over the years. It donates substantial funds to mainstream parties, including $63 000 to the Liberals in 1995 and $92 000 the previous year.[33] A number of Senators sit on tobacco boards, as did Finance Minister Paul Martin until he became an MP in 1988. Presidents and other executive members of various riding associations have strong ties to the tobacco industry, and tobacco companies have made substantial campaign contributions to individual candidates.

The tobacco story offers a number of insights into pressure group activity in Canada. It illustrates how influential and well connected business groups can be, as previously discussed. But it also demonstrates, in support of pluralist views of policy making, that other interests — in this case from the health field — can also mobilize and make an effective case. Even with all of its connections, the tobacco lobby was unsuccessful in blocking a second attempt at government legislation banning advertising, introduced in late 1996. But continued pressure has apparently weakened the resolve of the Liberal Government, and it is now talking about amending the legislation and phasing in some of the new restrictions.

Concluding Observations

This chapter has provided an extremely brief overview of political parties and the political spectrum. It in no way constitutes an adequate examination of this topic. It is up to you to build from this introduction. Find out more about the political parties and where they stand on the issues that concern you. The next federal election is almost certain to come sometime in 1997. Do you have an informed basis for exercising your democratic rights?

---

[33]*Ibid.*

When you look at the parties and the promises they make, you should also consider carefully the assumptions they are making about the role of government — in other words, where they fit on the political spectrum. Where you want them to fit is your call. But this Guide offers a reminder that — as with all things in life — a balance must be maintained in the size and scope of government. It may well be that government had grown too large and too intrusive. If we over-react to this perceived situation, however, we may pay the price for scaling back too much the role and contribution made by government. We may aggravate social divisions and widen the gap between the haves and have-nots. We may find ourselves with not only a leaner government but a meaner society. It's up to you, and all Canadians, to monitor the actions of our governments and our political parties, and to maintain a desirable balance between the scale of government operations and that of the private sector.

Besides participating through political parties, you may wish to join pressure groups that deal with issues that concern you. But recognize that governments can't always respond to the interests of your particular group(s), no matter how well expressed. Nor would such a response necessarily be desirable, unless one assumes that the "public interest" is little more than the sum total of the various, separate pressure group interests.

The Last Word

Definition of Terms and Concepts

Interest Group: [See also Pressure Group.]
A number of individuals who come together because of their common interest in a particular issue or activity.

Left Wing:
Term to describe political views which support a major role for government in the management of the economy and the provision of programs and services to support individuals and families.

Lobbyist:
Someone who specializes in attempting to influence government, either as an employee of a particular organization or as a professional who works for a variety of different clients.

Political Party:
Organization dedicated to recruiting candidates and electing members, with the objective of forming a government and carrying out their policies and objectives.

Pressure Group:
An interest group which interacts with government in an attempt to influence its policies. All pressure groups are interest groups, but not all interest groups become (or stay) pressure groups.

Right Wing:
Term to describe political views which hold that minimum government is best in terms of individual freedom and development. Also a term used to depict a strong (punitive?) position on matters of crime and punishment.

Points to Ponder

1. Where do you place yourself on the political spectrum, and why? [Don't be surprised if you decide that you are left wing in some respects and right wing in others. This doesn't mean that you are schizophrenic. You might, for example, hold right wing views on law and order (such as favouring the return of capital punishment) but left wing views on social programs and their importance.]

2. In considering which party you support, is that support based on:
   a) a positive view of the leader of the party,
   b) a negative view of the alternatives, or
   c) positive feelings about specific policies of the party?

3. Identify any current political issue, observe how it is handled, and attempt to identify the pressure groups involved, their activities, and their apparent degree of success in promoting their viewpoint.

For Further Reading

For a good overview of political parties and the philosophies of conservatism, liberalism and socialism, see Robert Jackson and Doreen Jackson, *Canadian Government in Transition*, Scarborough, Prentice Hall Canada Inc., 1996, Chapter 10. There is also a more extensive treatment of this topic by these authors in *Politics in Canada*, 3rd edition, Scarborough, Prentice Hall Canada Inc., 1994, Chapter 10. See also C. Campbell and W. Christian, *Parties, Leaders and Ideologies in Canada*, Whitby, McGraw-Hill Ryerson Limited, 1996, and Michael Whittington and Richard Van Loon, *Canadian Government and Politics*, Whitby, McGraw-Hill Ryerson Limited, 1996, Chapters 13 and 14.

A series of short articles on Canadian political parties and their roles and philosophies is found in Paul Fox and Graham White (eds.), *Politics: Canada*, 8th edition, Whitby, McGraw-Hill Inc., 1995.

For an overview of the much more limited activity of organized political parties within local government, see C. Richard Tindal and Susan Nobes Tindal, *Local Government in Canada*, 4th edition, Whitby, McGraw-Hill Ryerson Limited, 1995, Chapter 8.

Pressure groups are discussed in many texts including A. Paul Pross, *Group Politics and Public Policy*, 2nd edition, Toronto, Oxford University Press, 1992, the previously-cited Whittington and Van Loon text, Chapters 16 and 17, and the previously cited texts by Jackson and Jackson.

A good discussion of whether or not business groups enjoy privileged access to government is found in the articles by William Coleman and W. T. Stanbury in Mark Charlton and Paul Barker (eds.) *Crosscurrents: Contemporary Political Issues*, 2nd edition, Scarborough, Nelson Canada, pp. 336-363.

Chapter 8

Don't Fight Them, Join Them

Objectives and Highlights

♦ To describe various ways you can participate in the activities of government.

♦ To identify the barriers which tend to restrict the availability of candidates for political office.

♦ To distinguish the main techniques of direct democracy and to assess their value.

In October 1995 hundreds of thousands gathered in Montréal to profess their love for Canada and their desire to see it stay together — an action credited by many with having generated the razor-thin victory for the pro-Canadian forces in the referendum of October 31. Three years earlier, Canadians had turned out in large numbers to vote in a referendum on constitutional reform, in which they rejected the advice of their political leaders and the Charlottetown Accord. These events suggest that the traditional image of Canadians as deferential and apathetic about matters political no longer applies, if it ever did.

This chapter explores various ways in which Canadians can participate in government. Consistent with its purpose as a "Guide," it includes information on requirements for voting and candidacy, as well as information on the laws governing election financing. It also explores participation through appointment to advisory bodies, membership in interest groups and such direct democracy concepts as the referendum and the recall. It concludes with a reminder of the importance of retaining participation through elections, parties and established governing instututitons, no matter what other forms of participation are embraced.

T here are many ways for Canadians to become involved with their governments. One of the strengths of our democratic system is that there are few limits on our rights to participate through voting, joining groups and lobbying, joining and working for political parties, serving on appointed committees and boards, and running for office. This chapter will describe the legal rights and restrictions which apply to your participation in government, and will suggest ways of enhancing that participation.

I. Voting and Candidacy

It may surprise you to learn that the *franchise* (that is, the right to vote) has been universal only since 1960.[1]

At the time of Confederation, the franchise was based on provincial laws and restricted to male property owners. Plural voting was allowed in that citizens could vote in each area in which they owned property. There was no single election day and government staggered voting so that results came in first from their strong areas to develop a bandwagon effect.

In 1885, balloting was brought under federal jurisdiction, but a new restriction was added with the disenfranchisement of Asians. In 1917, Canadians of Central European descent lost their vote. Females, if relatives of soldiers, were given the right to vote, along with native Indians serving in the Armed Forces. The following year, all women were granted equal voting rights. Canadians of Asian descent, however, were not granted normal voting privileges until 1948, and Inuit — who were disenfranchised in 1934 — didn't have the right restored until 1950. Religious conscientious objectors, mainly Mennonites, who had been disenfranchised as early as 1920, did not regain voting rights until 1955. The last group to receive voter status was reservation Indians, and that as late as 1960.

---

[1]The summary which follows is based on Robert Jackson and Doreen Jackson, *Politics in Canada*, 3rd edition, Scarborough, Prentice Hall Canada Inc., 1994, p. 479.

 Today, we enjoy a universal franchise at all levels of government. Every Canadian citizen, 18 years of age or older by polling day, who meets the specified residency requirements, and who is not otherwise disqualified, is eligible to vote.

Amendments to the Canada Elections Act in 1993 broadened the **federal** franchise[2] by removing disqualifications for several groups, including judges, persons who are "restrained of their liberty of movement or deprived of the management of their property by reason of mental disease" and inmates serving sentences of less than two years in a correctional institution. Provision was also made for Canadians to vote if they are absent from Canada for less than five consecutive years and intend to return to reside in Canada, or if they are temporarily outside of the country or outside of their electoral district.

There are very few persons still prohibited from voting. These include the Chief Electoral Officer, returning officers in each riding, individuals disqualified by law for corrupt or illegal practices, and inmates of penal institutions serving a sentence of more than two years. The latter group **may** have the right to vote in the next election as a result of a Federal Court ruling at the end of 1995. It struck down the current restriction on voting rights for prisoners serving sentences of two years or more, but left the door open for a new more narrowly focused law.[3]

Ontario legislation states that persons are eligible to vote if they have resided in Ontario for twelve months prior to polling day, and are ordinarily resident in the electoral district in which they intend to vote. A 1984 amendment to the Election Act gave the vote to judges, returning officers, election clerks, and inmates of mental hospitals or homes for the mentally incompetent.

---

[2]*Ibid.*

[3]Jim Bronskill, "Denying prisoners vote unfair, judge rules," *Kingston Whig Standard*, January 6, 1996.

To be an elector at the **municipal** level, one must be a Canadian citizen, 18 years of age or older by polling day, and a resident in the municipality — or an owner or tenant of land in the municipality or spouse of same.[4] It is possible to vote in more than one municipality. For example, someone may live in one municipality, own a business in a second municipality, and have a summer cottage in a third municipality.

Becoming a Candidate

Most Canadians would probably never consider becoming a candidate for political office. This reservation is not because of legal requirements, which are fairly minimal. Rather, it is because of a number of other "unofficial barriers" which tend to limit the availability of candidates. Before examining these barriers, let's look at the legal requirements involved.

Legal Requirements for Candidacy

The federal requirements are outlined below. Provincial requirements are similar, but you should consult the legislation in your particular province for the specifics.

1. You must be eligible to vote.

2. You must be a resident of Canada, but not necessarily a resident of the riding in which you seek to be a candidate — although candidates who are "parachuted" into a riding with which they have no past association are often rebuffed.

3. You must not be disqualified from seeking federal office by the provisions of the Canada Elections Act. This category includes persons guilty of corrupt election practices, members of a provincial legislature and inmates in penal institutions — although there are some Charter challenges with respect to this latter restriction.

---

[4]These are the provisions with respect to municipal elections in Ontario. A number of amendments to the Municipal Elections Act were passed in December 1996 as part of Bill 86, the Better Local Government Act.

4. You must have the signatures of 100 fellow electors. [But, if you decide to run some day, be sure to get 102 or 105 signatures while you're at it. If you have only 100 names and it then is determined that one of those people is not an eligible voter in your riding, and the nomination period has closed, you are out of luck! Don't take that chance. Have some margin for safety.]

5. You must pay a deposit of $1000. This payment is intended to discourage frivolous candidates, and it is returned to all those who receive at least 15% of the votes cast in the ensuing election.

As mentioned, the provisions for provincial elections are very similar. For example, the requirements for Ontario include the same 100 signatures. A financial deposit has only been required since 1984 and it is for $200, not the $1000 required at the federal level.

In the case of municipal elections (again using Ontario as the example), you must be eligible to vote, must not be disqualified from being a candidate (such as by being a member of the Legislative Assembly of Ontario or the Federal House of Commons) and you must not be an employee of the municipality or of defined local boards — unless you obtain a leave of absence. A new requirement for a deposit for municipal candidates (expected to be $100) is being introduced in Ontario, a change very much in line with federal and provincial provisions.

Barriers to Candidacy

So far, so good. There aren't many legal barriers to becoming a candidate for office at any level in Canada. But we have been ignoring two significant hurdles which have to be overcome, even though they are not legal requirements. First, there are a variety of what might best be termed socio-economic variables which tend to reduce dramatically the potential pool of candidates. Second, those seeking office at the federal and provincial levels have the added task of becoming nominated by a political party — since there is little chance of being elected as an independent candidate. A closer look at both of these types of barrier will reveal the real limitations on public participation through standing for office.

Socio-Economic Limits on Candidacy

Perhaps as little as 20% of the Canadian population would ever consider themselves "candidate material" or would be accepted as such by their fellow electors. What are the factors which so severely restrict the pool of potential candidates?

a) *Age*

Once elected, a candidate can be re-elected any number of times, without too much attention being paid to the advancing years. However, a first time candidate who was a senior citizen might be considered too old by the electorate. At one time, first time candidates also faced the possibility of being rejected as too young, but over the past couple of decades we have seen a dramatic increase in the number of youthful candidates being elected at all three levels.

b) *Sex or Gender*

This has been a factor, but it too appears to be lessening. In the recent past Canada has had a female Prime Minister, albeit for a brief period. The federal NDP replaced one female leader with another in the fall of 1995. Women have also been gaining more prominent positions in provincial politics. BC had Canada's first female Premier in 1991, the last election in Prince Edward Island returned a female Premier (although she recently stepped down from that position), and the leader of the NWT Government until the fall of 1995 was a woman. Perhaps most dramatic of all has been the number of women heading municipalities, including (in Ontario alone) present or recent past Mayors of Mississauga, London, Kingston, Ottawa, Toronto, Vaughan, Kanata, Vanier, St. Thomas and East York.

On the other hand, there is some evidence from the provincial and federal levels to suggest that the gains by women are not always sustained and that, in particular, they have more difficulty than men in retaining support when they are in leadership positions. For example, the mid-term resignation of PEI Premier, Catherine Callbeck, is blamed by some on pressure from "backroom boys," Lynda Haverstock was forced out as Opposition

Leader in Saskatchewan by a caucus revolt last year, and Lynn McLeod is gone as Liberal leader in Ontario after that party's failure in the June 1995 provincial election.[5] In all cases, they have been replaced by men. The pattern of reversal has been particularly striking in Ontario, which not long ago featured an NDP Government in which 40% of the members were female. There are now only four women in the Conservative Cabinet and almost 85% of the legislature is male.

c) *Race and Religion*
Historically, these factors almost always related to the French-English and Catholic-Protestant features of the "two founding races" of Canada. However, Canada, especially in its urban areas, has become increasingly cosmopolitan. Many races and religions are now to be found and may influence a candidate's chances for success in particular ridings.

d) *Type of Employment*
There is a widespread, if ill-defined and even subconscious, perception that shift workers, labourers, semi-skilled workers and others in what used to be termed "blue collar" jobs would not be suitable candidates as elected members. Conversely, those in "white collar" positions like lawyers, bankers, business managers and other professionals are regarded as better qualified.

e) *Educational Level*
This is, to some extent, a perception issue like the preceding one. It refers to the fact that people are likely to question the suitability of a high school dropout, especially if the alternative is a college or university graduate. The requirements of elected office will mean that most members will be called upon to communicate with the public frequently. Whether fair or well founded, the perception is that the higher the educational level, the more likely a member will write and speak in a polished and articulate manner

---

[5]This discussion is based on "Why don't female leaders last in Canadian politics?" *Ottawa Citizen*, November 29, 1996.

and will present an image in keeping with what most people think
an elected member should be.

f)   "Social Class"

This factor is similar in some respects to the "blue collar-white
collar" distinction made earlier and also reflects one's educational
background. However, it can be much more. While Canadians
like to think of themselves as a classless society, there is still a
strong sense of living on the "right side of the tracks." Some families are prominent in a community; they have enjoyed social
standing for decades — perhaps back through several generations.
Other people are felt to come from uncertain or dubious origins.
They lack the same pedigree. Much of this, of course, is little
more than snobbery. It may be quite inaccurate and unfair. But,
perception is reality, and nowhere more so than in politics.

g)   Money

The income level a candidate for office enjoys is largely a product
of the preceding three factors: type of employment, educational
level, and social class. It can influence the availability of candidates in two contradictory ways. If those with limited incomes
should consider running for office (in spite of all the other barriers listed above), they may be attracted by the prospect of the
salary and expense allowance paid to an elected member. The
majority of prospective candidates, however, are likely to hold
reasonably well paid positions already; for them, the politician's
salary is likely to offer a reduction in income and a disincentive.

   Whatever their existing income, most prospective candidates
think twice when they contemplate the expenses that they face —
first in contesting the election itself, and second if they should
win the election. Campaign expenses, and sources of funding for
these expenses, are discussed later in this chapter. The extra expenses which arise after an election victory come particularly
from the need to maintain two households (in the riding and in the
national or provincial capital) and from the unending list of chari-
ties and worthy causes which will expect (demand) financial support from a public figure.

Municipal politicians who operate businesses in their municipality often face two further difficulties relating to finances. They may lose business opportunities with the municipality because of a perceived conflict of interest. They may also find that some ratepayers shun their business if unhappy about some municipal policy or service. This may sound petty, but it is all part of the "goldfish bowl" atmosphere of municipal political life.

h) *Impact on Personal Life*

This impact can be expressed very simply — you won't have a "personal" life. It has been said that public figures can't have private lives. It is true that the public is entitled to know about private matters which may affect the public performance of an elected member or may place the member in a conflict of interest situation.

Under a Microscope

But, they do not need to know personal details of a member's private life or of the private lives of the member's family. Yet with increasingly aggressive investigative journalism now in vogue, "health records, past academic performance, youthful peccadillos, friendships, family life, holiday activities, entertainment preferences, and all else are now fair game...."[6] The thought of being placed under a microscope, or of having one's family background probed by overzealous media investigators, may be enough to eliminate a good number of potential candidates.

The demands of the job also take their toll on one's personal life. Members are separated from their families throughout much of the year. They are not present to share in the important events in their children's lives — from school plays to sporting events to first dates. When members are home (mostly on weekends), they are expected to be "out and about" —being seen in the riding and available to take calls from constituents who have some problem

[6]John Meisel, "Decline of Party in Canada," in Mark Charlton and Paul Barker (eds.), *Crosscurrents: Contemporary Political Issues*, 2nd edition, Scarborough, Nelson Canada, 1994, p. 241.

which the member should solve. It has been said that "politics is a demanding mistress" and one of the unfortunate consequences of elected office is a number of broken marriages — presumably fuelled by the long separations of partners and the constant demands on the time and energies of the elected partner.

These eight points are not a definitive list of the factors which tend to inhibit people from becoming candidates for political office. Some may dispute the validity of some of these points and the way they are described. The fact remains that factors such as these dramatically limit the pool of Canadians who would ever give serious consideration to becoming a politician — and who would be taken seriously by the rest of the public if they decided to run. One result, as discussed in Chapter 6, is that the make-up of the House of Commons does not represent the characteristics of the overall Canadian population. If it did, it would have more members under the age of 35, far more women members, and many more unskilled workers. We sometimes decry the fact the House of Commons is not more representative of "ordinary" Canadians, but it is uncertain that we would elect significant numbers of such Canadians if they could be persuaded to stand for office.

The Limitation of the Party Nomination

There is no legal requirement to obtain the backing of a political party to run for office at any level of government. Official party endorsement is not even an issue at the municipal level, except in the handful of Canadian cities in which political parties vie for seats on council. Even though they run as independents, however, many candidates for municipal council benefit from the fact that they are known to be associated with one political party or another. They also benefit from the campaign support they may receive from "the party machine." In fact, Canadians have a rather perverse view about party politics in municipal government. They accept quite willingly that municipal councillors are actively involved with political parties. They just don't accept that councillors should make this fact official by running on a party label.

However, elections for the federal and provincial level are fought on party lines. The political parties raise and spend large sums of money on behalf of their platforms and their candidates. The chances of an independent candidate being elected are extremely slim — almost nonexistent.

> But, the chances are not absolutely impossible. In 1974, a former Mayor of Moncton, New Brunswick, Leonard Jones, was elected as an independent MP. The circumstances were most unusual. He had originally been chosen as a Conservative candidate, but the leader of the Conservative Party, Robert Stanfield, refused to sign his nomination papers — which meant he could not contest the election on behalf of that party. Stanfield refused on the grounds that certain anti-French sentiments and statements expressed by Jones were unacceptable and unwelcome in the Conservative Party. The response of Jones was to run anyway, as an independent candidate. Because of the high profile and personal popularity which he enjoyed, as a former Mayor, he was elected anyway. However, he served only one term. Being an independent member in the House of Commons is a pretty lonely life.

If success at the provincial and federal levels presupposes a party affiliation, how does a prospective candidate go about obtaining a party nomination?

Party candidates are selected at nomination meetings called by each local *riding association*. This means that the decision on a candidate is usually made locally, by the party members in a particular riding who attend the nomination meeting. On the surface, this is a very democratic process, in which the candidate who attracts the largest number of supporters to the meeting carries the day. Some riding associations dictate that party memberships must have been held for some defined time period prior to the meeting — in an attempt to guard against some group packing the meeting with "instant members." The candidate who sells the most memberships (before any such deadline), and who gets out the votes, wins the nomination.

Most ridings are large and diverse. To become well known across such a riding, a candidate may have to spend several years working with the riding association and assisting in election campaigns.

Parties like candidates to have "earned" the right to represent them.

While special issues may dictate some riding outcomes (for example, an ethnic candidate or an anti-abortion takeover), normally the local riding will select someone well established in the community and in the party. Obtaining the nomination, therefore, is to a large extent a matter of good timing and good luck. For example, if you would like to seek the nomination in a riding in which your party has a sitting member, you have almost no chance. If you are a Conservative seeking election in a riding which has returned Liberals since Confederation, your prospects aren't great. But, if you are a Liberal, living in a riding which has had a popular Liberal member who is not seeking re-election, your timing could hardly be better. There is an opening for you to win, in a riding which your party holds. Lucky you.

Changes in the Canada Elections Act have increased the role of the federal party leaders. Revisions in 1970 require that each candidate's party affiliations appear on the ballot. It is necessary for parties to identify their own candidates so that they will qualify for benefits under the legislation, including expenditure reimbursement (discussed below). A statement signed by the party leader or designate confirming the party's endorsement must be filed with a candidate's nomination papers. This provision allows party leaders to reject candidates nominated by the local riding. (As discussed above, it was this provision that allowed Robert Stanfield to block the candidacy of Leonard Jones.)

♦ Something to Think About

How much say should the party leader have in the selection of candidates?

Prior to the 1993 election, the Liberal Party gave its leader the authority to hand-pick (prior to a nomination meeting) a number of candidates for the upcoming federal election.The rationale was that discretion would allow the leader to ensure a good balance among candidates and to field a strong team to attract the voters.

Jean Chrétien used this power on several occasions. One early example was his selection of former Toronto Mayor Art Eggleton as the candidate for a Toronto-area riding. Eggleton was elected and became a member of the Liberal Cabinet. Chrétien received a good deal of criticism (from within the Liberal Party itself) for what was perceived as high-handed and undemocratic actions.

What do you see as the pros and cons of giving a party leader the authority to select a limited number of candidates (let's say no more than 20) for the party?

Election Costs and Financing

As noted above, money — or the lack thereof — can be one of the factors limiting the availability of candidates. This issue is directly linked to that of party endorsement, since becoming a party candidate gives one access to additional sources of funding. Over the years, however, there have been widespread concerns about where parties receive the increasingly large amounts of funding required to mount election campaigns and how such funding might influence the decisions made by parties and their members.

Much of the increase in costs coincided with the growing use of television advertising. Media costs from all sources became a very significant portion of total election costs. For example, in 1979 the Liberal media advertising campaign (T.V., radio and newspapers) was estimated at $2.25 million, the PCs at $2.5 million and the NDP at $1.2 million. These figures represented 71%, 62% and 61%, respectively, of the three parties' total campaign expenditures. The 1988 PC advertising campaign was reported at $4.7 million, with the Liberals spending $3.8 million and the NDP $3.1 million. These expenses as a percentage of total campaign spending by each party were 59%, 56% and 44%, respectively.[7]

By the 1993 election campaign, it was estimated that:

◆ The national parties spent $45 million (comprising $10.6 million each by the Liberals, Conservatives and NDP — their limit under

---

[7] From the Report of the Chief Electoral Officer Respecting Election Expenses, 1988, as quoted in Jackson and Jackson, *op. cit.*, pp. 487-487.

the election financing legislation — $6 million by Reform, $4 million by the Bloc, and $2 million by the National Party).

♦ Candidates spent $50 million in the 295 ridings across Canada.

♦ Some $30 million was spent on pre-election spending and indirect expenses (notably polling), much of it by the then cash-rich Conservative Party.

♦ **More than half** of the expenditures were on advertising, about 70% of it for television ads.

As the costs of campaigning escalated, we faced the prospect of candidates having to be wealthy or having to rely heavily on others for donations. Neither alternative is particularly healthy for a democratic system. There were growing concerns about sources of funding and what "strings" might come with the money being provided. The legislation of the time did not result in full disclosure, and when the public doesn't know, it fears the worst!

What was known was the two old-line parties (Liberals and PCs) had traditionally relied very heavily on big business for their campaign donations. Both parties utilized a "Finance Committee" composed of leading business people, and they focused their fund raising efforts on Toronto, Montreal and Vancouver — where the head offices of most corporations were located. They relied upon very large contributions ($50 000 was not unusual) from a relatively small number of donors — mostly corporations and wealthy individuals. The NDP was also beholden to an economic interest to an unhealthy degree, since it relied for much of its money on donations from unions.

The federal Election Expenses Act of 1974 (and associated legislative reforms) was substantially successful in overcoming a number of the concerns about election financing. It introduced ceilings on the amount of money which could be spent by a party and a candidate, tightened the rules governing financial disclosure and accountability, and made donations income tax deductible so as to attract financial contributions from a broader cross-section of Canadians. The main reforms are summarized in **Appendix A** of this chapter, along with a brief discussion of their strengths and shortcomings.

One of the continuing problems and concerns relates to so-called "*third party*" spending. This potentially confusing term does **not** refer to spending by political parties but by various interest groups which may wish to support or oppose various issues during an election campaign. Since the legislative reforms discussed above are quite strict in limiting parties and candidates as to how much they could spend and when, they also initially restricted (indeed outlawed) spending by these so-called third parties. There was a legitimate concern about the possible influence of "political action groups" which have been very prominent in the United States.

However, a court challenge led by the National Citizens' Coalition led to the ruling that such restrictions violated the Charter. Freed from any legislative controls, business groups spent between $2 million and $10 million during the 1988 election campaign, promoting the free trade agreement (and, therefore, promoting the PCs, the only party which supported this agreement). We don't have a more precise measure of how much was spent because there are no requirements on these groups to file audited financial reports. They aren't even prevented from advertising on election day — unlike the political parties.

The politicians tried again, in April 1993, passing a law (Bill C-114 or the "Gag Law" as its opponents quickly dubbed it) which made it an offense for anyone except political parties to purchase more than $1000 in advertising during an election campaign. Once again, a court challenge was mounted, with opponents arguing that this law repressed individual rights and impinged upon democracy by allowing political elites to control the flow of ideas during an election campaign. Once again, the courts rejected the attempt to restrict advertising — on the basis of the Charter.

As a result, we have a system under which there are strict limits on how much money can be spent by candidates and parties, and no limits on what anyone else can spend during the same election. The latest example of the inequities that can arise occurred when Sheila Copps resigned over the GST issue and ran in a by-election in Hamilton East in mid-1996.[8] The National Citizens' Coalition and several anti-GST groups spent thousands of dollars campaigning against

[8]Joan Bryden, "Gag laws: Over-reaction or Necessary Evil," *Kingston Whig Standard*, August 19, 1996.

Copps, thereby augmenting the funds spent by her opponents.

On the other hand, third party spending restrictions could lead to extreme limitations or abuses, such as we have witnessed with the charges which were laid under Québec's referendum law against non-Québecers who helped to organize the huge unity rally in Montréal during the fall 1995 sovereignty referendum. While we may deplore unfettered spending by big business, it seems at least as unacceptable to have laws which could prevent Canadians from trying to save their country. Yet we either limit third party spending or we don't. It is hard to see how we can have it both ways.

♦ Something to Think About

How do we reconcile the notion of individual freedom of expression with the concern that those with unlimited funds should not be allowed unrestricted opportunities to sway public opinion?

How could legislation of this sort be drafted in a way which would avoid a successful Charter challenge?

One would assume that the basis for a compromise on this important issue might be found in the Charter provision that the basic rights and freedoms within it are "subject to such reasonable limits prescribed by law as can be demonstrably justified in a free and democratic society." On this basis, it ought to be possible to craft a law which allows third parties some spending, but within reasonable limits. One might have thought that the federal government's 1993 legislation with its $1000 limit would serve this purpose, but the courts rejected it.

II. Serving as a Citizen Appointee

Another opportunity for participation is provided by the many openings for citizen appointments to committees, boards and advisory bodies. In many respects, this option represents something of a middle ground between the relatively passive and infrequent exercise of voting every three or four years and the very active and demanding role of being an elected member.

Openings for citizen appointments exist at all levels of government. However, there are fewer openings and more formalized appointment procedures at the provincial and federal levels. Most of us will not have an opportunity to apply, or be seriously considered, for a position as a member of the Atomic Energy Commission of Canada, the CRTC (Canadian Radio, Television and Telecommunications Commission), the Niagara Parks Commission, or the Liquor Control Board of Ontario. In some cases there are qualifications to be met (at least unofficially). For example, people appointed to the Ontario Municipal Board tend to be lawyers, experienced municipal councillors or senior staff, or others whose backgrounds make them familiar with the kinds of issues which come before the Board for consideration.

Since most of the appointments at the federal and provincial levels are made by the Cabinet or a Minister, party politics also comes into play. While you don't have to be an active member of the party in power to be considered for an appointment, it helps. If you are an active member of a different party, however, your chances of appointment are slim.

In contrast, there are a wide range of openings for citizen involvement at the local government level, and usually far fewer constraints affecting the appointment process. The situation varies from province to province, with Ontario leading the pack in terms of the number of separate agencies, boards and commissions found at the local level. There are also variations from municipality to municipality, depending on its size and whether or not it uses standing committees as part of its governing arrangements.

In most municipalities, however, you will see a notice in the local newspaper inviting applications from citizens interested in serving on a list of local committees and boards. These might include such bodies as library boards, committees of adjustment, recreation committees, community centre/arena boards, theatre boards, and planning advisory committees. While some boards are "popular" and attract many applicants, municipal councils often have difficulty finding enough interested citizens to fill all the positions available.

However, like the patronage appointments at the senior levels of government, municipal appointments may also include some favouritism. Indeed, the Land Division Committee (the county body in Ontario which hears applications for severances to create new lots) is sometimes referred to as "The Senate" since so many former heads of county council serve on it.

Serving as a citizen appointee to one of these bodies is an excellent way to participate in government. Besides making a contribution to the particular body on which you serve, you inevitably become more aware of the whole system of government of which you are now a part, and even of some of the intergovernmental linkages as they may affect your particular area. You experience some of the challenges and satisfactions (and frustrations) faced by elected politicians — but without having to face the rigours and uncertainties of the election process. You may even use this experience as a training ground and prerequisite to a run for office. Seeking and accepting such an appointment allows you to make an important contribution to your community. That contribution may be needed more than ever in the coming years, with municipal governments facing decreased revenues and, in some cases increased responsibilities, as a result of cutbacks and downloading from the senior levels.

III. Joining a Group

Yet another way of participating in government is by joining one or more interest or pressure groups whose views are similar to your own. As discussed in the previous chapter, these groups range from long-standing national organizations with ample resources and access to government, to temporary groups which spring up to fight a particular battle and then disappear, to groups which share a common interest but rarely move beyond that interest to any kind of interaction with government.

Ironically, membership in the larger and more prominent interest groups may be the least satisfying experience in terms of citizen participation in government. Because these groups are so large and well financed, they have full time staff to carry out their research and present their reports. Your role as an individual member would seldom go beyond paying your annual membership fee and reading occasional newsletters and reports. You have the satisfaction of knowing that your group's voice is heard, but you may also not feel very much part of that process.

In contrast, membership in a local group — even a temporary and obstructionist one — can be a real education in the ways of government. You are likely to find yourself very actively involved. Such groups have next to no resources other than their membership. You may find yourself attending municipal council meetings, researching issues for the group, preparing or presenting briefs or any number of other activities. You will learn more about municipal governments in the process and about the increasingly tight financial circumstances under which they operate. You will come to a grudging appreciation of why governments can't always do what you want them to do. Whether your group wins or loses on the particular issue which prompted their creation, you will be richer for the experience. Ideally, you will use your increased understanding of the ways of government to continue to play a more active role. Society needs such ongoing, positive involvement on the part of its citizens, not just temporary and negative involvement when we are strongly opposed to something.

IV. Techniques of Direct Democracy

Even more direct ways of participating in the affairs of government are possible using features of what is usually termed "*direct democracy*," a concept which gained renewed interest in recent years. The key features involved are the referendum, initiative and recall.[9]

---

[9]The discussion which follows is largely based on the articles by Boyer and Charlton in Charlton and Barker, *op. cit.*, pp. 304-335.

Use of a *referendum* involves submitting a policy question or proposed law to the electorate for approval or rejection. The referendum can be binding or it can be consultative only, to provide guidance to decision makers. The latter type of exercise is usually called a plebiscite in Canada. Canada has had a few highly publicized and emotionally charged referendums over the past couple of decades, including the two votes relating to Québec separation (in 1980 and in 1995) and the vote on the Charlottetown Accord in 1992.

The *initiative*, which is common in many American states, allows citizens to propose new laws which are then submitted to voters for approval. Support, in the form of a specified number of signatures from the electorate, is required before a proposal can be placed on the ballot. This process essentially allows the public to initiate a referendum exercise on their own, without having to rely on government putting a question to the voters.

The *recall* is the most dramatic of the three instruments of direct democracy. It allows the public to remove from office an elected representative whose performance is felt to be unsatisfactorily. If a petition is filed with sufficient signatures, a vote has to be held on whether or not the individual can continue in office.

Much of the interest in these forms of direct democracy stems from public disillusionment with our existing governing institutions. The House of Commons is regarded as far from representative of "typical" Canadians, as noted in an earlier chapter. The mainstream political parties offer little in the way of distinctive policies or clear choices. Members of Parliament largely ignore the wishes of the electorate because of the requirement to follow the party line in voting. An added concern, which fuelled the populist movement in Western Canada in the 1920s and 1930s, was a feeling that the national government was overly preoccupied with the economic interests of Central Canada, to the neglect of the interests of farmers and workers and outlying regions. An agrarian-based protest party known as the Progressives won 65 seats in the federal election of 1921, placing it second in the standings. Provincially, the United Farmers won power in Alberta in 1919 and the Social Credit party was victorious in 1935, both on platforms which emphasized direct democracy. Once in office, however, both parties functioned much like any other parliamentary government.[10] In a fascinating parallel, another western-based party pledging more democratic, accountable operations swept into Ottawa in 1993 with 52 seats, just two shy of second place. That party, of course, is Reform, which in many ways is a reincarnation of the Social Credit party; just as its leader is the son of the former Social Credit leader, Ernest Manning.

♦ Something to Think About

Do we need more elements of "direct democracy" in Canada's political system?

Would selective use of the referendum, the initiative, and even the recall, encourage greater citizen participation in the affairs of government and add greater legitimacy to the decisions which are made?

As already indicated, these are not new concepts, and they have been more widely used in Canada than is commonly realized. Notable examples include the 1942 plebiscite on conscription, the 1988 plebiscite on the fixed link connection between PEI and the mainland, and the 1992 vote in the Northwest Territories concerning the creation of a new separate territory in the Eastern Arctic.[11] Referendums are also used in Britain and Australia, both with the same form of parliamentary government as Canada, and are extensively used in the United States.

Proponents of direct democracy claim that the public becomes educated and informed because a referendum process involves "the politics of engagement."[12] Under traditional governing arrangements, Canadians have no real say in the decisions that are made, so why should they make the effort to become informed and involved. "Why

---

[10]*Ibid.*, p. 334.

[11]All cited in *ibid.*, pp. 308 and 310.

[12]A term used by Boyer, *ibid.*, p. 309.

study for an exam if nobody is going to ask you the questions?"[13] In contrast, when Islanders were given an opportunity to vote on the fixed link issue, the ensuing debate made residents active and much better informed participants in this important issue affecting the future of PEI.

Some support for this position is found in the initial experience of Rossland, British Columbia, which has been experimenting with forms of direct democracy.[14] Concerned about the growing rift between citizens and their governments in the aftermath of the collapse of the Meech Lake Accord, the Rossland council gave their citizens three avenues to participate more directly in city government. First, there would have to be a referendum for any change to be made to the new constitution by-law of Rossland. Second, either council or the citizens (providing that 20% of them signed a petition) could subject a council decision to public confirmation by initiating a referendum within 30 days of the third reading of a by-law. Third, members of the community (again with 20% backing) could initiate a referendum to force council to take action on an issue.

Early experiences with the new arrangements have been largely positive. Of the first six referendums initiated, three were put forward by council and three by the public. The most notable involved a proposed $100 tax increase to finance an improvement in the municipality's drinking water, which was approved. More important than the number of referendums or their outcome, however, has been the apparent change in community itself. Instead of just complaining about council action or inaction, more people are discussing policy issues. Because they have been given some say in municipal decisions, they feel a greater responsibility to be informed and to exercise their new power thoughtfully. To re-phrase an earlier quote: "You feel motivated to pay more attention to the questions if you are going to have to answer them on an exam."

---

[13] *Ibid.*, p. 310.

[14] The discussion which follows is based on C. Richard Tindal and Susan Nobes Tindal, *Local Government in Canada*, 4th edition, Whitby, McGraw-Hill Ryerson Limited, 1995, pp. 358-359.

The limited experience in Rossland is far from conclusive. Nor does it necessarily follow that what may work in a small Western Canadian municipality could be successfully transplanted to large cities, much less used on a province-wide or Canadian basis. It is noteworthy, however, that Alberta provides for local referendums with respect to a number of actions by school boards and municipal councils.[15] In addition, changes introduced by the Ontario Government in December 1996 give municipalities expanded authority to hold referendums — although in an ironic twist, that same government has declared that it will pay no attention to the results of the referendums being conducted in March 1997 in all or most of the Metro Toronto municipalities on the issue of amalgamation and the creation of one "megacity."

Evidence from the referendum experience of other jurisdictions raises doubts about how much the voter becomes involved and empowered through this exercise. In countries such as Switzerland and the United States where direct democracy is a common feature, voter turnout is disappointingly low. It has averaged only 35% for referendums and initiatives in Switzerland in recent years.[16] American studies indicate that referendums have little drawing power in getting out voters when held in conjunction with elections and even less success with voter turnout when they are held separately.

Whatever the turnout, some observers express doubt that referendums provide a vehicle which stimulates greater participation on the part of the general public. Issues get placed on the ballot only if they receive the required number of signatures. The experience of jurisdictions such as California is that the task of obtaining such signatures has increasingly shifted from civic groups and volunteer organizations to professional firms who pay petitioners for each signature gathered.[17] As a result, the petition and referendum process has be-

---

[15]Jack Masson (with Edward Lesage Jr.), *Alberta's Local Governments*, Edmonton, University of Alberta Press, 1994, pp. 301-306.

[16]Charlton and Barker, *op. cit.*, p. 323.

[17]*Ibid.*, p. 324.

come dominated by special interest groups who can afford the expensive petition-gathering process. This domination has been furthered by the decision of the U.S. Supreme Court that quashed restrictions on campaign spending by interest groups. The same position has been taken by the Supreme Court in Canada, leaving interest groups without limits on their spending as well. As a result, there is reason to expect that referendums will be dominated by the educated and the wealthy, the same groups that have long dominated our other democratic institutions and processes as well.

Concluding Observations

This chapter is far from a thorough examination of the many facets of public participation. But it does demonstrate that Canadians have a number of ways in which they can participate in the activities of their governments. In some respects, the more avenues there are for public participation, the more open and democratic the governing system may appear to be. This conclusion presupposes, however, that Canadians participate widely through all or most of these avenues. Instead, recent years have seen some evidence that a growing number of Canadians are "turning off" and "tuning out" their traditional avenues for democratic expression, centred on the election process and the operations of Parliament. Many are joining pressure groups so that they can push for the particular issues that most concern them, and many others are demanding an even more direct say in decision making through the direct democracy tools discussed above.

The Canadian democracy is based on the principle of representative government. It is a system in which we elect individuals to represent us and make decisions on our behalf. In almost all instances, these individuals are also members of political parties. If there are imperfections in this representative and party system — and there most certainly are — then they should be directly addressed and resolved. Modest examples in this direction include past reforms which provide more support for constituency offices in each riding, which increase research funds and provide more support staff for parties and members, and which increase the opportunity for consideration of private members' bills. To the extent that Canadians give up on the parliamentary system and find ways of working around it (such as through the direct democracy tools), they ignore the central core of our democratic system.

It may well be appropriate to use referendums on very infrequent occasions when fundamental issues are at stake. Amendments to the constitution would fall into this category, and the 1992 vote on the Charlottetown Accord may have established a precedent in this regard. It is certainly appropriate for citizens to become involved with interest groups and to use whatever other means they can to express their views and concerns. These avenues, however, should be seen as a supplement to, not an alternative for, the traditional methods of participation centred on elections and political parties.

Whatever you do, don't stay on the sidelines, complaining about government or ignoring it. The only way to have "government of the people, by the people, for the people," is through "the people" becoming active participants.

Appendix A
Reforms in Election Financing

As noted earlier in this chapter, the federal Election Expenses Act of 1974 (and associated legislative reforms) attempted — with considerable success — to overcome many of the concerns which then existed about election financing. The main provisions are outlined below, followed by a brief summary of the legislative provisions governing provincial and municipal elections. These provisions are:

1   A requirement that parties register (with the Chief Electoral Officer of Canada) to be eligible for the benefits available under the Act.
2   A requirement that registered parties designate those agents who are authorized to receive and spend money on their behalf.
3   A dollar limit (based on a formula related to the number of voters in the ridings being contested) on the amount of election expenditures by a party.
4   A dollar limit (based on a similar formula related to the number of voters in the particular riding) on the amount of election expenditures by a candidate.
5   A requirement for audited financial reports — annually by a party and after each election by individual candidates.
6   A requirement that the names of donors who give more than a total of $100 must be disclosed.
7   Candidates receive a partial reimbursement of their expenditures, if they receive 15% or more of the popular vote (and if they have complied with all of the requirements of this legislation).
8   Donations are made tax-deductible, to attract a broader base of support.
9   There are limits to the period of advertising, from 29 days to 1 day before an election.
10 Six and one-half hours of free T.V advertising time are divided among the registered parties, according to a formula. As discussed below, a Charter challenge led to a change in the time allocations for the last federal election.

Assessment of these Financing Reforms

Generally, these reforms have brought a considerable improvement in addressing the concerns about the high costs of elections and the lack of disclosure about the sources of financing.

There has also been a considerable broadening of the support base for the parties, as evidenced by the following statistics concerning the total number of donors in two different election years.

Party	1974	1980
NDP	27,910	62,428
PC Party	6,423	32,720
Liberals	9,882	17,670

Not surprisingly, the NDP continued to have the largest number of separate donors, but particularly striking is the fivefold increase in Conservative donors in the first six years following the new legislation. The Liberals were much slower to make the transition contemplated by the new legislation — partly, it is alleged, because during his long years as leader Trudeau largely neglected head office and "housekeeping" types of activity. This neglect was certainly one of the factors contributing to the financial problems which plagued the Liberal Party right up until its election victory in 1993.

Legislative Loopholes

There are, however, some loopholes in the election financing legislation. For example, the spending limits in the legislation apply only to **election** expenses, not **campaign** expenses, like volunteers' expenses or polling research. The limits also don't apply to annual, ongoing expenditures. So, parties can transfer expenditures to this category if they are in danger of exceeding their election spending limits.

There have also been problems and court challenges relating to two matters. One of these, the issue of third party spending, was addressed earlier in this chapter. The other relates to the fairness of the allocation of the six and one-half hours for free broadcasts during an election campaign. In the past, this time has been apportioned on the basis of each party's popular vote and number of seats won in the last election. The Reform Party successfully challenged this formula in court — essentially arguing that it obviously favoured the incumbent and long-established parties and disadvantaged newer and smaller parties.

Provincial and Municipal Election Financing

Provincial provisions are for the most part similar to those found at the federal level. For example, the Election Finances Act of Ontario provides that:

♦ Candidates must register — with the Commission on Election Finances — in order to accept and spend money.
♦ There are limits on how much can be spent by a candidate and on how much fund-raisers can accept from any single contributor. The latter restriction is not found in the federal legislation.
♦ Candidates must make public the names and addresses of everyone who donated more than $100 to the campaign.
♦ An auditor must be appointed to examine and report on the candidate's campaign financial statement.
♦ Campaign advertising is limited to a period of 21 days, ending two days before polling day.

Municipal arrangements understandably vary somewhat from province to province but still exhibit some common themes. Several provinces require or allow provision for financial deposits. For example, section 29 of the Local Authorities Elections Act in Alberta allows a municipality to require a financial deposit of $100 or $500, the amount depending on whether the municipal population is under or over 100 000 — although only Edmonton has used this provision.[18] Candidates for municipal office in Nova Scotia must pay a deposit of

---

[18]Masson, *op. cit.*, p. 308.

$200, unless council has specified a lesser amount or eliminated the deposit altogether.[19]   Recent changes in Ontario under the Better Local Government Act, passed in mid-December 1996, authorize the Minister of Municipal Affairs to establish by regulation the amount of refundable financial deposit which must be paid by candidates. It is understood that this amount will be $100.

These financial deposits are usually justified on the grounds of discouraging frivolous candidates. For that purpose, the deposits may or may not be successful, but they can deter serious candidates who are without financial means. As Masson argues, "at a time when property qualifications for holding office and voting have become almost an anachronism, the erection of financial barriers to prevent 'undesirables' from running for public office is at the very least inappropriate."[20] Requiring a candidate's nomination papers to be signed by a significant number of fellow electors would appear to be a better way to ensure that candidates are serious, and yet the recent changes introduced in Ontario are removing the requirement for ten signatures which had been in existence.

Other requirements deal with such matters as limits on the amount of money which one donor can give to a candidate, requirements for candidates to file financial statements, and provisions for the disposal of surplus funds following an election campaign. For specific details, you should consult the legislation in your particular province.

---

[19]Kell Antoft (ed.),. *A Guide to Local Government in Nova Scotia*, 3rd edition, Halifax, Dalhousie University, 1992, p. 4.

[20]Masson, *op. cit.*, p. 309.

The Last Word

Definition of Terms and Concepts

→ **Direct Democracy:**
A series of techniques to allow the public to participate much more directly in the activities of government, as in the use of the initiative, recall and referendum.

Franchise:
The right to vote in public elections. Also known as suffrage. Canada is said to have universal suffrage because the right to vote is so widely held.

Initiative:
A technique which allows citizens to propose new laws that must be submitted to the voters for approval, if they can get a specified proportion of voters to sign a petition in this regard.

Recall:
A process under which voters can file a petition demanding a vote on an elected representative's continued tenure in office.

Referendum:
A process under which a policy question or proposed law is submitted to the electorate for approval or rejection. This process is also referred to as a plebiscite, although that term as used in Canada usually refers to referendums which are not binding and are only intended to provide guidance to decision makers.

Riding Association:
The local party organization found in each riding or constituency which, among other things, selects the candidate for each election.

Third Party Spending:
> This does **not** refer to spending by political parties but by others, usually groups and associations which seek to advance their point of view during an election campaign. Largely because of successful Charter challenges, there is no limit on spending by these outside parties.

Points to Ponder

1. What do you think of the list of eight socio-economic "barriers" to candidacy? Do you think that it limits those who might offer themselves as candidates? Would these factors influence you in your choice of a candidate?

2. Some have suggested that if "third party" spending during election campaigns can't be limited, then neither should spending by parties and political candidates be limited? What is your view? Does election spending, particularly for television ads, influence your voting decision?

3. What interest groups or pressure groups are you aware of that focus on issues that concern you? If you haven't already done so, consider getting information on any such groups, attending one or more of their meetings, joining, and becoming an active participant.

4. What do you see as the respective merits of direct democracy versus representative democracy, and why?

For Further Reading

See Mark Charlton and Paul Barker (eds.), *Crosscurrents: Contemporary Political Issues,* 2nd edition, Scarborough, Nelson Canada, 1994, for a good examination of the possible influence of business groups (Issue 17) and the pros and cons of direct democracy (Issue 16.)

Paul Fox and Graham White (eds.), *Politics:Canada*, 8th edition, Whitby, McGraw-Hill Inc., has a number of pertinent articles in two sections dealing with elections and voting behaviour and with parties and pressure groups.

Robert Jackson and Doreen Jackson, *Canadian Government in Transition*, Scarborough, Prentice Hall Canada, Inc., 1996, Chapters 10 and 11 provide a good treatment of elections and interest groups. Both of these topics are also explored in more detail in *Politics in Canada*, 3rd edition, 1994, Chapters 11 and 12, by the same authors and publisher.

Michael Whittington and Richard Van Loon, *Canadian Government and Politics: Institutions and Processes*, Whitby, McGraw-Hill Ryerson Limited, 1996, describes interest groups and their interaction with government in Chapters 16 and 17.

Chapter 9

Canada's Fiscal and Economic State

Objectives and Highlights

♦ To evaluate the government's performance in managing Canada's economy.

♦ To illustrate the economic limits on government actions and policies.

♦ To examine the causes of Canada's debt and to assess the appropriateness of government actions in response to the debt.

This chapter illustrates how closely politics and economics are intertwined. It outlines the kinds of actions taken by government to influence the economy **and** the kinds of economic circumstances which influence government actions. Nowhere are these links more evident than in the current issue of Canada's deficit and debt problems. Depending on which point of view one accepts, Canada got into its financial difficulties because of excessive spending (especially on social programs), tax concessions to business, or excessively high interest rates which magnified the cost of borrowed money.

However it happened, the high level of Canada's debt is certainly real. What is less clear is what needs to be done about it. Those advocating drastic cuts in government spending are currently in the ascendancy. It would appear, however, that much of the cutting essentially involves reducing transfer payments to the next level of government below, which leaves municipal governments to bear the brunt of this form of "fend-for-yourself" federalism.

It may also be, as critics claim, that many of the current cuts are short-sighted and will cost governments even more money within a few years. This issue is explored not only in this chapter but in the subsequent two chapters dealing with health and social services.

Introduction

A s we move toward the end of this decade and this century, Canadians are deeply concerned about the health of our economy and its ability to provide sufficient jobs, especially in the face of increased international competition highlighted by *free trade* agreements with the United States and Mexico.

For the past half century, governments in most Western nations have accepted responsibility for trying to manage their economies. Economic problems have become increasingly difficult to solve, but it is clear that citizens still look to their governments to "make things right" and take a dim view of governments that fail the test of economic management. A few examples will illustrate this point.

When Bill Clinton, as Governor of Arkansas, sought the U.S. presidency as the Democratic Party candidate in 1992, he had a sign posted prominently on his campaign bus and in his campaign offices. It read simply, *"It's the economy, stupid."* This constant reminder helped keep the focus of his successful campaign on the single item that was identified as being most important to the voters.

Jean Chrétien, Leader of the Liberal Party of Canada, similarly focused his party's successful federal election campaign of 1993 on the economy. His Liberal "Red Book" highlighted economic issues of importance to Canadians, particularly *"Jobs, Jobs, Jobs,"* a theme which has been revived as the expected 1997 election draws near.

The Progressive Conservative Party of Ontario was the third party in the Ontario Legislature and in pre-election polls when the 1995 provincial election was called. Under leader Mike Harris, the party swept to power with a majority government on the basis of its political manifesto labelled the "Common Sense Revolution." The CSR stressed the party's desire to reduce the deficit and to get Ontario's economy back on track.

Local politicians are similarly elected on the basis of their promises to keep property taxes down and to attract new business to their communities. The debt and deficit, inflation, jobs, taxes, are all economic themes of concern to the citizen, and are critical to the success of politicians at all levels of government.

Economic Constraints on Political Action

Under the circumstances, it is remarkable that we have reached the ninth chapter of this Guide without examining more directly the subject of economics. It is really inseparable from the study of government. The most obvious link, as already mentioned, is that governments are expected to pursue policies and actions which will help the economy to grow and prosper. But a link of at least equal importance is the way economics limits what governments may do.

This pattern was evident in Canada from its earliest stages of development. We have always been a trading nation, dependent on external markets for our products. Long before Confederation, Canada developed primarily as a supplier of certain staple commodities such as fur, cod and timber. After Confederation, the "National Policy" of Sir John A. Macdonald (emphasizing state-subsidized railway construction and immigration policies geared to settlement of the wheat-growing Prairies) reinforced Canada's role as a resource-producing hinterland in the international division of labour.[1] We did gradually develop our secondary manufacturing, but mainly on the basis of foreign — mostly United States — investment, which brought outside influence and control over the operations of our domestic economy. Over 70% of Canada's import and export trade was accounted for by the American market, even before the Canada-U.S. free trade agreement of 1988 ensured the further integration of our two economies.

Being drawn so extensively into the economic orbit of the most powerful nation on earth has left Canada with limited freedom to pursue independent policies — on the economy or on anything else! The *"globalization"* of the economy and the increase in "footloose" multinational corporations less and less tied to any particular country has exposed even more dramatically the limited scope for government actions. Governments in developed nations like Canada find it difficult to pursue policies contrary to the interests of "big business." If they do, they face threats from these businesses to pull up stakes and

---

[1]This discussion is based on Stephen Brooks, *Public Policy in Canada*, Toronto, McClelland & Stewart Inc., 1993, Chapter 3.

to switch operations to another jurisdiction which is more accommodating.

Bearing in mind, then, that there are many economic factors and
forces (barely touched on above) which severely constrain the actions
which governments can take — on any front — let us turn to the
"other side of the coin" and look at the actions which governments do
take and should take with respect to the economy.

To understand how governments attempt to manage the economy
on our behalf will involve the introduction of a variety of economic
terms and concepts. While an attempt will be made to explain these
terms in everyday language, they are also included in the usual definitions section found at the end of this chapter.

Objectives of Economic Management

While the specific mix and emphasis of economic policies and objectives will fluctuate with changing economic conditions, governments
of Western nations have focused on **four main economic goals**: full
employment, economic growth, price stability, and a balance of international payments. As we discuss each of these briefly in the following section, it will become clear that these goals are not only difficult
to sustain, they are not mutually compatible. For that reason, tough
choices have to be made, and it will be argued that our governments
have made some questionable choices by giving far too little attention
over the past two decades to the goal of full employment.

1. Full Employment

The single most important economic issue facing Canadians is unemployment. The *unemployment rate* in Canada remains at close to 10%
of the labour force. This represents a very weak recovery from the
11.8% unemployment recorded at the peak of the 1990-91 recession
— in fact, it has been described by some analysts as a "jobless recovery." Businesses continue to trim their workforces as a way of
increasing their international competitiveness. Governments have also
been announcing plans to reduce significantly the number of civil ser-

vants as part of their deficit reduction strategies. For example, the federal government, in its February 1995 budget, stated that it would be reducing the federal public service by 45 000 jobs over three years. Further expenditure cuts were announced in the 1996 budget, which are expected to result in 10 000 further job losses. Since its election in June 1995, the Harris Government in Ontario has talked of public service downsizing of anywhere from 13 000 to 27 000 jobs.[2] Municipalities in several provinces, especially Ontario, have undergone or are facing major amalgamations, one key result of which is expected to be staff downsizing as well.

Under the circumstances, it is not surprising that the public is so concerned about jobs. The *Maclean's* magazine year-end survey for 1996 found that unemployment was identified as by far the most important issue facing Canadians, more than twice as important (31% versus 15%) as the second issue which was the *deficit*. This preoccupation was most pronounced in Québec, where a whopping 42% of respondents listed unemployment, followed by 19% for the deficit and only 11% for national unity.[3]

The Unemployment Rate

If concern about unemployment is very clear, the meaning and significance of unemployment figures is not. Let's take a closer look at the unemployment rate. It refers to the percentage of the labour force out of work **and actively seeking a job**. People enter and leave the labour force for a variety of reasons, leading to changes in the "participation rate." For example, the great increase in the number of women entering the labour force has in turn increased the participation rate and the need for jobs.

People tend to drop out of the labour force when there is a severe depression and job prospects are bleak, and people often enter the labour force when there is rapid growth and jobs seem plentiful. As a result, the unemployment rate may appear better than it really is (dur-

---

[2]*Toronto Star*, January 25, 1996.

[3]Anthony Wilson-Smith, "Future Imperfect," *Maclean's*, December 30, 1996, p. 18.

ing a depression) or worse than it really is (during a period of rapid growth). Consider the following simple example:

Population	Participation Rate	Number seeking jobs	Number with jobs	Unem-ployed
1 000 000	50%	500 000	450 000	10%
1 000 000	55%	550 000	475 000	13.6%

Even though 25 000 more jobs were created for the same total population, the unemployment rate increased substantially in this example because the participation rate went up by 5%.

The unemployment rate is usually quoted as a national average, which conceals great fluctuations across this country. When unemployment was at a nine year peak of 11.8% in 1990-91, it ranged from 7.4% in Saskatchewan to 18.4% in Newfoundland.[4]

Because the unemployment rate focuses on the proportion of unemployed, it fails to track important changes which may be occurring in the pattern of jobs and employment. For example, in September 1995 there were 500 000 more jobs in the Canadian economy than there were in 1990, but these represented an increase of 1.3 million in jobs for people with a post-secondary degree or diploma and a decrease of 800 000 jobs for those with lesser credentials.[5]

2. Economic Growth

The best hope for more jobs and reduced unemployment is a growing economy. This objective is not without its detractors, however, who worry about the impact of *economic growth* on the consumption of limited and often non-renewable resources and on the environment. Concerns about various forms of pollution and about the thinning of the ozone layer protecting us from the sun reflect the views of those

---

[4]According to the *Canada Year Book*, 1994.

[5]*Financial Architects*, Winter 1996 Newsletter.

who believe in limits on growth. Rapid growth can also lead to economic problems if demand for goods and services exceeds their supply, triggering price *inflation*. This type of demand-pull inflation has traditionally been referred to as "too much money chasing too few goods." While most people may recognize and appreciate all of these concerns as valid in the long term, we have a tendency to focus on today, and for jobs and material benefits now. How has Canada measured up in providing economic growth?

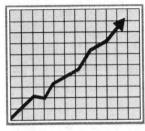

Prolonged Growth until Recently

The economic history of Canada has been dominated by prolonged economic growth. This growth has been tempered occasionally by *recessions* and even, in the early 1930s, with the Great Depression. Prior to World War II, the "unmanaged" economy went through recessions and booms for "natural" economic reasons. Since the war, the economy has been managed by government policy — sometimes successfully and sometimes not so successfully. Governments have adopted policies to prevent or shorten recessions and to counteract *inflation*.

Managing Economic Growth according to Keynes

From the end of World War II until the early 1960s Canada experienced sustained growth, reasonably low unemployment, and a low degree of inflation. Much of the credit for this success went to governments following the policy of economic management prescribed by economist John Maynard Keynes. In simplest terms, Keynesian economics started with the position that government policies could be adopted to smooth out fluctuations in the economic cycles which countries experience. Because of the cyclical nature of economic activity, with growth gradually followed by decline, and then by renewed growth, governments were expected to face at one time only one of the following key economic problems:

♦ an increase in unemployment as growth declined **or**

♦ an increase in prices or inflation as the economy took off again.

Keynesian policies addressed each of these as a separate problem. Faced with high unemployment, governments should pursue *fiscal policies* which "prime the pump" by increasing government spending and/or introducing tax cuts to stimulate spending by consumers and businesses. In either case, the result would be a deficit budget, but the spending stimulus would lead to economic growth and the resulting tax revenues would allow the government to balance its budget again. *Monetary policies* to create "easy money," notably through a lowering of interest rates, would also help to stimulate growth.

Faced with high inflation, governments could dampen down economic activity and reduce the upward pressure on prices by decreasing government spending and/or increasing taxes to discourage consumer and business spending. The result would be a surplus budget, which would have the effect of taking money out of circulation and helping to "cool off" the economy. The accompanying monetary policy in this case would be "tight money" reflected in higher interest rates, which would tend to discourage business investment and consumer spending.

Economic Stabilizers

In addition to these deliberate adjustments to fiscal and monetary policies to manage the economy, governments also developed a number of what were known as *"automatic stabilizers."* Most of these took the form of income maintenance programs that helped to ensure incomes and therefore purchasing power in the hands of Canadian consumers, which — in turn — would help to ensure consumer spending and economic growth.

An excellent example of an automatic stabilizer has been unemployment insurance. (This was recently renamed the "employment insurance program," as discussed in Chapter 10, even though most people still use the former name.) When the economy is booming, employment is high, more and more people are paying unemployment insurance premiums, and the surplus in the U.I. fund is increasing. The U.I. payments, by taking money out of the economy, can be seen as helping to slow down the pace of economic growth and to reduce the upward pressure on prices (inflation). When the economy delines, unemployed workers draw upon the fund, thereby increasing their purchasing power and helping to maintain spending and economic growth. Thus the fund expands and collapses automatically in ways which help to offset, automatically, whatever economic forces are underway.

The family allowance program, historically known as the "baby bonus" and recently replaced by an expanded child tax credit, was another example of a stabilizer. It provided additional funds to families with children, bolstering their purchasing power and helping to maintain consumer spending.

Social assistance (welfare) and various forms of income maintenance programs can be seen in the same light. Whatever their merits as a humanitarian initiative, most of the social programs of the postwar period were also supported by governments because they helped to shore up incomes and spending which, in turn, helped to stimulate ongoing economic growth.

The annual rate of real economic growth (that is, adjusted for inflation) for members of the OECD (Organization for Economic Cooperation and Development) averaged 5% between 1950 and 1970. Unemployment and inflation both averaged in the 2 to 3% range during this period. As the 1970s unfolded, however, economic performance declined, and disillusionment with Keynesian economics increased. Between 1974 and 1983 the rate of annual growth for member countries of the OECD was only 2.1%, unemployment was 6% and inflation averaged 9%. Western nations, including Canada, found themselves facing the spectre of "*stagflation*" (high unemployment and high inflation), a combination that wasn't supposed to arise according to Keynesian economics. By the 1980s, government policies were almost entirely focused on the problem of inflation.

3. Price Stability

Price stability is particularly related to the maintenance of low inflation. Inflation is generally defined as a significant and continuing increase in prices. As with unemployment, however, inflation is a vague and imprecise measure which may gloss over underlying developments in the Canadian economy.

Consumer Price Index

Inflation is usually measured in terms of changes to the *Consumer Price Index* (CPI). This index is a composite measure that expresses the change over time in a weighted average of prices paid by a typical Canadian household. The CPI measures monthly changes in the retail price of a selected "basket" of about 300 commodities ranging from haircuts to dental fillings. To understand a change in the CPI, imagine that the index was 100.0 in January, 1991 and 125.0 in January 1996. This means that consumer prices have risen by 25% on average during this period.

Because the basket is mainly based on household expenditures in urban centres, it may not give an accurate picture for those living in rural areas or even small urban centres. The index takes little account of improvements in the quality of the commodities being purchased. The index further assumes that people keep buying the items in the basket regardless of what happens to the prices. Realistically, people often substitute less expensive items — chicken for beef, for example.

Whatever its imperfections, the Consumer Price Index and the rate of inflation derived from it have preoccupied the Canadian government for the past couple of decades. Inflation began to rise after 1970, influenced by such factors as the quadrupling of oil prices following the creation of OPEC[6] in 1973. After peaking at 10.8% after the first oil shock, inflation rose to a new high of 12.5% in 1981, and remained stubbornly high throughout the decade.

Inflation is certainly a cause for concern. It erodes the purchasing power of Canadians, especially those on fixed incomes. It can force up prices to the point where Canadian products are less competitive in international markets. The latter development, of course, is a major concern of the business community which, in turn, appears to have ready access to government, and influence over government policies.

From the mid-1980s, the *Bank of Canada* became increasingly

---

[6]OPEC stands for oil producing and exporting countries and is essentially a cartel which was established to limit the supply of oil made available for sale and thereby to force up its price.

focused on a goal of not only reducing inflation but achieving "zero inflation." Its policies were to limit growth in the money supply and to keep interest rates high (to discourage excess spending which might drive up prices). There were two very significant side effects of such monetary policies: **(1)** they contributed to higher unemployment in Canada and **(2)** they increased the cost of borrowing for the government and, therefore, the cost of financing its debt.

TAKE YOUR PICK!

Less Inflation but More Unemployment and Higher Debt Charges

As the economy slid deeper into recession by the end of the 1980s, inflation all but disappeared, with the Consumer Price Index rising less than 2% a year. But, unemployment soared to close to 12% (or more than 1.6 million Canadians looking for work) and interest payments on the debt of the federal government were becoming greater than its spending on pensions, health care, welfare and education combined! By 1995, the inflation percentage change in the CPI annually had gone from a high of 13% in 1981 to a low of less than 1% — but only at a "price" of higher unemployment and higher debt charges. Yet decision makers remain fixated on inflation as the one and only economic evil to be controlled. For example, figures released in early September 1996 indicated a significant increase in jobs in the Canadian economy the preceding month. Commentators immediately began to worry about the prospect of strong growth figures also appearing in the United States. This, they claimed, would raise the spectre of possible inflation and would put upward pressure on interest rates again.

It is remarkable that fear of inflation so dictates our every economic move. Yes, inflation erodes the purchasing power of Canadians — but not having a job at all has an ever more dramatic impact on one's purchasing power. If there are moves to slow down the economy every time it shows any signs of economic growth and job creation, there is little hope of us improving on the disgraceful unemployment rate of close to 10%. This dilemma is explored further in a later section of this chapter.

4. Balance of Trade

Canada has been a trading nation since its very beginning, when Europeans traded tools and fabrics with native people in exchange for fur and meat. Today Canada sells more than one-quarter of its goods and services abroad, and imports what it needs from countries around the world. The United States is by far Canada's most important trading partner, taking three-quarters of our exports in the early 1990s.

The main reason that countries trade is that the earth's resources are not equally distributed across its surface and therefore each nation must trade with others to acquire what it lacks. International trade allows each party that enters into a trading arrangement to benefit from the exchange. In any voluntary exchange both parties must gain, or at least expect to gain, something from the transaction. Otherwise, why would both parties agree to the trade? Trade brings about mutual gains by redistributing products in such a way that both parties end up having a combination of goods that better meets their preferences than the goods they held before the trade.

Free Trade Agreements

Canada has been involved in a number of free trade agreements over the years, beginning with Commonwealth preference treaties with Britain. Since 1948 it has been a member of the General Agreement on Tariffs and Trade (GATT), an organization which has negotiated gradually lower trade barriers among its member nations. In 1965 Canada entered in an Auto Pact agreement with the United States which provided for free trade in cars, trucks, buses and auto parts. 1988 saw the signing of the very controversial free trade agreement with the United States. This was followed by an agreement with the U.S. and Mexico in 1992 which ushered in the North American Free Trade Association (NAFTA), the largest trading area in the world accounting for nearly 30% of the global economy.[7] The elimination of tariffs and other barriers to free trade under NAFTA over a fifteen

---

[7]This discussion is partly based on James John Guy, *How We Are Governed*, Toronto, Harcourt Brace & Company, 1995, p. 417.

year period will have an impact on a number of economic sectors, including the auto industry, agriculture, forestry and fisheries, textiles and apparel, metals and minerals, machinery and equipment, services such as transportation, business and professional services, telecommunications services, and financial services.

Pros and Cons of FTA and NAFTA

Proponents argue that the 1988 deal was critical to ensure Canada's continued access to its largest market, in the face of growing *protectionist* sentiment[8] in the United States — although there have certainly been continuing challenges from the Americans about a number of Canadian exports to that country. More generally, they contend that the free trade agreements give Canadian companies unrestricted access to much larger markets in which they can grow and prosper. The resulting economic expansion, they argue, will strengthen Canadian sovereignty and our ability to sustain our social safety net.

Critics worry about the massive adjustments which are occurring in the economy of Canada as resources are shifted to respond to the new trading arrangements — adjustments which are creating considerable unemployment, at least in the short term. Part of this unemployment arises from U.S. branch plants in Canada closing down because they can now ship products from their head offices into Canada without having to contend with a tariff wall. Critics also worry about the potential loss of Canadian independence as we become increasingly intertwined with the United States economy.[9] Free trade supporters respond[10] that Canada's culture is not even mentioned in the free trade agreements, and that the provisions leave our governments free to take whatever actions they feel are necessary with respect to

---

[8]Protectionism is the opposite of free trade. It involves the use of tariffs which make imported goods more expensive and encourage consumers to purchase domestic products.

[9]This is certainly not a new fear. The Liberals lost the election of 1911 when they ran on a platform of reciprocity or free trade with the U.S.

[10]Guy, *op. cit.*, p. 418.

such areas as our environment, energy and natural resources. But Canada's culture remains vulnerable, as evidenced by the January 1997 ruling of the World Trade Organization (which replaced GATT) that policies to protect our magazine industry from American competition violate international trading rules. It remains to be seen if this ruling, as many fear, will expose Canada's entire cultural sector to global forces.

For some, the free trade agreements are part of a globalization of the economy which is undermining the importance of individual national governments and elevating the power of multi-national corporations. As the whole world becomes their marketplace (thanks, in part, to the collapse of communist regimes), these corporations gain great bargaining leverage. With modern technology, it matters less and less where their head office is located, allowing them to extract concessions from national governments, all in the name of maintaining their international competitiveness.[11]

Because Canada is a major trading nation, we have an "open" economy, one very much influenced by developments around the world. This openness makes it difficult for the Canadian government to pursue effective policies on its own. To take one example, a considerable portion of Canada's debt is owed to foreign lenders. Money goes wherever it can make a profit, which means that Canadian interest rates must remain high enough to continue attracting foreign money into Canada. If interest rates go up in other countries, and especially in the United States, Canada has virtually no choice but to follow suit. If we allow our interest rates to look unattractive compared to those in the United States, the result would be a flight of capital out of Canada, upward pressure on the value of the U.S. dollar (because its supply would be insufficient to meet the demand for it), a corresponding downward pressure on the Canadian dollar, and a resulting increase in the cost of living for all Canadians as we pay for our heavy volume of imported goods with devalued dollars.

---

[11]This point of view is clearly and passionately presented in Maude Barlow and Bruce Campbell, *Straight through the Heart*, Toronto, Harper-Collins, 1995.

The Deficit and the Debt:
The Determinant of Economic Policies Today

There have already been several references in this chapter to the deficit and the debt. These are the result of past government policies and actions and they also limit future government policies and actions. It's time we had a closer look at these phenomena. We begin with some basic definitions.

Deficit:	The result of an excess of government spending over revenues in any one fiscal year.
Surplus:	The result of an excess of revenues over government spending in any one fiscal year. [Yes, the federal government used to have surplus budgets, but not since 1973.]
Debt:	The total of all net deficits (not offset by surpluses) accrued by the federal government over time.

The precise amount of Canada's *national debt* is difficult to pin down, since it includes debt of provincial, territorial and local governments as well. However, we have more than enough debt to "play with" if we just deal with that of the federal government. Consider the following figures, to put things in perspective.

Canada's national debt is currently some $600 billion. The federal government is apparently now on track to achieve a balanced budget by at least the year 2000. By that time, however, our national debt will have increased to about $650 billion. "How is this possible?" you exclaim. It's not "the new math." This happens because even though we may move toward a balanced budget, each year that we still have a deficit means a further increase in the cumulative national debt.

What would it take to eliminate that total debt? Well, if we ran a budget surplus of $5 billion a year throughout the 21st century — a target which is neither achievable nor necessarily desirable — we would be debt free in 131 years. This is about the time that Captain Jean-Luc Picard of the Enterprise should become Prime Minister of the Galaxy!

"Why doesn't the government just stop spending so much money?"you say. According to the critics, and there are many, governments are wasteful and extravagant. Why if only they were in charge for a day, they could eliminate much of this waste and cut the government back down to size. But, it's not that easy. It seems that every government program has clients who are determined that their program must not be cut. There are also other complications and rigidities. The result is that **deficit reduction is like chastity**. Everyone is in favour of it in theory. But in practice, they prefer that it applies to someone else, not them. It has also been said that "when it comes to budget cuts, everyone wants to go to Heaven, but nobody wants to die."[12]

What Would You Do If You Were Minister of Finance?

Let's see how you would do if you were Minister of Finance. In 1994-95, the federal government spent just under $161 billion. Given that much spending, there must be lots of "fat," lots of potential for making cuts with all that money involved. Well, more than 1/4 (26%) of all that spending went (as it must by law) to pay interest on past government debt. On the following page is a summary of the main categories of program spending for the $118.7 billion that was left.

You are the Minister of Finance, and you have been asked to cut $5 billion dollars from the budget. Where will you wield the axe? Find out just how easy it is to cut expenditures.

---

[12]Remark attributed to Jean Chrétien quoted in David Olive, *Canadian Political Babble*, Toronto, John Wiley & Sons, 1993, p. 24.

Total Program Spending by the Federal Government, 1994-95
(Department of Finance, *The Economic and Fiscal Update*, December 6, 1995)

Major transfers to persons	(billions of dollars)
Elderly benefits	$ 20.5
Unemployment insurance	14.8
Veterans' pensions/allowances	1.4

Major transfers to other governments

Health, social assistance, education[13]	17.4
Notably equalization payments for "have not" provinces	9.3

Subsidies and other transfers

Business subsidies	3.7
Indians and Inuit	3.7
International assistance	2.9
Canada Infrastructure Works	0.4
Other transfers and subsidies	7.0

Crown Corporations

CBC	1.1
CMHC	2.0
Other	1.9

Defence	10.7
All other spending	21.0

---

[13]These payments have been made under Established Program Funding (EPF) and the Canada Assistance Plan (CAP), but are now combined into a new Canadian Health & Social Transfer (CHST), which has fewer strings attached to its use, but is being reduced in amount over the years ahead.

How did you make out? Don't forget that you have to take your recommendations to a Cabinet meeting and sell them to all your Cabinet colleagues — like those from Agriculture, Defence, Health and Welfare. Then you have to face the opposition parties across the floor of the House of Commons, the questions from the media, and the outraged reactions from all of the interest groups whose programs you cut. Keep in mind that much of the savings you achieve will have to be at the expense of public service jobs. Have you the stomach to lay off employees? How real will the savings be if displaced staff can't find other work?

So, what will it be?

◆ The biggest "chunks," the first two categories, involve spending on social programs. Do you really want to cut benefits to the elderly or support for hospitals, health care, post-secondary education and the like?

◆ The next biggest is spending on defence, but it has already sustained several cuts in recent years. Further reductions would jeopardize our continuing role in United Nations peace-keeping efforts, not to mention our capacity to provide even the most minimal defence of this nation. In any event, cuts can also be counterproductive in many instances. For example, closure of an army base has a very adverse impact on the surrounding regional economy.

◆ Cuts in international assistance might look tempting — after all, we have to help the poor at home. But it would arguably be very selfish for a country as fortunate as Canada not to provide foreign aid and other programs which assist underdeveloped nations. Unless these countries are helped to develop, they won't be able to provide a market for Canadian exports. Moreover, much of the assistance we provide is "tied-aid" which ensures that it is spent on Canadian goods and products. Once again, the issue is never as simple as it first appears on the surface.

Are you sure that you want to be Minister of Finance, or any member of the federal Cabinet for that matter? It doesn't get any easier if you switch to being a provincial Cabinet minister or a municipal councillor. Governments at all levels are now confronting very difficult decisions about what expenditure cuts to make, especially given that the public appears to have reached its limit of tolerance concerning tax levels. But is it possible that our focus is misplaced, that our interpretation of the "problem" and the necessary "solution" is faulty? It is important for you to appreciate that there is more than one way to analyze the economic and financial situation facing Canada and its governments.

Causes of the Debt

As discussed in the next two chapters, many of the government cutbacks have centred on our social programs, reflecting a viewpoint largely advanced by the business community that it is the cost of these programs which has aggravated our debt problems. Yet as these later chapters point out, blaming the debt on Canada's social programs is open to dispute. Wolfe notes that no new social spending programs have been instituted in Canada since 1975. The cost of the programs already in place increased mainly because of recessions in 1981-83 and 1989-1992 — recessions which some would argue were prolonged and made worse by government high interest rate policies overly preoccupied with curbing inflation to the neglect of unemployment. Moreover, according to Wolfe the key factor in explaining the growing debt has been the unwillingness of the federal government to increase the level of taxation, especially of business and the wealthy, to keep pace with expenditure growth.[14] This, in turn, reflected a concern that Canadian tax levels not get too out of line with those in the United States, providing yet another example of the external constraints on Canadian economic policy making.

Research by the federal finance department indicates that the growth of the debt has been almost entirely due to the compounding

---

[14]David Wolfe, "The Politics of the Deficit," in Bruce Doern, *The Politics of Economic Policy*, Volume 40 of the research studies for the Macdonald Commission, Toronto, University of Toronto Press, 1985, p. 141.

of interest on the original debt — much of this attributable to the high (arguably excessively high) interest rates maintained by the Bank of Canada until the past couple of years. Interest payments took up 11% of government revenues in 1975, the equivalent of 2% of the *Gross Domestic Product* (GDP). By 1991 interest payments were claiming one-third of government revenues, the equivalent of 6% of the nation's GDP.

Statistics Canada studies show that government spending, and specifically social spending, held steady from 1975 to 1991. The increase in deficits after 1975 was caused, **not by any surge in spending**, but by a drop in federal revenues relative to the growth of the GDP and rising debt charges.[15] Revenues dropped partly because of a variety of tax concessions introduced by the federal government, particularly concessions to business. These are usually referred to as *"tax expenditures"* to reflect the cost they impose on the federal treasury and they have amounted to many billions a year over the past couple of decades. As Bakker argues, the debt problems can be attributed to "the failure of the federal government to bring its revenue-raising capacity in line with its expenditures," and to "various tax breaks and deferrals" that have resulted in a significant revenue loss.[16]

Shifting Views of Social Programs

There is no simple answer to the causes of our current economic difficulties or to the solutions which should be followed. But, even from this brief discussion it should be evident that there are several possible answers and solutions, even though our governments seem to have focused in on one main one — the cost of our social programs. It is ironic that many of these programs, like unemployment insurance and the now-abandoned "baby bonus," were introduced in support of economic policies. They were seen as shoring up personal and family incomes, thereby main-

[15]Figures from Barlow and Campbell, *op. cit.*, p. 82.

[16]Isabella Bakker, "The Politics of Scarcity: Deficits and the Debt," in Michael Whittington and Glen Williams (eds.), *Canadian Politics in the 1990s*, Scarborough, Nelson Canada, 1995, p. 57.

taining purchasing power and consumer spending and helping to support economic growth. Yet our current economic policies, focused on deficit and debt reduction, have now led to an attack on social programs, as an expensive luxury we can no longer afford.

Have We Gone Too Far?
The Dangers of Downsizing

For the moment, those advocating further cutbacks in government spending and further downsizing still hold centre stage. The "conventional wisdom" is still that governments must do whatever it takes to avoid any increase in taxes. Throughout the 1980s, governments claimed that they were unable to do much about unemployment because they had to deal with the apparently greater evil of inflationary pressure. Years of high unemployment have helped to bring down inflation, but now the government finds itself unable to deal with unemployment in the 1990s because it must fight yet another greater evil — this time that of the deficit and the debt. Moreover, the government (and more particularly the Bank of Canada) remains fixated on preventing any return of inflation.

Private Sector Now Expressing Doubts

It is ironic that governments often justify their cuts by explaining that they are just following the example of the private sector in getting their expenditures and their labour forces under control. Yet the private sector is starting to question whether it has gone too far, whether downsizing has become an end in itself, rather than a means to improved productivity. One of the most influential "gurus" of the downsizing mentality, Stephen Roach, the chief economist for Morgan Stanley, has had second thoughts about the gospel he preached for the past decade.[17] He claims that there were actually three ele-

---

[17]Bill Sass, "Sultan of Sack says downsizing must stop," *Kingston Whig Standard*, May 30, 1996.

ments to his corporate vision: (1) downsize, (2) use the saved cash to rebuild the company for global competition, and (3) re-hire, re-educate and invest in workers. He concludes, however, that companies got so busy counting the money from step one that they forgot to follow through with the other two. As a result, many companies are now suffering from a serious shortfall in experience and expertise. It has also become apparent that masses of laid-off workers are hardly in a position to buy the products of the slimmed-down, more efficient companies — a glaringly obvious point that seems to have been slow to penetrate the corporate boardrooms.

Economists and others are also increasingly questioning the wisdom of the economic objectives pursued by government. A recent report from the Chief Economist at CIBC Wood Gundy Securities Inc. concluded that fiscal restraint at the federal and provincial levels reduced economic growth by 3.5% since 1994 and cost the country almost 500 000 jobs.[18] Keynesian economics may have been out of fashion for some time, but its underlying logic remains intact. In an economy plagued by high unemployment, the appropriate fiscal policy would be government spending to "prime the pump" and stimulate economic growth. Instead, our governments have continued to cut expenditures sharply, pursuing deflationary policies which help to undermine economic growth.

Also being called into question more and more is the appropriateness of the strong anti-inflation policy which Canada has pursued for the past decade. On September 7, 1996, the *Toronto Star* editorialized that "We pay a big price for zero inflation," while the *Globe and Mail* of the same date carried an article by William Thorsell entitled "A Higher Inflation Rate Would Lubricate Our Stagnant Economy." Economist Pierre Fortin[19] argues that Canada's much weaker economic performance in comparison to the United States can be explained by an overly tight monetary policy compounded by fiscal restraint

---

[18]Quoted in Tom Fennell, "Revenge of the Scalpel," *Maclean's*, September 9, 1996, p. 30.

[19]Pierre Fortin, "Raise the Inflation Target and Let Canada Recover," *Globe and Mail*, September 26, 1996.

brought on by the sharp cuts in government expenditures. He points out the U.S. Federal Reserve has been content to achieve an inflation target of 3% which has not stood in the way of growth and relatively full employment in that country. In contrast, the Bank of Canada's actions in pursuit of its goal of 1% inflation has been the major cause of unemployment rates remaining almost double those found in the United States.

Interest rates have been lowered steadily since the middle of 1995, and have approached record lows through 1996. But the response of consumers and business has been quite restrained. This should not be surprising. While tight money can kill off an economy quite effective-ly, easy money doesn't necessarily revive it. No matter how low the rates, consumers don't buy new appliances or cars, much less new homes, if they are worried about becoming part of the next wave of lay-offs. Businesses don't invest in new buildings or equipment, no matter how low the rates, if they lack confidence in the economy. With governments and business in a race to see who can become leanest, fastest, is it any wonder that low interest rates aren't enough by themselves to jump-start the economy. Over 46 000 public service jobs disappeared in 1996, and as Anna Guthrie, senior economist with the TD Bank commented: "efforts to balance the budget, shrin-king the public service...tend to depress things."[20] Further evidence of this pattern is found in recent figures from the Ontario Ministry of Finance. The 90 000 new jobs created in 1996 were well below the 145 000 promised in the Conservative Party's Common Sense Revo-lution and were partly offset by 10 000 jobs lost in the public sector.[21]

The current obsession with no tax increases also needs to be ques-tioned. Of course we would all prefer to pay less in taxes, not more. But do we really want to avoid tax increases by having the govern-ment take over from organized crime as the major promoter of gamb-ling in society? In 1995 almost 4% of provincial revenues came from

---

[20]Quoted in Brad Evenson, "National Unemployment Rate plunged in August," *Kingston Whig-Standard*, September 7, 1996.

[21]William Walker, "Boom time, say Tories," *Toronto Star*, February 7, 1997.

New Tax Office

lotteries, casinos and electronic games.[22] Mike Harris campaigned for office in 1995 with a promise to scrap the province's fledgling casino trade if the new casino in Windsor didn't work out. Instead, the Conservative Government is instead getting into the gambling game in a big way by introducing 20 000 VLTs (video-lottery terminals) at race tracks, bars, restaurants, hotels and charity sites. Nova Scotia derived 5.6% of its revenues in 1994 from gambling, and such results will inevitably tempt onto the gambling bandwagon the five provinces and two territories that have so far resisted. Yet Statistics Canada reports that in 1992 those who spent the greatest portion of their income (1.2%) on gambling were households which earned less than $20 000 a year — confirming the criticism that lotteries are nothing more than a regressive form of taxation.

Do we really want to avoid property tax increases at the municipal level by facing instead a barrage of user charges every time we turn around? User charges have their place, and can obviously provide a direct link between payment and benefit received. They can also be beneficial in rationing and influencing behaviour in socially desirable ways. Probably the most familiar examples in that regard are "tipping fees" at the landfill site and "bag tags" for garbage bags, both of which encourage reduction, reuse and recycling of garbage.

But how far do we go with user charges? There have been reports of municipal fire departments which will charge for using the "jaws of life" to extricate a non-resident (and, therefore, non-municipal taxpayer) from a car accident. Picture the scene. The spectacular crash, the sirens screaming to the rescue, the tension as the jaws of life do their work, the smiles of relief from the assembled crowd, and then — as quickly as the victim can be revived — the time-honoured question: *"Will that be cash, or charge?"*

---

[22]Brad Evenson, "Governments bet on gambling for new jobs," *Kingston Whig Standard*, September 5, 1996.

Far-fetched, you say. Perhaps a little. But Ontario municipalities have been give expanded powers to levy user charges under Bill 26 (The Savings and Restructuring Bill) passed in January 1996. They have been strongly encouraged by the Ontario Government to exploit these powers as a way of coping with the cuts in provincial transfer payments which will continue. As a result, there has been widespread discussion about the possibility of police fees, firefighting fees, library fees, fees for the use of arenas and skating rinks, higher charges for death certificates and marriage licenses, even tolls on municipally controlled roads.[23] The possibility of expanded user fees has become even more likely as a result of Provincial proposals at the beginning of 1997 that will shift costs for such services as libraries, airports, highways, public transit and ferries to the municipal level.

Concluding Observations

One of our recurring themes in this book is that "everything connects." Nowhere is this more evident that with respect to economic problems and policies. Efforts to stimulate economic growth can trigger inflationary pressure; efforts to curb inflation can push an economy into a recession. High interest rates can attract foreign capital into Canada and help to sustain the value of the Canadian dollar; but these high rates increase the cost of borrowed money for the Canadian Government and add to its deficit and debt problems. Cuts in social programs bring savings in the short run; these cuts may actually increase government expenditures in the longer term. It has been said that "if all the economists in the world were laid end to end, they wouldn't reach... a conclusion." Perhaps you have somewhat more sympathy for economists now, when you contemplate the wide range of often contradictory choices we face in attempting to deal with the economy.

---

[23] William Walker, "From Libraries to Firefighting, Municipalities look at User Fees," *Toronto Star*, January 25, 1996.

The Last Word

Definition of Terms and Concepts

Most of these definitions are taken from William J. Baumol, Alan S. Blinder and William M. Scarth, *Macroeconomics: Principles and Practices*, 4th edition, Toronto, Harcourt Brace & Company, 1994.

Automatic Stabilizer:
Any arrangement that automatically supports aggregate demand when it would otherwise sag and holds down aggregate demand when it would otherwise surge ahead; thus it reduces the sensitivity of the economy to shifts in demand.

Bank of Canada: (See also monetary policies.)
Canada's central bank, responsible for control of the money supply and interest rates and, therefore, a key player in the government's management of the economy.

Consumer Price Index (CPI):
The most popular index number for the price level. Its weights are based on the spending patterns of a typical urban household.

Deficit: (See also national debt.)
The amount by which the government's expenditures exceed its receipts during a specified period of time, usually one year.

Economic Growth:
The growth that occurs when an economy is able to produce more goods and services for each consumer.

Fiscal Policies:
The government's use of its spending and taxing powers to stimulate or slow down the economy.

Free Trade: (See also protectionism.)
    The free movement of goods and services between countries without any government-imposed barriers to trade.

Globalization:
    The increasingly open world market in goods and services which promotes international trade, provides growing opportunities for trading companies and nations, but also limits the scope for independent decision making by any one country and government.

Gross Domestic Product (GDP):
    The sum of the money values of all final goods and services produced in the economy during a specified period, usually a year.

Inflation:
    A sustained increase in the general price level.

Monetary Policies:
    Actions taken by the Bank of Canada to create "easy money" (reflected in lower interest rates) or "tight money" (higher interest rates) so as to stimulate the economy or slow it down.

National Debt:
    The federal government's total indebtedness at any given moment in time; results from the accumulation of previous deficits.

Protectionism: (Same as Tariffs)
    The opposite of free trade, involving the use of tariffs to make imported goods more expensive, thereby encouraging consumers to purchase domestic products.

Recession:
    A period during which the total output of the economy declines.

Stagflation:
    An economic situation which combines elements of stagnation and inflation (high unemployment and high prices).

Tax Expenditures:
Revenues not collected by the government because of various tax concessions provided to individuals and organizations.

Unemployment Rate:
The number of unemployed people, expressed as a percentage of the labour force.

Points to Ponder

1. Are you one of the many Canadians who holds the view that excessive government spending is the main cause of our deficit and debt problems? Has this chapter caused you to reassess your thinking in regard to this issue?

2. Why have government efforts not focused more on the issue of unemployment? Do you find these reasons acceptable?

3. While government actions influence the economy, the economy has even more influence over government actions. Provide examples to support either or both sides of this statement.

For Further Reading

The best source of information about government actions concerning the Canadian economy is found in Canada's media, its daily newspapers and news broadcasts and news magazines like *Maclean's*.

There are a large number of economics textbooks which examine the issues touched on in this chapter, and several are likely to be found in your public library.

Chapter 10

The Unravelling Social Safety Net

Objectives and Highlights

♦ To describe Canada's main social programs and to evaluate their effectiveness.

♦ To assess the link between social spending and Canada's national debt.

♦ To debate the merits of entrenching social rights into the constitution.

According to its defenders, Canada's social safety net is unravelling, as more social programs lose their universality and/or have their financial support reduced. According to its critics, the safety net has become a hammock, encouraging dependency and inviting abuse.

For those preoccupied with deficit and debt reduction, social programs must be cut if government is to get its expenditures under control. Even those who support social programs have to concede that they have not been very effective in keeping Canadians above the poverty line and in narrowing the gap between the "have-nots" and the "haves" in Canadian society.

At the same time, critics of the cuts have a strong case when they argue that reduced financial support in areas such as junior kindergarten and day care will simply result in increased costs later for such programs as health, policing, courts and prisons.

Obviously, we are dealing with a complex subject and one about which emotions often run high. This chapter will attempt to "unravel" the issues involved and give you a basis on which to judge the appropriateness of government actions in this area.

Introduction: Safety Net or Hammock?

An issue of the *Kingston Whig Standard* in the Fall of 1995 illustrated vividly the changing perceptions about welfare or social assistance in society today. The page full of angry letters had been triggered by a story about a family on welfare who were distressed by the welfare cuts being introduced by the newly elected Conservative Government in Ontario. The family had been on welfare for the past six years and the husband, 38, was starting to think that he would have to give up on a job in his chosen field and take any kind of work. During this six year period on welfare, he and his wife had three more children, bringing their total to nine. The family were receiving social assistance of $31,000, and were paying rent of $995 monthly.

Angry respondents pointed out that they worked long and hard to make "take home pay" equivalent to the money being given to this family, that houses were available to rent for much less than $995 a month and, most of all, that it was totally irresponsible of this couple to have more children if they couldn't afford to take care of the ones they had. In their view, the behaviour of this couple was the very reason Mike Harris had to get tough on welfare recipients and break the cycle of dependency.

Premier Harris didn't let them down. In September 1995, Ontario sliced 21.6% from its basic welfare rates as part of a series of measures intended to get the province's deficit and debt under control. Soon stories of other welfare families began to circulate through the media — stories of families who no longer had a place to live because they had to choose food for their children over rent payments, stories of more and more children living in poverty in the wealthiest province in one of the wealthiest countries in the world.

What is happening to our so-called social safety net, why is it happening and are the changes necessary or justifiable? In an attempt to understand this very complex and controversial issue, we will begin by outlining the main components of Canada's social services.

The Evolution of the Welfare State

At a time when many seek to dismantle the *welfare state*, or at least conclude that its dismantling is unavoidable, it is useful to recall why and when it was established.

The decline in individual self-sufficiency and the rise of dependence on government coincided with fundamental changes in the nature of the Canadian economy and society inherent in the shift from an agricultural and rural society to an urban and industrial one. It was the Great Depression of the 1930s, however, and the almost total collapse of the Canadian economy, which dramatized the need for government intervention and support for those in need. Consider the following images from that period.[1]

> Atlantic Canada was devastated. Fish exports plummeted and unemployment soared. Unemployment in Ontario rose from 2% in 1929 to 36% in 1936. The collapse in the Prairies was aggravated by drought and shrinking world markets for wheat. By 1936, one-third of Saskatchewan farmers were on relief; two-thirds by the following year. In some districts every single family was on relief. At the height of the Depression, half of the wage earners in Canada were on some form of relief.
>
> The "relief" referred to was administered by provinces and municipalities, who were generally punitive in their approach. There was a terrible stigma attached to the "dole." To be eligible for relief, a family had to demonstrate that it was nearly destitute. Inspectors would come to the home, and if they found any signs of food, new clothes, liquor or, in some cases, even a radio, relief was denied. Most municipalities had a one year residency requirement even for emergency health care, and immigrants were not only turned down for help but deported for requesting it. Medical aid was scarce and far too expensive for many Canadians and, of course, there wasn't any universal health care.

As the Depression deepened and dragged on, the federal government gradually assumed some responsibility for unemployment relief,

---

[1]The description which follows is based on Maude Barlow and Bruce Campbell, *Straight Through the Heart*, Toronto, HarperCollins Publishers Limited, 1995, pp. 14-16.

in part to bail out provincial governments which were virtually bankrupt from trying to make these payments. Many municipalities had gone bankrupt — defaulting on debt obligations incurred for expansion of roads, water and sewer systems and other infrastructure during the boom period of the "Roaring Twenties." The Depression eventually ended because of the upsurge in economic activity associated with World War II, and by the end of the war most Western nations were embracing the economic ideas of John Maynard Keynes. Central to Keynesian economics was the view that governments could pursue deliberate policies which would help to minimize unemployment and maintain rising incomes, stable prices and other desirable economic objectives. As a result, government payments to the unemployed and other forms of income support gained favour, not as a form of welfare, but as a stimulus to the purchasing power of Canadian citizens and thus to economic growth. Consider these developments:

1941	Introduction of a federal unemployment insurance program
1945	Family allowance payments ("baby bonus") introduced
1952	Old age pension of $40 per month to Canadians 70 and older
1965	Canada Pension Plan, payments at age 65 to contributors
1966	Comprehensive public assistance plan, Canada Assistance Plan or CAP, to coordinate provincial plans
1966	National health care program ("Medicare") introduced

Thus over about a twenty-five year period many of the key components of Canada's modern welfare state were put into place. They were established during a period in which the Canadian economy enjoyed almost continuous growth and revenue sources for government seemed inexhaustible. Since then, we have gone through the "stagflation" of the 1970s and several economic downturns in the 1980s and 1990s. The federal government has not been able to balance its budget for over 20 years. Both the federal and provincial governments have become increasingly preoccupied with deficit and debt reduction. Under these changed circumstances, a number of issues and concerns have arisen concerning the nature of the welfare state in Canada.

In particular, there has been growing debate about two fundamental issues:

1. That Canada's social programs have become overly costly and must be cut if government deficits and debt are to be brought under control.
2. That our social programs are overly generous and have created a harmful dependency which also introduces rigidities into our economy and inhibits normal adjustments.

For both of these reasons, critics call for a scaling down of social programs and for targeting expenditures more to those who are most in need. The remainder of this chapter is largely concerned with an examination of these issues and their apparent validity.

The Size and Cost of the Welfare State

The exact cost of the welfare state is difficult to calculate, since there is no precise definition of what programs or payments should be included within it. Some indication of scope is provided by the tabular summary on the preceding page. The "big three" are usually considered to be health, education and welfare, although some programs provide cash benefits and others provide specific services. Whatever definition is used, there is no doubt that social spending is sizeable, amounting to close to two-thirds of total program spending by the federal government and as high as three-quarters of such spending in provinces such as British Columbia and Saskatchewan.[2]

As discussed in the previous chapter, the business community and the various interest groups representing it have mounted a very effective campaign to persuade Canadians that Canada's debt problems are

---

[2]John Richards, "The Social Policy Round," in William G. Watson, John Richards and David M. Brown, *The Case for Change: Reinventing the Welfare State*, Toronto, C. D. Howe Institute, 1994, pp. 37-38.

intertwined with our overly generous social programs and can only be addressed by curtailing social spending. Typical of this viewpoint is a C. D. Howe publication which states that Canada's social programs are too elaborate and expensive. "They may not have caused Canada's current huge debt problem, but they are too large a component of public expenditure not to be part of the solution."[3] Since the free trade agreement with the United States, businesses have also attacked social programs and their costs as an impediment to Canadian competitiveness.[4]

♦ Something to Think About

Have social programs become too costly and too heavy a burden on business in the new global economy? Do we have to reduce expenditures in these areas to deal with our deficit and debt problems?

Is there any truth to the claim of some that we have to cut social programs in order to save them?

However costly they are, it is not the business community which has been paying for Canada's social programs, partly because of the significant shifts which have been occurring in the **burden** of taxation in Canada. In the early 1950s, revenues from personal and corporate taxation were roughly in balance. Since then, the balance has swung heavily against personal taxpayers. This pattern intensified during the Mulroney years in the 1980s. One study of this period notes that after the Conservatives came to power in 1984, corporate taxes increased by only 8%, income taxes by 45%, and the sales tax (not counting the GST) by 67%.[5]

---

[3]William G. Watson, "The View from the Right," in *ibid.*, p. 1.

[4]This aspect of the business community's posture on social programs is well explored in Barlow and Campbell, *op. cit.*

[5]Isabella Bakker, "The Size and Scope of Government: Robin Hood Sent Packing?" in Michael Whittington and Glen Williams (eds.), *Canadian Politics in the 1990s*, Toronto, Nelson Canada, 1990, p. 444.

Brooks points out that at the federal level direct taxation of personal income currently accounts for about half of state revenues. Individuals also have social security taxes (U.I. and Canada Pension Plan contributions) deducted from their pay. The conclusion is inescapable according to Brooks:

> The welfare state has been financed mainly by the users of public education, public health services, and income security programs. The idea that business has been squeezed to finance politically popular programs is **a gross misrepresentation of the facts.**[6]

A recent book by McQuaig provides some striking statistics and arguments about the causes of Canada's deficit and debt problems and the extent to which they have been caused by social spending. She cites a 1991 study by an official in Statistics Canada that calculates how much each social program contributed to the growth of the federal debt.[7] The study found that unemployment insurance was responsible for only 1% of the debt problem, welfare 4.5%, and old age pensions 6%. It found that family allowance benefits had been cut so severely after 1975 that they had helped to **reduce** the debt growth by 11%. Overall, the study found that Canada was spending roughly the same portion of its Gross Domestic Product on social programs in 1991 as it had been in the mid-1970s, when the debt was considered small and manageable.

The Real Culprit!

Interest Charges Caused Half of Debt Growth

How, then, do we account for the large increase in Canada's debt over this period? The Statistics Canada study found that larger spending increases had occurred in areas that had not been singled out for public criticism. For example, about 8% of the debt growth was attributable to spending on protection to persons and property, a category which included the military, the police and

---

[6]Brooks, *op. cit.*, p. 205.

[7]Linda McQuaig, *Shooting the Hippo*, Toronto, Penguin Books, 1995, pp. 56-58 and p. 117, on which this section is based.

prison systems. But by far the biggest cause of the debt was rising interest costs, which accounted for 44% of the growth of the national debt between 1974-75 and 1988-89. In the fiscal year 1988-89 alone, interest charges accounted for 72% of the deficit. As discussed in the previous chapter, these interest costs were largely the result of deliberate government policies directed toward eliminating inflation, an objective strongly urged by the business community. Under the circumstances, it is rather remarkable that the business community continues to blame Canada's debt problem on our social programs and to advocate their curtailment.

The Effectiveness of Social Spending

The preceding section examined, and raised serious doubts about, the charge that excessive social spending is the primary cause of Canada's current debt problems. What about the second key issue, that of whether or not all of this social spending is effective? The evidence here is, at best, mixed. It is disappointing to find that the distribution of income has remained virtually unchanged. In 1951 the top 20% of income earners in Canada accounted for 42.8% of total money income and the bottom 20% accounted for 4.4%. In 1990, the top 20% accounted for 40.2% and the bottom 20% generated 6.9%.[8]

On the other hand, evidence of the redistributive effect of government spending is found in a publication of the Fraser Institute, a Vancouver-based business "think tank."[9] It examined how much various income groups benefited from government spending programs and found that the lower the income group, the more it benefited. Those on the lower income levels clearly received more in government benefits than they contributed through their taxes, but families receiving $45 000 and up received less in benefits than they paid in taxes. Indeed, those in the top income group contributed $34 000

---

[8]*Brooks, op. cit.*, p. 190.

[9]This publication is quoted and discussed in McQuaig, *op. cit.*, pp. 270-271.

more than they received in benefits. While this pattern might not please the wealthy clients of the Fraser Institute, it reflects the way social programs are supposed to work. The private marketplace distributes resources very unequally. Social programs are intended to reduce this inequity.

Poverty Amidst Plenty

Whatever social programs accomplish in reducing the extremes of the inequitable distribution of income in our society, they haven't been very successful in keeping Canadians from falling below the *"poverty line."*[10] The National Council on Welfare reported in 1995[11] that the number of people living in poverty in Canada grew to 4.8 million in 1993, up from 4.3 million in 1992. As a result, the poverty rate increased from 16.1% to 17.4%. Poor single mothers were the most impoverished, averaging $8500 below the poverty line. In fact, 90% of families headed by a single mother were below the poverty line. The Council reported that more than 1.4 million children, representing 20.8% of all Canadians under 18, were below the poverty line — the highest level ever recorded.

The statistics have not improved, but the possibility of a new federal-provincial program to address child poverty has been receiving increasing attention at the beginning of 1997. The general approach being discussed is to integrate the existing federal child tax credit with the portion of provincial welfare payments earmarked for children.[12] The objective would be to make the same benefit available to all poor families, whether working or not. This would end one of the worst features of existing welfare programs — the fact that parents

---

[10]Defined by Statistics Canada as when at least 56.2% of income goes to pay for food, shelter, and clothing — in contrast to the Canadian average of 36.2% of income spent on those items.

[11]*Globe and Mail*, April 6, 1995.

[12]This summary of the new approach is based on Andrew Coyne, "Equality at the heart of child benefit," *Kingston Whig Standard*, January 14, 1997.

who find work must pay a penalty in the form of lost welfare benefits for their children, which at low rates of pay can make them worse off than they were before.

A combination of factors have come together to produce some momentum for this new initiative. First, the federal Liberals find themselves well ahead of their deficit reduction target and in a position to direct some new funds to this area. Such action, however sincerely motivated, would also work well in recasting the Liberals as social reformers. This had been the hallmark of the party but had received little consideration since the 1993 election victory, because of the preoccupation with deficit and debt reduction. A child poverty initiative would serve to remind the public of the Liberal commitment to social reform before the impending election in 1997.

Another factor is that five provinces — British Columbia, Alberta, Saskatchewan, Québec and New Brunswick — have already announced or implemented new social programs for working poor families with children.[13] The timing is good for a joint initiative which would also serve to demonstrate the flexibility of federalism, thus providing some ammunition for the federalist side in the ongoing struggle over Québec separation. This point is certainly not lost on the Minister responsible for the federal discussions, Pierre Pettigrew, one of those specifically recruited by Prime Minister Chrétien to bolster the federalist cause.

Whatever the underlying motives and influences, one can only hope that the proposed new child poverty initiative proceeds.

Regional Disparities and Rigidities

Our social programs have also had limited success in reducing the regional economic disparities in Canada. In spite of past efforts, the three "have" provinces (Ontario, B.C. and Alberta) remain the same and the four Atlantic provinces remain the poorest of the poor. Some economists, such as Courchene, contend that continued high unem-

---

[13]Jeffrey Simpson, "What's the price, political and financial, of fighting child poverty," *Globe and Mail*, January 15, 1997.

ployment in Canada generally, and in particular regions, is actually caused by harmful government policies.[14] Among these, he cites restricted labour mobility because of interprovincial trade barriers, excessive expenditures on passive income support for the unemployed and a neglect of training needs of those entering the labour force without necessary skills.

The Canadian economy needs to adapt rapidly in the face of accelerating pace of change. To the extent that income security programs discourage people from moving between sectors or between regions of the economy, they are viewed by many economists as a drag on the international competitiveness of our economy.

It is also widely held that unemployment remains high because people can make more money by staying on welfare than they can by taking a job at minimum wage. In 1992, in a landmark report, the National Council on Welfare calculated that a single parent on welfare in Ontario with one child could receive $16 999 per year; that is, $4685 more than a job of 40 hours per week at minimum wage would provide.[15] Even with the cuts recently made by the Harris Government, a single parent remains marginally better off staying on welfare. The same report pointed out that a single-earner couple with two children in Manitoba could receive $20 519, which was $9047 more than the minimum wage in that province. These findings suggest that the system seems perversely designed to discourage work and self-improvement.

From Welfare to Workfare?

Frustrated with this situation, governments throughout North America are turning to "*workfare*," requiring that able-bodied welfare recipients work for their cheques. Ideally, according to the proponents of workfare, it will ease welfare recipients into the workforce, restoring

---

[14]Quoted in John Richards, "The Social Policy Round," in Watson, *op. cit.*, p. 44.

[15]Mary Janigan, "Wading into the Welfare Mess," in *Maclean's*, November 27, 1995, p. 34.

their self-confidence and upgrading skills made rusty by inactivity. Premier Klein of Alberta has decreed that welfare recipients will be cut off if they refuse jobs in programs such as Community Employment, which provides up to 26 weeks of work performing such tasks as tree-planting.[16] Québec offers higher benefits to those who accept work or training and New Brunswick has a workfare program.

The Ontario Government launched a workfare program in 1996 and in June promised that by the end of September 54 000 people would be working for their benefits in 20 pilot municipalities. The Ontario experience to that point is revealing in terms of the potential of this much-touted program. When the end of September came, **not one job** had been found for those supposedly able-bodied welfare recipients that the Harris Government had promised to put to work.[17] Interviews with 17 of the 20 pilot municipalities revealed that only about 5000 welfare recipients would be on workfare in 1997.

While workfare may have its merits, it appears to stem from an underlying premise or insinuation that welfare recipients are lazy and unmotivated and must be forced to work. Instead, there is evidence to suggest that most are anxious to get any kind of work. Consider these two examples.

♦ General Motors announced in January 1995 that it was accepting job applications at its Pickering location.[18] There were no current openings, but the company anticipated hiring about 700 people over the next year. That prospect was enough to prompt people to begin camping out in sub-zero weather on Friday, to become part of what turned into a line-up of 25 000 people when the doors opened Monday morning.

♦ A similar event occurred just before the Ottawa Senators moved into their new hockey home in The Palladium (now the Corel Centre) in January 1996. More than 3000 people, including uni-

---

[16]*Ibid.*

[17]Phinjo Gombu, "Workfare falls short of Tory targets," *Toronto Star*, September 29, 1996.

[18]The description of this incident is from McQuaig, *op. cit.*, p. 36.

versity graduates and out-of-work public servants lined up over-
night the previous November to apply for 1000 part time jobs at
The Palladium paying $7 per hour.[19]

Defenders of social programs contend that the real problem is not
motivation of welfare recipients or overly generous welfare payments;
it is the lack of jobs in our economy. Here again, the free trade agreement and the globalization of the economy are key factors. To increase their international competitiveness, companies have been
downsizing. Unemployment has remained at or near double digit
figures in Canada for more than a decade. Periodic economic upturns
feature "jobless recoveries."

One of the best ways for governments to reduce social spending
and dependence on the state would be to stimulate job creation in the
economy. Political parties often campaign on this platform but, upon
election, decide that deficit reduction must be their first priority and,
in any event, putting their fiscal house in order will lead to economic
growth and jobs. The result is that while parties come and go, the
priorities of government remain much the same.

Is the Safety Net Unravelling?

While concern about social programs has increased recently, the
programs have been losing ground for the past decade or more. The
two most important universal income security programs, old age security and family allowance payments (recently abolished), have long
been treated as income for tax purposes. The result is that lower
income recipients retain a larger share of these payments than do
higher income recipients. So, while these have been universal programs in terms of eligibility, they have actually been income-tested
programs in terms of their effects. The family allowance program was
abolished in the early 1990s, and replaced with a child tax credit.

---

[19]Kaye Fulton, "A Bridge too far: Liberals' UI Reforms draw fire
from all sides," *Maclean's*, December 11, 1995, p. 23.

Bakker charges this latter action was one of a number of steps taken during the Mulroney years which transformed social policy "by stealth" and undermined the egalitarian goals of the welfare state.[20] She is critical of the replacement of family allowances with a targeted program of family assistance. She notes that targeted programs are difficult to maintain because political support for them only comes from that segment of the population that receives them. In contrast, *universal programs* that benefit all have a much stronger support base.

Cuts in Federal Social Transfers

As discussed in earlier chapters, the beginning of the 1990s saw a number of other federal actions which reduced financial support for social programs, in the name of deficit and debt reduction. The federal government introduced a two year freeze on its payments under EPF (Established Program Funding) in 1990-91 and then extended the freeze until the end of the 1994-95 fiscal year. According to calculations by the Government of Ontario the total loss to **all provinces** from these modifications to EPF amounted to $33.6 billion.[21]

1990-91 also saw the federal government place a cap on CAP (the Canada Assistance Plan) for the three "have" provinces of Ontario, B.C. and Alberta. This cap placed a ceiling of 5% on the growth of Canada Assistance payments to these provinces, regardless of their actual social assistance costs, and it remained in effect through 1994-95. As a result, while the federal government continued to pay 50% of the actual social assistance costs in the other provinces, the proportions for the "have" provinces were 28% in Ontario, 37% in B.C. and 47% in Alberta. Estimates by Ontario suggested that the cumulative

---

[20]Isabella Bakker, "The Politics of Scarcity: Deficits and the Debt," in Michael Whittington and Glen Williams (eds.), *Canadian Politics in the 1990s*, Scarborough, Nelson Canada, 1995, p. 66.

[21]Paul Hobson, "Current Issues in Federal-Provincial Fiscal Relations," in Watts and Brown (eds.), *Canada: The State of the Federation*, Kingston, Queen's University, 1993, p. 181.

loss to these three provinces over the planned life of the cap would exceed $4 billion, over $3 billion of it to Ontario alone.[22]

Further cuts in federal payments in support of social programs have been introduced since the election of the Liberal Government in October 1993 and were presented as part of Finance Minister Paul Martin's initiatives to deal with the federal deficit and debt situation. The 1995 federal budget announced that beginning in 1996-97, EPF and CAP would be replaced by a single transfer — the Canada Health and Social Transfer or CHST. It is a block fund, like EPF, meaning that the amounts transferred are not determined by provincial spending decisions. The provinces were given $29.7 billion in transfers for 1995-96, about the same as in 1994-95 to allow them a period to prepare for the change. Under the new CHST, funding to the provinces is being reduced from what it otherwise would have been in 1996-97 by $2.5 billion to $26.9 billion. It will be further reduced in 1997-98 by $4.5 billion to $25.1 billion.

Changes to U.I.

The Liberal Government has introduced a number of changes to the Unemployment Insurance program, including a new name — Employment Insurance program.[23] One of its objectives is to reduce the cost of the U.I. program by some $2 billion. The other main objective is to redirect some of these savings into measures to help people get back into the workforce. In proportional terms, the cuts will fall most heavily on claimants with family incomes above $50 000 a year. Low income U.I. beneficiaries with children will be entitled to special supplements, while benefits for high income recipients will be taxed back.

These changes move U.I. away from a universal program toward one that is means-tested. The Minister responsible for the changes, Lloyd Axworthy, freely admitted that he wanted to make work more

---

[22]*Ibid.*, p. 184.

[23]Edward Greenspon, "Axworthy undoes Mackasey's work," *Globe and Mail*, December 2, 1995.

rewarding and the collection of U.I. benefits less so. The reforms also targeted seasonal workers who will still qualify for U.I., but will take home less money and for a shorter time.

In a related initiative, the federal government has entered into labour market training agreements with a number of provinces, under which some $2.5 billion in employment insurance re-employment money will be transferred for use by the provinces. Alberta was the first to sign on, followed soon after by New Brunswick, and a deal is apparently close for Québec, Newfoundland and Prince Edward Island.[24] One observer feels that this change is less about helping unemployed Canadians find work as quickly as possible than it is about "tossing another trophy" to the provinces, especially Québec, to satisfy national unity critics.[25]

CPP stands for Canada's Pension Problem

Another social program facing challenge and change is the Canada Pension Plan. *CPP* pensions are paid entirely by contributions made by employers and employees, and are based on past earnings. These contributions have not been keeping up with the demands on the plan, especially with Canada's aging population. A recent report from the Federal Superintendent of Financial Institutions states that the Canada Pension Plan will be wiped out in 20 years, just as baby boomers start to hit age 65 — unless contributions are more than doubled or benefits somehow cut.[26] There have been reports that the government is contemplating both an increase in the amount of the contributions to the CPP and a delay in the age of eligibility to 66 or 67.

A meeting of federal and provincial finance ministers in early October 1996 failed to reach agreement on reform of the Canada Pension Plan. They released a statement of "common principles," which

---

[24]Janice Tibbetts, "N.B. agrees to shoulder load on services for unemployed," *Globe and Mail*, December 14, 1996.

[25]Giles Gherson, "Farewell to policy reform," *Kingston Whig Standard,* October 9, 1996.

[26]Quoted in the *Kingston Whig Standard*, February 25, 1995.

called for gradually increasing (over a maximum of eight years) the contribution rate to 10.1% from the current rate of 5.6%. Benefits would also be curtailed, with emphasis on modest cuts to disability and survivor benefits.[27] However, the provinces, led by Ontario, are demanding a reduction in U.I. premiums to offset the increase in pension premiums. They point to the fact that the U.I. Fund will have a $5 billion surplus this year and a projected $10 billion surplus in 1997. While both U.I. and Pension premiums are a kind of payroll tax, the federal finance minister doesn't see that they are linked, although he has not ruled out a reduction in U.I. premiums. As with so many issues in Canada, it appears that both U.I. and pension reform will require some delicate federal-provincial negotiations.

The 1995 Federal Budget also raised concerns about the Old Age Security (*OAS*) and Guaranteed Income Supplement (*GIS*) benefits, which cost over $20 billion and are expected to grow by 60% over the next 15 years as the population ages. In changes which take effect in 2001, the OAS and GIS programs will be replaced by a Seniors Benefit program.[28] It will be tax free and fully indexed to inflation, but the size of the benefit will be reduced for those with family incomes over $40 000 and eliminated for single seniors with more than $52 000 and couples with more than $78 000. Here again, the shift is from a universal program to one which is means-tested. The government claims that the new arrangements are fairer since they target those most in need, while keeping pension costs manageable.[29] It has also offered all those at least 60 years old as of December 31, 1995, a choice of the old or new pension arrangements, thereby increasing the "saleability" of the reform.

---

[27]Barrie McKenna, "Provinces block CPP reform," in *Globe and Mail*, October 5, 1996.

[28]The summary which follows is based on Gene Swimmer (ed.), *How Ottawa Spends 1996-97: Life Under the Knife*, Ottawa, Carleton University Press, 1996, pp. 27-28.

[29]Indeed, savings of $2.1 billion are expected by 2011. *Ibid.*, p. 28.

Provincial Cuts as Well

Provincial governments have been responding in kind. Faced with cuts in transfer payments from the federal level, they could presumably have increased their expenditures to make up the shortfall. But, most provinces have become equally concerned with deficit and debt questions. As a result, their reaction has been to make cuts of their own, including cuts in transfers to municipalities and other local governing bodies. Ralph Klein led the way in Alberta with a series of sharp cuts in funding for municipalities, school boards, hospitals and other social agencies.

Since his election in June 1995, Mike Harris has been doing his best to match the Alberta example in Ontario. The 21% cut in welfare payments has previously been mentioned. Further cuts were announced in a Fiscal and Economic Statement from the Minister of Finance in November 1995. As if imitating what the federal government had done to it, the Province announced that it would be giving municipalities a new unconditional grant, but one reduced in value. Three existing programs which made up about one-quarter of all provincial transfer payments to local governments were combined into a new Municipal Support Grant (MSG). It is being cut by 47% between 1995 and 1997 (and will then be eliminated). In addition, the Province announced substantial cuts in grants for such programs and services as libraries, public transit, education and child care spaces.

All of this was just a warm-up, however, for a massive series of changes introduced by the Ontario Government in January 1997. To offset the cost of education funding which it decided to remove from the residential property tax, the Province has shifted to municipalities 50% of the cost for welfare, family benefits, long term care for the elderly and child care, along with 100% of the cost for other social programs such as public housing. At this point, it is impossible to assess what the final financial impact will be of the massive shifts in responsibility being introduced, but few believe the Province's claim that it will be revenue-neutral. Moreover, even if that is the case for the municipal level of government overall, it will certainly not be the case for individual municipalities or areas of Ontario. It is well known that some social programs are disproportionately concentrated in large urban centres, which are likely to be very hard hit financially by the new arrangements.[30] Attempting to raise the funds needed from the regressive property tax will not be possible — which is why most Provinces have assumed greater, not less, responsibility for social programs, an arrangement recommended by numerous studies in Ontario but ignored by the Harris Government.

Holes in the Safety Net

If the present trend continues, we appear to be witnessing the gradual dismantling of the welfare state. Many are concerned that without federal requirements and conditions backed by federal money (reflected in such now-abandoned programs as EPF and CAP), it is difficult to see how national standards in social programs will be maintained. Without national standards, we may be left with a hodge-podge of programs across Canada and the danger that these programs will be weakest in the poorer provinces, where they are needed the most. A similar pattern could also emerge within Ontario as a result of the Harris Government changes outlined above.

One instance of a departure from national standards is provided by the example of British Columbia in imposing a three month residency requirement for welfare eligibility, in clear contravention of the provisions of the Canada Assistance Plan. As noted elsewhere, CAP has now become part of a block grant called the Canada Health and Social Transfer, but the federal government has insisted that it will continue to enforce the no-residency requirement. Its response has been to withhold some $46 million of that new block grant, an action which British Columbia has challenged in the courts. In the meantime, anti-poverty groups mounted a successful court challenge

---

[30]For example, Metro Toronto has 36% of the total social housing in Ontario and three-quarters of the social housing in the GTA, leaving it unfairly burdened with the provincial downloading of all costs for this service. John Barber, "Calculator or not, Harris's plans don't add up," *Globe and Mail*, January 16, 1997.

against the B.C. residency rules. However, the court did not rule that B.C. could not impose such a restriction, only that it must be done through proper legislation. The B.C. government has indicated that it will side-step this court ruling by imposing the residency requirements in another (more legally acceptable) manner, which suggests that the battle with Ottawa over this issue will continue.[31]

A potential threat to federally-imposed national standards was delivered in connection with the 37th annual Premiers' Conference, held in Jasper, Alberta in August 1996. The challenge came from Ontario's Mike Harris who, wearing cowboy boots, strode like John Wayne aboard the "Unity Train" carrying the Premiers to the meeting, with a copy of the Courchene Report in his back pocket.[32] This report, by Professor Tom Courchene of Queen's University, asserted that federal cuts to health care and social programs had left the federal government without the "moral authority" to tell the provinces what to do. It also suggested that reduced federal payments would soon be ineffective anyway in trying to force provinces into line. Instead, Courchene concluded that the provinces must accept a larger responsibility for preserving and promoting social Canada. While national standards would still be needed, he argued that these could be developed and enforced by the provinces themselves.[33]

These ideas generated a great deal of controversy before Harris could even address them at the Premiers' Conference. Premiers from a number of the poorer provinces predictably opposed what they saw as a weakening of the federal role (which would lead to a further reduction in federal funding) in these areas. However, all Premiers (except Lucien Bouchard) agreed with the idea of a joint council with

---

[31]This summary is based on Craig McInnes, "B.C. moves to restore welfare residency rule," *Globe and Mail*, October 5, 1996.

[32]This colourful description was provided by Richard Brennan, "The trial balloon that went over like a lead balloon," *Kingston Whig Standard*, August 27, 1996.

[33]Thomas J. Courchene, *ACCESS: A Convention on the Canadian Economic and Social Systems*, working paper prepared for the Ministry of Intergovernmental Affairs, August 1996.

the federal government, which would oversee the reorganization of social policies and ensure that the provinces as well as the federal level are involved in setting new national standards. To date, the federal government has not shown any indication that it is prepared to surrender its current role of enforcing standards such as those under the Canada Health Act to some form of dispute-settling mechanism under a joint council.[34]

Is a Social Charter the Answer?

One of the responses of those concerned with the gradual deterioration in the social safety net has been to advocate a *social charter* which would somehow provide constitutional protection of social rights just as the Charter of Rights and Freedoms protects other rights. This was a major objective of former Ontario Premier Bob Rae, who succeeded in getting a social charter included in the ill-fated Charlottetown Accord. Rae's position was that a national system of health care, an array of income support programs, free public and secondary education, and affordable post-secondary education had become common values shared by Canadians and expected from their governments.[35]

Proponents argue that entrenchment will prevent erosion of these rights by governments obsessed with deficit and debt reduction.[36] They claim that equality of treatment across provinces would be ensured, instead of the danger of harmful competition in which provincial governments would reduce social programs as part of a strategy to reduce taxes and thereby attract more economic growth — a possibility usually referred to as "the race to the bottom." They further

---

[34]Hugh Winsor, "Don't Wait for Québec, Klein urges," *Globe and Mail*, September 27, 1996.

[35]See Ontario Ministry of Intergovernmental Affairs, *A Canadian Social Charter: Making Our Shared Values Stronger*, September 1991.

[36]For an examination of this topic, see Issue Twenty-Three in Mark Charlton and Paul Barker (eds.), *Crosscurrents: Contemporary Political Issues*, 2nd edition, Scarborough, Nelson Canada, 1994, pp. 493-511.

argue that entrenchment would provide protection in the face of economic harmonization efforts, especially those related to free trade. Canadian businesses demanding "a level playing field" constantly pressure for tax reductions which, in turn, threaten established social programs.

Critics of the entrenchment concept argue that we can't/shouldn't bind future governments financially, and that guaranteeing certain social programs in the constitution would prevent future governments from responding to the preferences of their electorates. Such a step would further elevate the role of the courts and dilute the role and responsibility of elected legislatures. Entrenchment opponents also point out that the judicial process is slow, relatively inflexible and not accountable.

The social charter died with the Charlottetown Accord and little has been heard about it since. While it might not have been the answer, it is clear that something is needed to arrest the erosion of social programs which is occurring in Canada. Ultimately, the best protection lies in such strong public support that governments ignore or reduce them at their peril. That kind of public support has not been in evidence for many of our social programs, especially those involving social assistance to the less fortunate in society. The one dramatic exception has been medicare; surveys consistently show that Canadians attach great importance to our public health system. How that system is faring is the subject of the next chapter.

Concluding Observations

The expansion and contraction of Canada's welfare state illustrates a number of issues and themes addressed in this Guide. The intertwining of economics and politics is evident from the fact that many social programs were originally supported as beneficial for the economy because they were automatic stabilizers or otherwise helped to shore up the purchasing power of Canadians. That link is also evident in the recent reduction in, or abandonment of, many of the same programs, on the grounds that they are now seen as a primary cause of our public debt and, therefore, a negative influence on the economy.

The intergovernmental complexities of government in Canada are also revealed in the changing approach to social policies. The Great Depression of the 1930s led to a growing number of federal initiatives in social policy, even though this field was clearly allocated to the provinces under the constitution. The federal spending power was used to promote and enforce national standards in various social programs. These standards now seem in jeopardy, given the declining and less conditional federal funding being provided to the provinces. In a parallel development, concerns are now being raised about the preservation of provincial standards in various social programs in Ontario as a result of recent actions by the Harris Government to download all or substantial responsibility for funding these programs to the municipal level.

The erosion or potential erosion of social programs can be seen as one of the harmful consequences of an over-preoccupation with deficit and debt reduction. On the other hand, proponents of fiscal restraint can argue that it is only because of the federal government's concerted efforts to bring down the annual deficit that we are in a position to launch a long-overdue program to combat child poverty. Critics will respond that while this program is warranted, its discussion at this time has less to do with the validity of its need than with the Liberal Government's desire for a softening of its image prior to the 1997 election and for a successful federal-provincial initiative to demonstrate the flexibility of federalism. Such influences are the reality of political life.

The Last Word

Definition of Terms and Concepts

CPP:
Canada Pension Plan, which provides payments at 65 to those who have made payments into it.

GIS:
Guaranteed Income Supplement, which provides a supplementary pension to the elderly who have no means of support other than old age security.

OAS:
Old age security payments made by the federal government to all Canadians over 65 who meet basic residency requirements. (Not to be confused with the CPP which is only paid to those who have made contributions to it.)

Poverty Line:
The point at which at least 56.2% of income goes to pay for food, shelter and clothing.

Social Charter:
A constitutional declaration of certain social rights guaranteed to Canadians, similar to the Charter of Rights and Freedoms.

UI:
Unemployment insurance (now called employment insurance), which provides insurance — through contributions made by both the employer and the employee — against an interruption of income due to unemployment, illness or pregnancy.

Universal Programs:
   Social programs provided to all Canadians regardless of need or circumstance — in contrast to targetted or means-tested programs, which are provided only to those who qualify.

Welfare State:
   A network of government programs providing comprehensive social services for the population.

Workfare:
   Government programs designed to require able-bodied welfare recipients to accept some form of employment (usually through community projects) in return for their cheques.

Points to Ponder

1. Are our social programs a primary cause of the deficit and debt problems of government, or have they been unfairly singled out?

2. What do you think of the concept of targeting social programs more specifically, so that the money gets to those most in need? What do you see as the pros and cons of universal versus targeted programs?

3. Do we need a strong federal commitment, including funding, to ensure national standards, or could such standards be set and maintained by the provinces?

4. What are the benefits of having greater provincial involvement and discretion with respect to social programs?

5. How has Canada's federal system of government complicated the development and delivery of social programs?

For Further Reading

Maude Barlow and Bruce Campbell, *Straight Through the Heart,* Toronto, HarperCollins Publishers Limited, 1995, present their case that Canada's social programs are under siege.

Linda McQuaig, *Shooting the Hippo (Death by Deficit and Other Canadian Myths)*, Toronto, Penguin Books, 1995, offers a fascinating analysis of how we got ourselves into the debt and deficit mess we face.

William G. Watson, "The View from the Right," in William Watson, John Richards and David Brown, *The Case for Change: Reinventing the Welfare State*, Toronto, C.D. Howe Institute, 1994, provides the right wing perspective on Canada's social state, complete with numerous examples to illustrate the abuses of the system.

The pros and cons of entrenching social rights in the constitution are explored by Brian Howe and Janet Ajzenstat in Charlton and Barker (eds.), *Crosscurrents: Contemporary Political Issues*, Scarborough, Nelson Canada, 1994.

A series of articles exploring Canada's social service state is found in the June 1996 issue of *Policy Options*, Montréal, Institute for Research on Public Policy.

Issues relating to Canada's social safety net are raised on almost a daily basis in Canada's newspapers, and are frequently examined in newsmagazines and periodicals.

Chapter 11

How Healthy Is Our Health Care System?

Objectives and Highlights

♦ To appreciate the main determinants of health and to evaluate the appropriateness of existing health care policies in light of these determinants.

♦ To examine the factors putting pressure on our existing health care system.

The field of health care illustrates many of the key issues which are discussed throughout this Guide.

As with so many areas of government responsibility, health care is very much a divided jurisdiction. The basic constitutional responsibility is provincial, but there has long been extensive federal involvement, through both funding and legislation (the Canada Health Act). Local governments also play an important role in providing services and enforcing regulations in support of a healthy living environment.

Canada's existing health care policies might more properly be termed "sickness care," given their focus on doctors and hospitals and treatment of illness. Consistent with the pattern that governments somehow find it easier to devote resources to solving problems after they have occurred, rather than preventing them in the first place, barely 5% of our "health" expenditures actually go to public health.

There is also no better example than health care for demonstrating how we can take more personal responsibility for our fate, instead of relying on government. As this chapter will explain, the main determinants of good health are largely within our power to provide.

Introduction

The Conservative Government in Ontario spent the beginning of 1996 buffeted by increasingly angry reactions from the public about changes being introduced in its omnibus Bill 26 legislation (The Savings and Restructuring Bill). Of particular concern were the changes relating to health care. There were criticisms of the Government's plans to cut spending on hospitals, to force doctors to relocate to under-served areas of the province, and to allow and encourage an American-style "for-profit" health care system to invade Ontario. The Harris Government should not have been surprised at the negative reaction. It had been watching and emulating the deficit-fighting approach of fellow-Conservative Ralph Klein in Alberta, and should have noted that it was cuts to hospitals and health care that finally put a dent in his prolonged popularity with the voting public. Apparently undaunted, however, Ontario has pushed ahead with a Health Services Restructuring Commission, charged with recommending hospital mergers and closures, thereby intensifying public concern in that province.

There is always a strong reaction in Canada to any perceived threat to our health care system. For many, that threat is seen as the possible development of a *two tier* system, in which the majority of Canadians would be covered by an underfunded public system, featuring long waiting lists, while those with money would get immediate and superior medical care by paying for it in private clinics. Few things besides the Stanley Cup unite Canadians as much as their conviction that the existing national health care system is one of the defining characteristics of this country, one of the things which distinguishes us from the less civilized Americans.

Hockey and Health Care

As we will learn in this chapter, however, the health of Canadians doesn't extend to clear vision on this issue. Instead, we have been viewing the health care issue through "rose-coloured glasses." Two fundamental points must be faced at the outset.

1. We don't have a national health care system; we have a national sickness care system. The overwhelming emphasis of government policies (as reflected in the commitment of resources) is on the treatment of sickness not the maintenance of health.

2. Whatever we call it, our national and publicly funded system has been under assault for some time now and the spectre of a two tier system for the rich and the poor is already largely upon us.

Support for these rather strong assertions will be provided as we trace the evolution of the government's involvement in "health care" in the following pages.

Tracing the Responsibility for Health Care

"The greatest contribution to the health of the nation over the past 150 years was made not by doctors and hospitals but by local governments."[1] This perhaps surprising statement recognizes the importance of the original *public health movement*. This movement was largely concerned with the prevention of contagious disease and epidemics — that is, with preventing sickness by keeping people healthy. To achieve this objective required action by local governments in dealing with sanitation, sewage and the treatment of drinking water. One of the first actions of the City of Toronto after its incorporation in 1834 was to establish a Board of Health. In Toronto and elsewhere, the public works department grew out of the public health movement, as did urban planning, parks, housing and social service functions.[2]

As the 20th century unfolded, however, powerful diagnostic and therapeutic tools such as x-rays, antibiotics and effective anaesthesia

---

[1]Jessie Parfit, *The Health of a City: Oxford 1770-1974*, Oxford, Amate Press, 1986, quoted in Richard Loreto and Trevor Price (eds.), *Urban Policy Issues*, Toronto, McClelland and Stewart Inc., 1990, p. 189.

[2]Trevor Hancock, Bernard Pouliot and Pierre Duplessis, "Public Health" in Loreto and Price, p. 192. This section is heavily based on Chapter 9 of this text.

appeared in medicine. Clinical supremacy (what was often called the medical model) took over from the public health movement and better health became equated — in the minds of the public and their political leaders — with doctors and hospitals. In response, the senior levels of government became increasingly involved in supporting these newer tools of health care. As a result, expenditures and emphasis on traditional prevention programs declined.

Government health care was first introduced in Saskatchewan in the 1940s under the CCF Government of Tommy Douglas — a point always cited by those who suggest that giving provinces more say in social services would allow for experimentation and innovation. Provincial health insurance programs were then introduced in various other provinces, including Ontario starting in 1957. Health care as a national program was introduced by a Liberal minority government in 1966 and received all party support. From the outset, it has involved providing transfer payments to provinces to cover part of the cost of hospitals and physicians' services.

Upward Pressure on Costs

Expenditures on hospital construction, the acquisition of new technology, drugs and payments to physicians have expanded dramatically throughout the 20th century. In contrast, the proportion of government spending devoted to public health, to the maintenance of health and prevention of disease, has been less than 5% for many years.

New technology and increasingly sophisticated treatment techniques are not holding down medical costs. They are having just the opposite effect. These "advances" have contributed to the life span of the ill, without contributing to the "health" of society.

Another major cost pressure is the aging of the population. A 1984 study by the Canadian Medical Association estimated that between 1981 and 2001, population aging would result in a doubling in the demand for beds in hospitals and chronic-care facilities, a 28% increase in physicians' services, and a 64% jump in the demand for home-care services. Demand for all these services was also projected to double again between 2001 and 2021.

According to demographer Robert Evans, people over 65 use over half of the hospital days in Canada, undergo about half the surgical procedures, account for roughly one-quarter of the physician billings and use about 40% of all prescription drugs — even though they represent only one-eighth of the population of Canada.[3] In addition, Canada's medical system considers nearly half of its bed capacity to be the "permanent residence" of elderly patients. As the "baby boomers" age and make senior citizens an increasing proportion of the total population of Canada, the upward pressure on health (sickness) care costs will steadily increase.

Another upward pressure on health costs relates to the issue of physicians' incomes and medical practices. According to Brooks,[4] our publicly run health care system has not changed the fact that most doctors continue to operate as independent business people with relative freedom to determine who they will accept as patients, where they will practice,[5] and the sort (and therefore cost) of care they prescribe. The fact that patients no longer pay directly for most medical services has not changed the *produce-for-profit* orientation of health care. It is not meant as any insult or criticism of their motives to point out that the economic self-interest of non-salaried doctors lies in maximizing the number of patients they see, specializing in areas where fees are highest, protecting their monopoly on health care, and prescribing expensive medication and procedures for their patients. Brooks adds that this produce for profit orientation is reinforced by the dominant value of the medical profession — that of professional autonomy, including autonomy to maximize income status.

---

[3]Quoted in *Alberta Report*, September 25, 1995, p. 12.

[4]Stephen Brooks, *Public Policy in Canada*, Toronto, McClelland and Stewart, 1993, p. 200.

[5]With some restrictions in British Columbia and with restrictions introduced in Ontario in early 1996 under Bill 26 (The Savings and Restructuring Bill).

The difficulties involved in this situation are illustrated by Ontario's recent experiences. The Ontario Government imposed a cap on doctors' incomes in 1996, after research indicated that 1200 doctors were billing OHIP more than $400 000 a year. Doctors were to receive only a portion of each dollar they earn over specified caps or ceilings, which varied from $251 000 to $399 000. For example, family physicians would receive only 67 cents of each dollar billed above a $251 000 Ontario Health Insurance Plan ceiling, only 33 cents of each dollar billed over $276 000 and only 25 cents of each dollar billed over $301 000.[6]

The medical profession responded angrily, with "job action" of various sorts, most of it relating to refusal to take new patients or otherwise to reduce medical services available. Doctors made the case that they were not looking for pay raises, only for adequate funding for health care. They pointed out that such funding had been fixed at 3.2% below what it was in Ontario in 1992, in spite of a population increase of 700 000 — 150 000 over 65 years of age.[7] Under the circumstances, they argued that the system is underfunded and that overexpenditures are inevitable. Rather than a pay increase, claimed the doctors, what they were seeking was funding to match the amount of service the citizens of Ontario require. Whatever the logic of these arguments, they still amounted to a request for additional pay for doctors, and increased costs for the health care system.

In late October 1996, the Harris Government caved in to the pressure from the doctors and agreed to reduce by more than two-thirds the salary clawback, beginning on November 1st. A formal agreement was reached in mid-December, under which the planned clawback on gross billings of doctors was reduced from 10% to 2.9%, and the billing ceiling before clawback for family physicians was raised from $251 000 to $300 000 — concessions which added nearly $50 million to the health care bill. No sooner had the agreement been struck,

---

[6]All figures from Lisa Priest, "Ontario slaps cap on doctors," *Toronto Star*, July 4, 1996.

[7]Letter from Gregory Baran, President, Kingston Academy of Medicine, to *Kingston Whig Standard*, October 9, 1996.

however, than the Ontario Medical Association was announcing that the government only had until February 28, 1997 to come up with a new deal that will fully restore doctors' incomes. The issue is unresolved at the time of writing.

Paying for Health Care

As these upward pressures on health costs have intensified, governments have become less and less willing to find the necessary funds, given their preoccupation with debt and deficit reduction.

As noted in earlier chapters, the federal government's financial support for health care was provided until recently under Established Program Financing or EPF, a block grant introduced in 1977. In the first decade of EPF there were concerns about a decline in provincial contributions to health care (and education), as provinces took advantage of the relatively unconditional nature of the transfer payment to meet other priorities.

One of the federal responses was the passage of the Canada Health Act of 1984, with its financial penalty for provinces allowing *extra-billing* by doctors or user charges by hospitals. The Act provides for a reduction in provincial transfer payments by an amount equal to the total value of these "outlawed" activities. These reductions were applied against Ontario in the mid-1980s, forcing the Ontario Government to confront extra-billing, precipitating a strike by doctors in 1986, but ultimately resulting in compliance with the federal requirements.

Ten years later, this scene was repeated, with Alberta agreeing not to allow private health care clinics to extra-bill patients seeking essential medical care, after a nine month standoff that cost the province almost $4 million in penalties.[8] The relatively modest size of the financial penalty reflects the erosion in federal transfers for health which has occurred over the past decade — as summarized below.

---

[8]Brian Laghi, "Alberta gives in to Ottawa on billing," *Globe and Mail*, May 31, 1996.

The declining federal support for health care was consistent with the thrust of Bill C-69, a very important piece of federal legislation passed quietly at the end of 1990 when most Canadians were pre-occupied with the Middle East war.[9] This legislation set out the federal government's plan to phase out totally its cash transfers in support of health care. Because of variations in the funding formula which need not concern us,[10] the pace of this withdrawal would vary by province. But plans underlying C-69 anticipated the elimination of all federal cash transfers for health care for most provinces by around the year 2000. This prospect raised the concern that if the federal government didn't have any money to withhold, it would hardly be in a position to enforce the Canada Health Act.

Presumably in response to this widespread concern, the federal Liberal Government elected in 1993 has guaranteed a minimum cash transfer as part of its latest changes in federal support for health care. Under these changes, announced in the budget of February 1995, both EPF and the Canada Assistance Plan (CAP) have been lumped together into a new unconditional payment called the Canada Health and Social Transfer (CHST) beginning in 1996-97.

During the transition year of 1995-96, the transfers to the provinces for health and social services are $29.7 billion, essentially the same amount as would have applied under the old EPF and CAP programs. However, in 1996-97 funding to the provinces under the new CHST is $2.5 billion less than it would have been under the old arrangements. A further reduction of $4.5 billion will occur in 1997-98. The federal government has committed to a minimum or "floor" contribution of no less than $11 billion a year under the CHST, as an assurance that it will continue to have the financial leverage to en-

---

[9]This discussion is based on remarks by Ted Ball, *Will Our Medicare System Survive Federal and Provincial Reforms?*, June 13, 1991.

[10]EPF transfers were a combination of cash and "tax points" which gave the provinces money by way of additional tax revenues. Since income levels and tax yields vary by province, so does the point at which diminished federal transfers would be totally covered by the tax points — without any federal cash payment required.

force the Canada Health Act (and, for that matter, the prohibition against residency requirements for welfare eligibility which had been part of the Canada Assistance Plan).

The provincial governments have been responding in kind. They have been cutting their expenditures on health care, partly through reducing the number of hospital beds and through closing some hospitals. Alberta had been in the forefront of this activity, although increased public resistance seems to have convinced Premier Klein that he has gone as far as he can with health care cuts for the moment. The NDP Government in Saskatchewan, the birthplace of government-funded health care, has closed 52 hospitals, mostly in rural areas, but has recently announced a $40 million increase in its 1996-97 health budget.[11] By coincidence, Manitoba has cut its health care budget by $40 million and is closing some 400 acute care beds, mostly in Winnipeg hospitals.[12] The Québec Government announced several hospital closings in Montreal within days of the referendum on separation. The Ontario Government has announced that funding for hospitals will be reduced by $1.3 billion over the three years from 1996-97 to 1998-99, and Bill 26 (The Savings and Restructuring Bill passed in January 1996) gives the Minister of Health new powers to close hospitals by executive decree. A number of hospital closings and mergers have been announced in Ontario during 1996, and more are pending as a result of the ongoing work of the Health Services Restructuring Commission.

Reduced Access to Health Care?

As federal financial support declines, and as the provinces gain new freedom under the Canada Health and Social Transfer block grant, there are fears that we will see a return to extra-billing, opting out and

---

[11]David Roberts, "Provinces take opposite approaches to health," *Globe and Mail*, August 22, 1996.

[12]*Ibid.*

other measures which the federal government had previously out-lawed by threatening to withhold transfer payments. Ontario has in-troduced new user charges related to health care. Seniors earning more than $16 000 a year as singles and $24 000 as families are for the first time forced to pay a $100 per year user fee, plus up to $6.11 per prescription. Welfare recipients and low income seniors pay a $2 prescription fee. Through such means the Government presumably hopes to recoup some of the $1.3 billion it spends annually on drugs for seniors and welfare recipients.[13]

Ontario's Bill 26 (The Savings and Restructuring Bill) gives the Minister of Health extensive new powers to control where doctors may locate, to decide which medical services it will insure, and for each one insured, to decide the payment that doctors will receive. For example, Bill 26 would allow the government to make cholesterol testing an insured service, but only for people over 50; it could de-clare cholesterol testing to be insured, but set the payment at zero.[14] Since doctors respond to prices like everyone else, these provisions give the Minister of Health the power to force doctors to practice medicine as he deems appropriate. While the objective of limiting health costs is laudable, people are understandably nervous about politicians and bureaucrats dictating or influencing what medical ser-vices their doctors provide for them.

We are also witnessing a sharp increase in privately operated ambulatory clinics and the prevalence of private labs — both sug-gesting that a two tier health care system is already evolving. Accord-ing to critics, Ontario's Bill 26 legislation will lead to a proliferation of American for-profit health care clinics, altering fundamentally the public health care system which has been a central feature of Cana-dian life. They point to provisions in Bill 26 which would allow American for-profit companies to tender bids to establish independent health clinics alongside Canadian nonprofit organizations. Critics also worry about the plans to allow drug prices to be deregulated and to be

---

[13]These figures are all from William Walker, "U.S.-Style Health Care Heads North," *Toronto Star*, December 9, 1995, B4.

[14]Examples for Editorial in the *Toronto Star*, January 27, 1996.

market-driven as they are in the United States. There are close to 1000 non-hospital clinics in Ontario, funded by OHIP, and providing services that include diagnostic tests such as ultra-sound and tuberculosis and pneumonia tests, plus treatment facilities for laser dermatology, plastic surgery, and gynaecological surgery.[15] The Independent Health Facilities Act has given preference to Canadian, non-profit companies in the tender process for these non-hospital clinics. Bill 26 removes that preference — to open up the market and to provide a level playing field, according to the Government.

The Klein government in Alberta has argued for increased privatization of the system. It allowed private clinics for cataract surgery to operate and charge patients $1000 over the provincial reimbursement fee. Premier Klein stated that he might sell some of Alberta's surplus hospitals to private companies which could offer "for-profit health care" for Americans. [16]

Two Tier Already Here?

Delegates to the Canadian Medical Association's annual meeting in August 1996 came close to endorsing a two-tier system for health care. Proponents argued that such a step would recognize that Canadians and their private insurers are increasingly paying for their medical treatment. These private expenses — for everything from drugs to physiotherapy to long-term institutional care — exceeded $20 billion in 1994. That figure represents more than 28% of the total spending on health care that year, and demonstrates that Canadians don't get equal "one-tier" care under the existing medicare system. Cutbacks have led to "passive privatization" that hurts the poor most. A Canadian Medical Association background document indicated, for example, that people are waiting longer for publicly insured physiotherapy and psychotherapy. There are frequent media reports about

---

[15]This section is based on Walker, *op. cit.* p. B1.

[16]Joan Price Boase, "Trends in Social Policy: Toward the Millennium," in Christopher Dunn (ed.), *Provinces: Canadian Provincial Politics*, Peterborough, Broadview Press, 1996, p. 467.

long waiting lists for surgery and various forms of medical treatment.[17]

♦ **Something to Think About**

If passive privatization is occurring anyway, should we face reality and plan for a two tier system of health care, public and private?
What are the pros and cons of such a step?

Under a two-tier system, patients would continue to have access to publicly funded, "free" core medical services, but could obtain treatment from private clinics if they wanted to pay for it, either from their own pockets or from private insurance. The private clinics, proponents argue, would divert some patients away from the overloaded public health care system. Since governments aren't going to provide more money for health care, the only answer is to move to a two tier system. Those with money will "jump the queue" and obtain faster service from private clinics. But their departure will reduce the current overload on the publicly funded system.

However, any scheme which introduces fees or charges for medicare touches a nerve for many Canadians. Critics claim that "the direct charge concept is an idea whose time has gone." According to most literature on the subject:

> extra billing, user fees, and the like impede equality of access to medical care, deter utilization by the poor, redistribute the burden of paying for health care from taxpayers to the sick, violate the principles on which the Canadian health care system was established, do not make a contribution to overall expenditure control, and serve the interests of not the public, but providers, private insurance companies, and provincial governments."[18]

---

[17]Mark Kennedy, "Doctors eye two-tier system," *Toronto Star*, August 18, 1996, on which this section is based.

[18]Mike Burke and Michael Stevenson, "The Politics and Political Science of Health Care in Canada," in Paul Fox and Graham White (eds.), *Politics: Canada*, 8th edition, Whitby, McGraw-Hill Ryerson Limited, 1995, p. 570.

Critics of a two tier system also argue that it inevitably leads to a deterioration of the first or public system.[19] Doctors would steer their patients toward the second or private system because it would pay them more. Patients, in turn, would take out private insurance to cover their costs for this second tier. Gradually, they would resent having to pay taxes for those left behind in the first tier, and would be inclined to support candidates and parties promising to cut funding for that tier. As a result, the first tier would deteriorate and waiting lists would get longer, not shorter.

The fierce Canadian attachment to medicare may reflect more myth than reality.[20] We find our identity (and our distinctiveness from Americans) in a health care system that may exist more in theory than in the reality of hospital closings and waiting lists for medical services. It is also true that public and private systems co-exist in a number of other jurisdictions. For example, Great Britain has a network of private hospitals, Sweden still imposes user fees, France allows private hospitals and over-billing, and 10% of the German population uses private health services.[21]

On the other hand, the best-known example of private health care, that found in the United States, is hardly an inspiring one. According to the most recent figures from the Organization for Economic Cooperation and Development, Canada in 1994 spent 9.8% of its Gross Domestic Product on health, compared to 14.2% for the U.S.[22] Even

---

[19]This section is based on Editorial, "Two tier system not the answer," *Toronto Star*, January 3, 1997.

[20]Although reality may be intruding, given the fact that (as discussed in Chapter 1) almost half of those responding to the *Maclean's* year-end survey for 1996 were reconciled to the emergence of a two tier health care system and found it "acceptable." Joe Chidley, "Reduced expectations," *Maclean's*, December 30, 1996, p. 23.

[21]According to Alain Dubuc, as quoted in Lysiane Gagnon, "Courchene plan crumbled before the unity train arrived in Jasper," *Globe and Mail*, August 24, 1996.

[22]David Crane, "Myths, money interests fuel bid to gut medicare," *Toronto Star*, August 24, 1996.

with the much larger proportion of expenditures, the American "system" leaves 35 million people without any health care coverage (since they do not have private plans). Moreover, health statistics show that, on average, Canadians are healthier than Americans.

Before we congratulate ourselves, however, we must face the fact that Swedes and Japanese are healthier than Canadians and yet spend much less on health care than we do.[23] Instead of simply focusing on the costs of health care, or the merits of public versus private systems, we need to address the underlying question of what factors influence our health.

Understanding the Determinants of Health

While they are the focus of almost all health expenditures, we need to face the fact that hospitals and doctors have very little to do with our health — except to the extent that they may provide some education or counselling about maintaining a healthy lifestyle. Hospitals and doctors provide valuable, even life-saving, treatment of sickness or illness, but they are not are involved in health care.

According to the 1986 Ottawa Charter on Health Promotion, the prerequisites for health include peace, shelter, education, food, income, a stable ecosystem, social justice and equity. The Premier's Council on Health, Well-Being and Social Justice in Ontario came to similar conclusions. According to the Chair of the Determinants of Health Committee of the Premier's Council, *"Canadians should be more concerned about job creation than hospital bed closures, if we are to improve the health of our population."*[24] The findings of this Committee are that human health and longevity are clearly linked to national wealth, household income, employment status, social support networks, level of education, early childhood development and the quality of our natural and built environment.

---

[23]*Ibid.*

[24]Dr. Andrew Pipe, in a Press Release dated January 20, 1993.

A report in the *Canadian Medical Association Journal*[25] drawing on 15 years of global research finds a strong link between unemployment and health. Job loss brings a greater risk of physical and mental illness and also a greater risk of mortality. According to the report, unemployed people are more likely than employed people to visit physicians, take medication or be admitted to hospital.

Dr. Fraser Mustard, a member of the Ontario Premier's Council on Health, emphasizes that health gains can best be achieved by integrating social and economic policies. He points out that life expectancy in Scandinavian countries, where governments have consciously used social policy to provide equal opportunities, is higher than in countries with higher average incomes, such as the United States. He adds that research has shown that when income gaps are narrower, such as in Japan and Sweden, the population as a whole is healthier.[26]

Past experience indicates that health care costs can be curbed by such actions as compulsory use of seatbelts in cars, measures to discourage smoking and to reduce the exposure of non-smokers to second-hand smoke, campaigns for moderation in drinking, and the pursuit of healthy lifestyles, including a nutritionally sound diet and regular exercise.[27] A study in Alameda, California disclosed the remarkable results that men lived an average of 11 years longer if they followed at least five or six of the rather common sense behaviours listed below, as compared to men who followed only one.

i) eat regularly and not between meals
ii) eat breakfast
iii) get seven or eight hours sleep every night
iv) keep 'normal' weight
v) refrain from smoking
vi) drink only moderately
vii) exercise regularly

---

[25]Quoted in *Kingston Whig Standard*, September 9, 1995.

[26]Quoted in Press Release, *op. cit.*

[27]Crane, *op. cit.*

To take one more example, there is considerable scientific data to show that the care provided to infants has a profound influence on the physical development of their brain, their coping skills and their social behaviour, with long term implications for how well they do in school and later life and how healthy they are as adults.[28]

The evidence is overwhelming. Instead of waiting until people get sick, we need a health care system which focuses on keeping people healthy. We need to allocate our resources to the prevention of sickness, not its treatment. Of course there will always be a need for doctors, hospitals and medical research, to combat illnesses which cannot be avoided. But so much of the health care problem could be avoided through different government policies and through individuals taking more responsibility for their own health.

For the most part, unfortunately, government policies are tragically misdirected. Consider the shocking fact that the United States ranks 20th in the world in infant mortality, ahead only of Greece among industrialized democracies.[29] The average hospital cost for low-birth-weight babies is $500 000, at least 250 times the average cost of medical care during pregnancy. Careful medical studies prove that preventive care during pregnancy saves money; estimates range from $2 to $10 for every $1 invested. Yet 20 million women and infants in the United States have no health insurance. Even so, President Clinton's efforts to introduce a national health plan were defeated early in his term after public support softened in the face of powerful lobbying efforts, many on behalf of large private health companies, health insurance companies and the like.

The record is scarcely better in Canada, with government policies which have directly contributed to sickness and increased health care costs. The federal government has actively promoted unemployment in Canada over the past decade or so, first by a high interest rate policy related to its obsession with fighting inflation, and then with its spending cuts related to the new objective of fighting the debt and

---

[28]*Ibid.*

[29]This example is taken from David Osborne and Ted Gaebler, *Reinventing Government*, New York, Penguin Books, 1992, p. 220.

deficit. Provincial governments, led by Alberta and Ontario, have recently adopted a "slash and burn" approach in support of their debt reduction targets. They will claim that they must get spending under control as a prerequisite to growth and job creation. However well motivated, their actions are undermining the very features which are widely held to be the key determinants of health!

Once again, we are struck by the fact that, in government, "everything connects." As David Foot reminds us, "a mountain of evidence exists to prove that unemployment and poverty are the prime causes of poor health, yet this fact is rarely discussed in the context of our health care system."[30]

Concluding Observations

Any reduction in hospital beds or closing of hospitals can mean a major inconvenience or a serious threat to someone who is already ill. But, as elements of an overall system of **health** care, it must be understood that hospitals and doctors are not key players. If we shift government resources from the traditional spending on the treatment of illness to job creation, education about nutrition and healthy lifestyles, pollution control, and provision of supports for the family and community, we can have a far greater impact on the long term health of the population of Canada, and at far less cost.

It is noteworthy that if we pursued this course of action we might also see a shift in the relative importance of the different levels of government and a return to the kind of prominent role which local governments played over 100 years ago during the first public health movement. As discussed at the beginning of this chapter, the medical model of health care brought a shift from the prevention of disease to the treatment of illness by doctors and hospitals, and a shift from the local government level to increasing provincial and federal involve-

---

[30]David Foot (with Daniel Stoffman), *Boom, Bust & Echo*, Toronto, Macfarlane Walter & Ross, 1996, p. 180.

ment. As the senior levels withdraw their funding and pass the buck to the lower levels, will local governments re-emerge to play a significant role?

To some extent, this has already happened. There has been a revival of the "healthy city" concept, beginning in Toronto in the mid-1980s and repeated in projects throughout Europe promoted by the World Health Organization.[31] As should be clear from the preceding discussions, a healthy city is as much a function of housing, transportation, urban design, public works, parks, economic development, education, police or social services as it is of the health care system, **if not more so**. In Toronto's case, a strategic planning exercise identified the need to reduce inequities in health care opportunities by addressing problems of homelessness, hunger, poverty, unemployment and illiteracy, creating physical environments for health through health-conscious urban planning, and creating supporting social environments.[32]

Ontario municipalities have been given an expanded role with respect to health care as a result of changes introduced by the Ontario Government in January 1997. A number of responsibilities and costs are being transferred to the municipal level to offset the increased education costs being assumed by the province. As part of this shift, municipalities will take on 50% of the cost of long term care and 100% of the costs for public health programs. But many other expenditure commitments are also being shifted downward. Given the near obsession that has developed at the local level about holding the line on any increases in the property tax, it remains to be seen what municipal capacity and commitment there will be to provide adequate financial support for these programs.

Ultimately, unless a better informed public begins to demand more intelligent priority setting and spending from government, we are apt to see a continued erosion of the traditional spending on sickness care **without** an offsetting increase in expenditures on the real determinants of health.

---

[31]This section is based on Hancock et al., *op. cit.*, pp. 199-201.

[32]*Ibid.*, p. 200.

The Last Word

Definition of Terms and Concepts

Extra-billing:
Charges by doctors which exceed the fee approved by the provincial health insurance program.

Medicare:
Canada's national health care program, under which Canadians receive "free" hospital care and physicians' services on the basis of financing provided by the provinces, supported by federal funding and legislated standards under the Canada Health Act.

Public Health Movement:
A series of initiatives related to the prevention of illness, through public education and promotion of a healthy living environment.

Points to Ponder

1. Are the main causes of our growing health care expenditures "internal" to the system (and caused by such factors as doctors' incomes) or "external" (and caused by such factors as advances in medical technology and an aging population)?

2. If Canada has already moved toward "passive privatization" and some elements of a two-tier system of health care, should we formalize this development and encourage private, fee-for-service clinics as a way of freeing up our over-extended public health care system?

3. What would you recommend as the key components of a new government initiative on "health care" for the 21st century?

4. How would you rate your personal lifestyle in terms of keeping you healthy and focusing on prevention of illness? (Be honest!)

For Further Reading

Stephen Brooks, *Public Policy in Canada*, 2nd edition, Toronto, McClelland and Stewart, 1993, examines health policy in the context of a general chapter (8) dealing with social policy in Canada.

Mike Burke and Michael Stevenson, "The Politics and Political Science of Health Care in Canada," in Paul Fox and Graham White, *Politics: Canada*, 8th edition, Whitby, McGraw-Hill Ryerson Limited, 1995, pp. 564-576, examines the current state of health policy and government support in Canada.

The article on public health by Hancock, Pouliot and Duplessis in Richard Loreto and Trevor Price (eds.), *Urban Policy Issues*, Toronto, McClelland and Stewart, 1990, pp. 189-206, provides a good explanation of the important role played by local governments in promoting and protecting health (as opposed to treating sickness).

Chapter 12

You and Your Governments: Lessons Learned and Actions Planned

Objectives and Highlights

- ♦ To summarize key findings of this Guide.

- ♦ To identify specific actions you can take to participate as an informed citizen in a democratic society.

One hundred years ago, Prime Minister Wilfrid Laurier proclaimed that the 20th century belongs to Canada. It has been a very good century in many ways, notwithstanding two world wars and a severe economic depression in between. Overall, Canada prospered and built a modern social services state which included various programs to help less fortunate citizens and less fortunate regions.

Our governing institutions also developed and matured throughout this period. For much of the 20th century, this development took the form of an increasing concentration of power within the executive branch, centred on the position of Prime Minister/Premier, the Cabinet and the bureaucracy. Over the past thirty years or so, various reforms have strengthened the watchdog role of opposition parties and redressed the balance of power somewhat within our legislatures. The Charter has helped to redress the balance in society, by shifting some power to groups which previously had little influence over Parliament and the parties and interests which controlled Parliament.

As Canada approaches the 21st century, however, it faces some fundamental choices about the kind of country it is and wants to be. The final chapter of this Guide serves to remind you of those choices and of the choices you can make as citizens in a democratic society.

Introduction

B y some measures, Canada has done very well for itself during the 20th century. The Canadian economy is seventh largest among Western industrialized nations, in terms of its total output of goods and services, the Gross Domestic Product. In 1992, total GDP amounted to $687.3 billion even after the recession of the early 1990s. On a per capita basis, this yielded Canadians the second highest incomes in the world, after the Americans. Moreover, in both 1992 and 1994, the United Nations human development index cited Canada as the most desirable place in the world to live.

The relationships between Canadian citizens and their governments are undergoing fundamental change at the present time, however. For the past 50 years or so, Canada has operated on the basis of an understanding or unwritten agreement that might be summarized as follows:

> Citizens made a contribution to work and to pay taxes in return for state-funded insurance against temporary unemployment, old age, poor health, and certain family responsibilities. The state committed to introduce policies that would ensure high levels of employment.[1]

As the 20th century draws to a close, however, it appears that neither side is living up to its part of the bargain.

On the one hand, citizens have convinced themselves that governments are so wasteful that they don't deserve our hard-earned tax dollars, thereby justifying various forms of tax avoidance and a flourishing "underground economy." Social programs that were intended as a temporary insurance against economic uncertainty are being claimed as entitlements by a certain portion of society which appears locked into government support stretching over lifetimes and even generations. On the other hand, governments have arguably done little to mount a concerted attack on Canada's serious unemployment prob-

---

[1]Judith Maxwell, "Rethinking Government," in *Perspectives on Public Management*, Ottawa, Canadian Centre for Management Development, 1994, p. 49.

lems, stretching back over a couple of decades. In addition, governments today stand poised to dismantle much of the social safety net built up over the past fifty years.

A substantial segment of the public appears supportive of, or reconciled to, the government downsizing underway, having embraced the prevailing philosophy that government is the problem and that a tax freeze represents the highest and best achievement to which politicians can aspire.

Governments Have a Purpose

One of the dangers we face at present is that people seem to have forgotten why we invented government, why it is desirable to have "public goods" which we all help to pay for through our taxes. Instead, too many have accepted uncritically the right-wing perspective that somehow virtually all spending by government is inherently less desirable than spending by and on the private sector. The less government, the better, is the refrain. The more money left in private hands, the better off we will all be, we are told.

We Need a Balance of Public & Private

Yet we should know by now that serious problems arise when we fail to maintain an adequate balance between public goods and private goods. In such a society, paradoxes abound. With taxes kept sufficiently low, people can afford increasingly fancy automobiles, even if the streets and highways on which these cars must travel are not well maintained. Children have ready access to television and various forms of entertainment, even if their schools are deteriorating and plagued by violence. People have no shortage of food, alcohol, cigarettes, and other "creature comforts," but lack adequate medical and hospital care when health problems arise from the excesses of consumption. The signs of this kind of dichotomy are increasingly present today, but the book which raised this issue of public-private imbalance is some forty years old! It is *The Affluent*

Society, by Canadian John Kenneth Galbraith, published in 1958.

Another perceptive analyst of government, Jim Sharpe of Oxford University, provides a vivid illustration of the value of public versus private goods in the local government context when he writes that:

> ... although the local government bill is not small, it provides education, public health, social services, highways, libraries, fire, police, refuse collection, and a whole range of other public services which most people need and demand, at a total cost that is no larger than the amount we collectively spend on such things as wine and beer, cigarettes, eye shadow, tennis rackets and a flutter on the horses.[2]

North Americans will spend more than a **billion** dollars this year on the latest video games and associated high tech reincarnations of "Pac Man." Yet we will continue to debate whether or not we can afford welfare, public housing, public health, environmental programs and other services which form part of a basic standard of living in a civilized society. Obviously, we can afford public services if we believe in them and are prepared to support them with our taxes.

What we cannot afford, paradoxically, is some of the tragically short-sighted spending cuts being made by governments today. A recurring theme of this Guide is that **everything connects**. Yet governments continue to take actions without apparent regard for the consequences or the longer term implications. Perhaps the best (worst) example is found in the misplaced priorities governments have in focusing on treating problems after they have occurred, rather than preventing problems before they arise. This pattern has been particularly evident in the health care field, where about 95% of government spending is actually directed to sickness care.

It is also reflected in government actions which slash social spending today in ways that will only serve to increase social problems and government spending tomorrow. Not only have governments failed to follow through with promises for a national day care program, but they have also cut support for day care spaces and for junior kindergarten programs. Leading experts, like Dr. Fraser Mus-

---

[2]L. J. Sharpe (ed.), *The Local Fiscal Crisis in Western Europe, Myths and Realities*, London, Sage Publications, 1981, p. 224.

tard of the Canadian Institute for Advanced Research, emphasize that quality child care, specifically pre-school care, is one of the three or four major social instruments for correcting the effects of bad parenting, severely dysfunctional family life, social trauma and violent behaviour.[3]

For some reason, we have difficulty getting through to politicians that what is invested in child care now carries a huge return down the road, saving great sums that would otherwise be spent on police, prosecutors, judges, and jails. Yet long term studies in the United States have concluded that $1 spent on quality pre-school care saves $7 that would have been spent later on welfare, policing, social services and prisons.[4]

♦ Something to Think About

How are we to judge an Ontario government on the eve of the 21st century which claims a need to cut funding for child care and education while embracing the concept of "boot camps" and "chain gangs?" If we can find the money to punish people after they get in trouble, why can't we find the money to support them when they are starting out in life?

By all means, let's demand that governments be careful with our money. Let's criticize examples of wasteful or excessive spending. Let's remind governments to set priorities and to concentrate expenditures where they can do the most good, rather than trying to be all things to all people. But we can do all this without succumbing to a mindless attack on all government spending, to a general support for any government cuts because somehow less government must be better. When we cut government spending we are also cutting pro-

---

[3]Michael Valpy, "Child Care: Why Politicians Still Matter," *Globe and Mail*, January 25, 1996.

[4]Michael Valpy, "Taking it out on Child Care," *Globe and Mail*, January 24, 1996.

grams and services being provided to us. When we reduce the number of politicians, we also reduce the number of elected representatives available to us in our democratic system.

This Guide has certainly not suggested that our government system is without flaws. There are reasons to be concerned about the concentration of power within our government system and also within our broader Canadian society. Strong interest groups, especially representing the business community, may wield undue influence over politicians and political parties — not least because of the extensive financial support they provide for election campaigns. Our disciplined party system may deliver too much power to any Cabinet in a majority government situation, thereby reducing the significance of the principle of responsible government and the effectiveness of the watchdog role.

It is understandable if you are disillusioned or cynical about government. But the answer is not to withdraw your involvement and participation. Whatever its faults, our government system is all you have to provide collective benefits for Canadian society.

What Difference Can You Make?

Even if you agree with many of the points raised in this Guide, you are apt to hold the view that one person can't make any impact. But you can make a difference — **if** you get involved. Whatever its faults, our government system is still a democratic one, in which the Canadian people have the ultimate say.

If you want evidence of that point, look no further than the incredible results of the 1993 federal election. The Progressive Conservative party, the party of Sir John A. Macdonald, the party which won back-to-back majority governments in the 1980s, was reduced to two seats in the House of Commons! Look at the more recent and even more dramatic example of the actions taken by thousands of Canadians on the eve of the Québec referendum in October 1995. Their strong show of support culminating in the huge rally in Montréal is held by many to have been a key factor in avoiding (barely) a yes vote for separation and all of the disruptive consequences that could have followed from that.

It is suggested that you (and I and all of us) can make a difference in two main ways:

1. by taking more personal responsibility for your own life and success; and
2. by taking more personal responsibility for the behaviour of your governments.

Take More Responsibility for Yourself

It is somewhat ironic or paradoxical to suggest that the first thing that can make a difference with government is to rely on it less. The fact remains that we have relied on governments too much in the past, which has not been good for individuals or for governments. While this Guide has tried to defend the value of government spending, it has also emphasized that we need to give more attention to preventing problems in the first place, rather than trying to solve them after they occur. Much of this prevention can take place through individuals practising more personal and self-responsibility, not waiting for governments to do something.

A few examples follow. They may appear obvious, almost trite, and they are not applicable to everyone. But, imagine the difference it would make if all those who could do so followed these examples.

If you are currently a student, stay in school. Finish your program of study. Complete sufficient education or skill training to help make you employable in the new information economy. If you are not currently in school, but lack job skills, take advantage of any opportunities to get those skills. Yes, governments should and can do more to help create jobs. But most of the jobs which are created will require education and training. Do your part to make yourself employable!

If you have been blessed with good health, do your part to stay that way. This is almost entirely within your control and it needn't cost much money. There is ample evidence to show that eating and sleeping regularly, exercising, not smoking and drinking only moderately are far more important in maintaining good health than any number of doctors or hospitals. We still need the latter for those suffering from illness, accidents or the infirmities of old age. If you are among the fortunate majority who have good health, however, it is largely in your hands — not the government's hands — whether or not you continue to enjoy it.

Take some responsibility for the quality of your neighbourhood. Are you involved in neighbourhood watch? Have you and your neighbours met recently with the police to discuss ways of minimizing crime, not just detecting it? Have you and your neighbours considered taking on any community projects, such as maintaining a neighbourhood park, looking after an outdoor ice rink each winter, painting the local bus shelter or laying sod for a new ball diamond. This kind of volunteer effort used to be widespread and is still found in many small communities. Are you part of that kind of self-help effort, or are you the kind who sits at home saying "why doesn't the government do something about...?"

You may feel that you've paid your taxes and it is now government's responsibility to provide the necessary services. Why should you have to volunteer time to do the government's job? Part of the explanation is that governments have gone from "doing more with more" to "doing less with less." But there is more involved than just supplementing or supplanting the traditional role of government. When you and your fellow citizens work on a ball diamond or a park, you develop a sense of ownership. The site becomes "your" park or "your" ball diamond. It always was, of course, even when built by government, but you didn't see it that way. With this new sense of ownership, a typical result is a reduction in vandalism. You and your neighbours won't stand for someone damaging "your" park.

However "preachy" it may sound, if we all took more personal and community responsibility, there would be fewer problems to divert the scarce resources of government.

Take More Responsibility for Government

You're too busy. You are juggling personal, family and work responsibilities. You're attempting to exercise more of the personal and community responsibility outlined in the previous section. Why do you have to keep an eye on government too? Isn't paying your taxes to support government services enough?

Since the government is spending **your money**, you should be keeping an eye on your investment. People who buy shares in private companies often look at annual reports and may attend shareholders' meetings. Should we not take at least as much interest in the shares we hold in government?

How Do You Rate?

Listed below are questions relating to **ten basic activities** that are part of public participation in a system of democratic government. Unless you can truthfully answer yes to most of these questions, you are not taking advantage of your rights and you are not fulfilling your obligations as a citizen.

1   Do you vote in each federal, provincial and municipal election?

Only a little over 2/3 of those eligible bother to vote in federal and provincial elections, fewer than 40% vote in municipal elections, and only about 1/5 vote in school board elections. Municipal and school board elections, at least in Ontario, have been shifted from December to November on the grounds that inclement weather was affecting the voter turnout. When the right to vote is granted in previously dictatorial nations around the world, it is impressive to see the news reports of people lining up for hours, sometimes with gunfire around them, usually with threats of violence, all for the opportunity to have a say in their government. Yet democracy in Canada is apparently too fragile to withstand an early winter snowfall!

2   Do you phone or write to your MP, MLA, or municipal councillor about any issues that concern you?

There is a growing cynicism about government and a widespread view that once in power politicians forget about us until the next election. But, how many people take the time to contact their elected members and to pass on their views and concerns? If you never try, how can you be sure that the politicians are uninterested and unresponsive?

Don't forget the *"Guide to Government"* Directory included in Chapter 2. Keeping a completed copy of that directory by your phone or on your desk provides you with a handy reference sheet when you want to contact someone in government.

3   *Do you ever sign petitions which are being sent to government?*

This is a particularly easy one to do — too easy in fact. Scarcely a week goes by that one does not encounter someone in a shopping centre or other main thoroughfare inviting signatures on a petition which will be going to "the government." The petition is usually in opposition to something, and it may well be that many who quickly sign as they hurry about their business have not given enough thought to the petition or to any other points of view which might be pertinent. Nonetheless, with all of its possible imperfections, it is a form of public participation.

4   *Do you ever attend government meetings?*

This is a broad question which could extend to attendance during "question period" at Ottawa or in your provincial capital, attendance during a committee meeting of the federal or provincial government or, most likely, attendance at a meeting of your municipal council or school board. (Catching a couple of minutes of your municipal council on cable television while channel-surfing doesn't give you a yes for this question.)

Attending a government meeting should extend beyond being part of a delegation to your municipal council. The trouble with delegations is that those participating present their concerns during their allotted time and then leave the meeting. This brief appearance doesn't give you any indication about how your municipal council conducts its business. It doesn't give you any opportunity to see and hear your elected representatives in action. It provides no insight into the issues and challenges that require local action. Attending a meeting means just that; it means staying through the meeting, or a least a good portion of it, whether or not you (or your group) are on the agenda as a delegation.

5   *Do you ever go to budget meetings?*

Here again, this question relates particularly to municipal governments, which in many instances have been holding open budget meetings for some years now. What an opportunity to educate yourself in the pressures and priorities which are found in your local community. A budget meeting will usually include high drama and low comedy, and a good mixture of pathos as well. It will be lengthy, confusing, ultimately exhausting. But it will also give you a new appreciation of the very difficult work done by our elected representatives. It will make you think twice before launching into the standard speech about all the waste in government. It might even make you concede, however grudgingly, that some increase in taxes now and then can be justified.

6   Do you ever attend a political party meeting or social event?

If meetings, especially municipal budget sessions, are not for you, there are options. The federal and provincial parties have constituency associations, made up of local people from your community. Depending on how active the party is in your constituency, there are likely to be at least annual functions. Many are social events also designed as fund-raisers and as ways of attracting new members. Attending such events is a way of participating in the political process while enjoying an evening out.

7   Have you ever joined a political party and worked for a candidate seeking the party nomination?

This is an extension of the previous point. As we discussed earlier in the Guide, those running for elected office provincially and federally almost always seek the nomination of a political party, without which their chances of victory are very slim. Most of these nominations are decided by the local constituency associations. So, besides attending an occasional social gathering, you can become much more directly involved in the political process if you work on behalf of a candidate. You will gain valuable experience and an increased appreciation for the demands of political office.

8   Have you ever campaigned for a candidate for elected office?

This may sound similar to the preceding activity, but it is different in one critical respect. Campaigning on behalf of someone who wants to win the nomination from a particular political party brings you into contact with people who share a common belief in that party — even though they may differ as to the best candidate to represent it. Going on to the next stage and campaigning for the successful party candidate brings you into contact with the public at large, with people who don't like your candidate or party, even with people who don't like any candidates or parties (or people knocking on their door).

While parties aren't usually involved, campaigning on behalf of a candidate for municipal office can be an equally challenging experience. It is all too easy to criticize politicians but when you "walk a mile in their shoes" on the campaign trail you gain an appreciation of the process through which they go to attain elected office.

9   Have you ever sought/obtained an appointment as a citizen member of a board or committee?

While such appointments are made by all levels of government, they are especially conspicuous at the local level. Most municipalities place ads in the local newspapers each fall, inviting applications from citizens interested in being appointed to serve on such bodies as planning advisory committees, industrial commissions, community centre boards and committees of adjustment. Being appointed to one of these local governing bodies is an excellent way of serving in government without the rigours of the election process. It allows public-spirited citizens to make an important contribution to their community and how it is governed.

10 Do you follow public issues and government actions on a regular basis?

To be an effective participant in government, you must be an informed participant. People often complain that government is secretive, that it rushes through ill-considered legislative changes, that it doesn't consult enough. Yet there is ample evidence to show that even when governments consult, even when there is massive media coverage about important public issues, the vast majority of Canadians remain blissfully unaware.

The sad reality is that most Canadians pay far too little attention to the activities of their governments. We can be roused on particular issues, especially when we feel that our interests are threatened, but a sustaining interest is much more difficult to achieve. Yet most of us find time to keep track of the daily sports scores and to exchange comments about our favourite comedy show on television from the night before. It takes no more time or energy to keep track of the activities of our governments and it is hard to imagine a more important way to spend our time in a democratic society. Imagine the difference it could make if most people redirected the energy they expend in complaining about government into more positive, active participation in government!

You Can Make the Difference!

It may be fitting to conclude with a quote from that famous political philosopher Pogo, who is credited with the saying: *"We have met the enemy and they are us."*

Our governments are far from perfect. This Guide raises a number of questions and concerns about the functioning of our government machinery, about the complexities and conflicts in our intergovernmental relationships, and especially about the kinds of priorities governments have chosen and the kinds of decisions they have made. But, cliché or not, it remains substantially true that we get the kind of government we deserve.

If you don't pay attention, if you sit back and grumble, if you contribute to the problems instead of preventing them from arising in the first place, you should look in the mirror when you want to allocate blame. If, instead, you take personal responsibility for your actions and for the actions of your governments, **you can make a difference**.

Index

A

B

C

G

H

I-J-K

W